Books by PHILIP KAPPEL

LOUISIANA GALLERY

JAMAICA GALLERY

NEW ENGLAND GALLERY

NEW ENGLAND GALLERY

NEW ENGLAND GALLERY

Philip Kappel

With an introduction by
WALTER MUIR WHITEHILL

BONANZA BOOKS · NEW YORK

LIBRARY OF CONGRESS CATALOG CARD NO. 66-14900

THIS EDITION PUBLISHED BY BONANZA BOOKS
A DIVISION OF CROWN PUBLISHERS, INC.,
BY ARRANGEMENT WITH LITTLE, BROWN AND COMPANY
a b c d e f g h

PRINTED IN THE UNITED STATES OF AMERICA

*To my sisters, Rose and Julie, who
share with me the good fortune of
a New England birthright.*

Introduction

This book is the diary of an artist's love affair with New England. This attachment is, however, a mature one of long standing that has survived the blandishments of numerous and more spectacular rivals, for Philip Kappel, in the course of his sixty-five years, has traveled widely and found congenial subjects for etching and drawing in every continent except Australia. His etchings are to be found in the print rooms of many American museums, as well as the Bibliothèque Nationale in Paris, while the sketches of his two previous books, *Louisiana Gallery* and *Jamaica Gallery,* have made his impressions of two very un-New-Englandish parts of the world familiar to a wide variety of readers. In an introduction to the latter book, the late John P. Marquand noted that, though he had known the artist since 1925, when he had a studio near Derby Wharf in Salem, Philip Kappel had "always possessed the instincts of an inveterate traveler" and that "no matter in what odd part of the world he may have paused, he has been artistically at home in it and in complete sympathy with its atmosphere and mood." So far as Essex County is concerned, this was neatly demonstrated in Philip Kappel's illustrations for John Marquand's *Timothy Dexter Revisited,* published in 1960.

For all his traveling Philip Kappel is a Connecticut man, born in Hartford and settled in New Milford. In *New England Gallery* he simply and modestly presents "New England as a New Englander looks at himself in it, feeling its pulse and making his report, calling his readers' attention to what he believes is pre-eminently attractive." This is neither history nor a guidebook, but rather one artist's sharing of those scenes "which lend themselves best to his working methods and which also contain the essentials for compositions of interest" in the six New England states. There are, of course, familiar scenes. The book opens with certain standard "sights" — Plymouth, Boston, Lexington, Concord, and Salem — but Mr. Kappel's choice of subjects is fresh and personal. When I first saw captionless proofs of the drawings here reproduced, I could only instantly identify about a third. Here are not only historic buildings and sites of national significance, but the varied elements of New England life — colleges, farmyards, granite quarries, fish piers, shipyards, apple orchards, cranberry bogs, tobacco fields, lobster pots, sugar houses, sand dunes, lighthouses, mountain lakes, lumbering, trout pools, dogs retrieving duck, the run of alewives, painters at work, and, above all, the houses and churches of shady villages and towns. And in the latter part of the book, where Mr. Kappel explores his own corner of Connecticut, there is much that will be new to many New Englanders.

A book like this needs no introduction; it speaks for itself. But John Marquand could not resist expressing his pleasure in Mr. Kappel's *Jamaica Gallery,* remarking: "When you view these pictures of Jamaica, you are seeing this varied and still not overexploited island through the eyes of an outstanding artist. Somehow, whether you are an expert in the graphic arts or not, you know that you are in good hands and that Philip Kappel will communicate to you, through his medium, the spirit of Jamaica and its people."

Alas, nobody could describe New England as "a still not overexploited" area. To reach *Mayflower II* and Plymouth Rock — the first two subjects in this book — from the main highway, the visitor has to run a horrendous gauntlet of commercial establishments, designed expressly to lighten his pockets. Mr. Kappel's drawings usually eliminate such nastiness, but in one instance (on page 87) he depicts something that is, at least to me, even more subtly unpleasant — the bowsprit pulpit, dedicated on May 22, 1961, that was contrived to make the Seamen's Bethel in New Bedford conform literally rather than figuratively to Herman Melville's description. This attempt to translate fiction into fact only corroborates Professor Daniel J. Boorstin's observation, in treating the "lost art of travel," that "in order to satisfy the exaggerated expectations of tour agents and tourists, people everywhere obligingly become dishonest mimics of themselves."

Were John Marquand still with us, he would, I am sure, share my feeling that *New England Gallery* vividly conveys the spirit of this place and its people. Perhaps today it is safer to travel in books like this than in Detroit-made automobiles.

WALTER MUIR WHITEHILL

Boston Athenaeum
April 19, 1966

x

Prologue

This is the story of New England as a New Englander looks at himself in it, feeling its pulse and making his report, calling his readers' attention to what he believes is preeminently attractive or simply stressing something historically significant and vital. No attempt was made to preempt the role of the historian; rather, I have tried to create a climate for the illustrations with appropriate supplementary data to provide an informative documentary — a living picture story of New England.

If noteworthy landmarks are conspicuously absent, their omission is not due to their lack of merit. It is the artist's prerogative to make those selections which lend themselves best to his working methods and which also contain the essentials for compositions of interest.

For many years a passive interest prevailed in our New England heritage. But more recently, in part owing to good public relations and the dedicated work of the historical societies across the land, the six New England states have discovered that selling the merits of their natural resources to the public or calling attention to their historic importance pays dividends. The automobile changed the pattern of communication; vast areas of beauty became accessible to the motorist via interlocking highway systems. Keeping roads open during the winter months turned winter sports into big business in our mountainous resort states, in need of a more elastic economy. The lakes and woods of New England have brought joy to fishermen and campers. People can roam at will and come to appreciate the dimensions of their New England heritage.

Hundreds of miles of coastline with variations of rocky ruggedness and clean sandy beaches have always been a magnet. The myriads of coastal inlets and deep-water harbors, where sailors and shipping sought anchorage, induced men to build shipyards, and nearly at the edge of the clearing stood the virgin timber for masts and keels. The die was cast for the contest to compete as a young nation with older ones for economic survival, and rugged individualism was born right then and there. The pioneers learned the art of survival through brotherhood and cooperation among themselves — there was no other way — and incorporated their faith in supreme guidance in such a manner that even the heathen look in the right direction when they scan a meetinghouse spire.

The Heritage Trails throughout New England can in a few days' trip unfold the chronicles of our past — especially the decisive challenge that came in 1775.

Every schoolboy knows the story. But it takes maturity and experience to evaluate the impact of the boldness and the courage of men and women who stood erect to be counted — willing to risk everything in a struggle from which there was no turning back.

Our New England villages, with their eighteenth-century houses and white churches with spires rising above ancient trees, were built and planted by men of vision and taste with an appreciation for open spaces, who are no longer here to protect what was to be for eternity. It would seem unthinkable that anyone should employ a bulldozer to level an old landmark, or equally ravaging and distasteful to rip an ancient tree from its roots, but it's being done! Everywhere the cry is for something more functional to fit the times; there must have been a rash of the same sentiments and inclinations in the eighties, or at the turn of the century, because everywhere, as if carried by a virus, monstrosities appeared. Look at the public libraries on numerous village greens, built in memory of donors who made much of fancy brick and granite, not small blocks of stone but chunks of it topped with meaningless ornamentation — bastions to imprison a few innocent books. Within the span of eighty years, more or less, nothing could have become more "old hat" and sad, in contrast with their earlier neighbors, than these nonconforming architectural impostors. What's more dismaying is that in most cases their donors left funds in trust to maintain them in perpetuity.

In spite of the availability of building sites outside of our villages, something new has appeared to further torment the tormented — the supermarket. It's here to stay. This byproduct of progress has replaced the local shopkeeper, in particular the village grocer, that colorful personality who never molested our vagrant fingers purloining tasty samples from his showcases, but in true Yankee fashion made sure what missed the scales didn't escape the family bill. It is becoming increasingly difficult to discourage big business from invading our village greens with their monstrous asphalt lots geometrically marked off for regimented parking.

Into the New England pattern is woven the spirit and enchantment of our past and the fight against stagnation. Not everybody relished the mundane task of divesting the fields of rocks scattered helter-skelter over the face of New England by the receding ice pack thousands of years ago. The lure of the sea held disquieting forebodings but the risk was worth it — the fortunate ones returned in their windjammers from far places with exotic cargoes. Our products in the nineteenth century found willing purchasers, and a new race of men with inventive genius became monstrously important and affluent. The *modus vivendi* no longer resembled the parsimony of the pioneer.

The shipowners fitted well into the new look and pattern with their New England-built and -manned square-riggers. New England boys spent less time in school and more on the high seas aloft in the rigging of those spectacular ships.

It became a certainty that sooner or later the cultures of ancient nations would infect us; those who carried the temptations of sophistication home created a yearning for something more satisfying than homespuns. The serious collector of Far Eastern arts in twentieth-century New England needs only to look in his own back yard for monumental things of quality, so numerous were the imports that came to our shores in the nineteenth century. It became a mark of status for the New England shipowners to have personal punchbowls in Chinese export porcelain bearing portraits of their ships, today among the most coveted antiquities of that great era of sail.

Salem, Portsmouth, Newburyport, Newport, New Bedford, Providence and New Haven became cultural centers along the seaboard with Boston predominantly host to all. Fragments broke away to take root throughout New England, each exploiting the prosperity that came its way; others were preoccupied with the soil. New England had much to offer, and by and large everyone with ambition won his keep, and more — fulfillment.

Every July Fourth fireworks and bell-ringing became a ritual to remind people of a great cause won, but the men who won the victories of the Revolution were no longer around. Speakers reminded their listeners who gathered around the village bandstands about their glorious past. The spell of the struggle for independence became vested in shrines like those of Lexington and Concord, where the first skirmishes took place for the struggle to attain independence; Yorktown, where Cornwallis handed over his sword to Washington; and Valley Forge, where the suffering, impoverished army relied upon spirit alone. A liberty-loving people can adjust themselves to many things and suffering was one of them.

New Englanders drove their energies into venturous domestic channels as any vigorous people would do, but the short relief of peace was destined to end in a rude awakening to crisis. Great and impassioned orators arose among us; each with a lusty voice loaded with persuasion for one cause or another tried to sway the minds of the people. Gently and softly at first, the evidence of something ominous and smoldering began to make itself felt, as if to test again the tempers of men, but this time it was horribly different and before long a vicious cacophony arose — men were shouting defiantly at each other in hatred, dividing and forcing the nation into a decision. Abolition and Slavery became dirty words depending upon where you lived, or whether *Uncle Tom's Cabin* could be found in the family library.

Good, bad or indifferent, our minds in the North were made up to face the inevitable, and the slaughter of brother by brother became a catastrophe and a shame. New England adjusted itself to the victory of the North in which her sons participated, while they returned home to explore the potentials of what lay ahead.

Eventually the products of an industrial New England began to revolutionize the mode of living everywhere. Soon small towns were no longer small and temperaments changed. The labor unions began to flex their muscles and what started as a noble ideal of abolishing the sweatshops and improving the lot of the laborer became a battle for shorter working hours. A hundred years have gone by since the Civil War, and those who were casually interested in labor now complain that the leisure the laborer won, and which he enjoys, makes it harder to get their own chores done.

New Englanders have fought for principles without territorial desire, responded without rancor or question whenever and wherever duty called. Their reflexes are responsive by inheritance and by pioneer conditioning; when their missions ended they spent little time waiting around to hear the panegyrics and effusions — there was work to be done to regain the lost years. To most New Englanders work is still a precious commodity and a pride. To the creative worker it's a compulsion. In general, New Englanders have been brought up to enjoy occupation, practice economy habitually, and be mindful of work. The New Englander also likes to have fun and enjoys a good story about himself at his expense — otherwise, why has he left unchallenged the legend of the wooden nutmeg? It's too intricate a piece of carving for the layman to fake realistically, and more time-consuming than profitable for a sculptor to be troubled with for pennies.

New England is the land of my birth. My forebears were not among those who stepped ashore on Plymouth Rock in 1620 — my father came to these shores two hundred and eighty years later. I might be called, if I may be facetious about it, a "Connecticut nutmegger" due to my father's recalcitrance to living elsewhere. Nonetheless, after years of roaming throughout the world I returned to my native state convinced I could never find greater happiness elsewhere. These pages proclaim the earnestness of my applause and gratitude, plus the recognition of the shrines of my adoption, left for all to inherit from those who felt in their day as you and I do in the present about our good fortune and opportunities.

P. K.

New Milford, Connecticut

Contents

NEW ENGLAND GALLERY

Massachusetts

Mayflower II

PLYMOUTH

There is no contemporary picture of the *Mayflower,* and nobody knows what she looked like. Also, the name was used by more than twenty ships in service in 1620; just why *Mayflower* was so popular a name is difficult to answer. The ship which brought the Pilgrims to Massachusetts was named after one of several plants that bloom in England in the month of May (in New England the term is applied to the trailing arbutus, the state flower of Massachusetts). The records are meager but it is certain that her tonnage was 180, with a length of 100 feet, that she had three masts and two decks and was larger than the average merchant ship of the day. Before 1616, the *Mayflower* hauled fish and lumber from Norway and later went into the Mediterranean wine trade.

Captain Christopher Jones was in command of the *Mayflower* when she sailed from Plymouth, England, September 6, 1620, arriving off Cape Cod November 9 and dropping her anchor in Provincetown Harbor November 21. On Christmas Day the Pilgrims weighed anchor in Provincetown Harbor to cross to Plymouth, but the wind was not in their favor and they had to put back. The following day a fair wind enabled them to enter Plymouth Harbor, remaining on board to spend the Sabbath before going ashore.

During the winter at Plymouth, the bosun, the cook, the master gunner, three mates and over half the sailors died. In spite of these handicaps, the *Mayflower* departed from Plymouth in April 1621 without cargo, riding high and in bad condition, and miraculously made an English landfall. She probably sailed up the Thames and moored at Rotherhithe, the birthplace of her skipper. It is not known whether the *Mayflower* ever sailed again. Scant information hints that she was broken up and some of the timber was ignominiously used in the erection of a barn.

Originally, the Pilgrims set out in two ships, but when the *Speedwell* proved unseaworthy her passengers were crowded aboard the *Mayflower* making a total of 102 passengers. Stowed away aboard the *Mayflower* was a large shallop capable of being rowed or sailed. This was assembled at Provincetown and used in exploration which ultimately led to the discovery of Plymouth, in Cape Cod Bay. Later, the shallop was pressed into coastal trading and fishing as far south as Connecticut and as far north as Maine.

The *Mayflower II,* moored at the State Pier near Plymouth Rock, was con-

PHILIP KAPPEL.

Mayflower II moored in Plymouth

structed in England from available dimensions of other vessels of the period to fit Governor Bradford's records. The *Mayflower II* is 181 tons burden, 104 feet long overall with a 78 foot 8 inch waterline, a beam of 25½ feet and a draft of 13 feet. Captain Alan Villiers set out from Plymouth, England, April 20, 1957, in *Mayflower II,* and fifty-five days later entered Plymouth Harbor from Cape Cod Bay, to an enthusiastic greeting from the multitudes who lined the shore.

Plymouth Rock
PLYMOUTH

Plymouth Rock might have been lost to us as the symbol of freedom and faith but for the prompt action of Thomas Faunce, who overheard a rumor that the rock was going to be moved away. He hurried to the waterfront and told the story of the landing of the Pilgrims as told him by his father. Faunce was ninety-five when he thwarted the removal of the rock, and died a short time afterward, at the age of ninety-nine.

The most famous rock in America had the "1620" inscription cut into it years after the landing of the Pilgrims. Had it not been put in safekeeping, souvenir hunters might easily have completely removed it bit by bit — as it was, two-thirds of the boulder had already been carried away before protective measures were taken.

Three hundred and forty-four years after the Pilgrims landed the interest in Plymouth is greater than ever. Visitors in tremendous numbers invade the town to pay tribute to the memory of the Pilgrims, to walk about the streets where history springs to life, or to drive a short distance south of the center of town where an authentic Pilgrim village has been reconstructed on a hill identical with Leyden Street. Plimoth Plantation is a nonprofit educational foundation; aided by exhaustive research, the image of the Pilgrims is indeed in keeping with fact.

The *Mayflower II,* moored every summer in Plymouth Harbor, is owned by Plimoth Plantation and will be berthed permanently at the Plimoth Plantation Eel River site.

Plimoth Plantation is a re-creation of the original Pilgrim Colony as it looked in 1627. Both sides of the street are lined with vertically planked houses with thatched or wooden shake roofs, and flowers in bloom everywhere. The oiled paper windows filter the daylight. Enormous stone fireplaces take up one entire wall of the tiny homes. All Pilgrim activities are shown with infinite care, even the process of making beer, which most Englishmen of the seventeenth century drank as a beverage instead of water because the water on shipboard was frequently contaminated — an appropriate excuse, even for Pilgrims.

The peristyle over Plymouth Rock

In a shed near the Samuel Fuller house it is possible to see how medicinal herbs were dried on poles after their removal from the herb gardens. Fuller was a seventeenth-century physician whose training was in the Galenic school of medicine — disease was believed due to disturbed tempers or disturbed humors, for which were prescribed certain herbal remedies or bleeding. Herbs were also used extensively in Pilgrim homes by the housewives as aromatic aids in storing clothes or strewn on floors to counteract cooking odors.

The Fort-Meetinghouse commands a sweeping view of the surrounding country from its hilltop site. The flat roof was built of thick sawn planks supported by oak beams upon which rest six cannon capable of shooting iron balls weighing four to five pounds each. The lower part of the building was used as a church.

Samoset, a friendly Indian, suddenly appeared in March 1621 and greeted the Pilgrims in broken English. He returned to the Colony later with another English-speaking Indian, Squanto. They made arrangements for Chief Massasoit to visit Plimoth Plantation, at which time a peace treaty was concluded which guaranteed the rights of both parties — a treaty that was honorably kept for over fifty years. The Colony could not have survived without the friendship of Massasoit and the Wampanoag Indians. They supplied the Pilgrims with corn and taught them how to plant it in hills with fish as fertilizer. Furthermore the Pilgrims were taught how to adapt themselves for survival in the wilderness.

Governor William Bradford declared a Thanksgiving feast in 1622, which was celebrated by families, their friends and neighbors, including Massasoit and ninety of his men who were entertained for several days on seafood, wild turkey and venison, together with an abundance of garden produce.

During the first winter half of the Pilgrims died and were buried secretly on Cole's Hill, overlooking the Rock. In the spring their graves were concealed by grain, planted to hide the decimation of the colony from hostile Indians. The bones of those who were buried on Cole's Hill repose in a sarcophagus today on that same hill. Everywhere in Plymouth there is evidence of Pilgrim stoicism, and some of the houses they knew still stand. In Pilgrim Hall, built in 1824 and rebuilt in 1880, you may see contemporary documents and books owned at one time by the Pilgrims. There are also furniture, portraits and articles of importance pertaining to the Colony.

The original fort on Burial Hill was dismantled after the end of King Philip's War, through which the Colony lived in terror. On Sandwich Street, the William Harlow house may be seen today, with its timbers taken from the old fort.

Longfellow brought lasting fame to John Alden's romance with Priscilla, and anyone can see where John Alden lived — the house still stands in nearby Duxbury, with all its simplicity and charm, in spite of having been built in 1653.

Because he was small of stature and quite peppery, Captain Myles Standish was called "Captain Shrimp," an irreverence to the memory of a competent soldier, but there is nothing small about the monument raised at Duxbury in his memory. Civil War cannon mark the grave of Myles Standish in Duxbury, six miles from Plymouth. No one is able to explain the incongruity of the stones erected to the memory of John and Priscilla Alden near the grave of Myles Standish, although the exact location of their graves is unknown.

Myles Standish engineered the erection of the fort on Burial Hill and organized the resistance against attack by unfriendly Indians; but now standing on Cole's Hill is an imposing statue of Massasoit — a reminder that all Indians were not unfriendly and that one of their race rendered the Pilgrims a service beyond measure.

Between the First Parish Church (Unitarian) and the Congregational Church of the Pilgrimage, a long and seemingly endless series of steps will take you to what I consider one of the most hallowed places in Plymouth. From the summit of Burial Hill, a vista of Cape Cod Bay may be seen between the spires of the churches. Many old stones mark the graves of the colonists, buried high above the rude houses thatched with swamp-grass that at one time lined Leyden Street, named for their city of refuge.

At one grave, without special emphasis to mark its importance, stands a tall slab of stone with a chamfered top, upon which is the following inscription:

UNDER THIS STONE REST THE ASHES OF WILLIAM BRADFORD A ZEALOUS PURITAN AND SINCERE CHRISTIAN, GOVERNOR OF PLYMOUTH COLONY FROM APRIL 1621–1657 EXCEPT 5 YEARS WHICH HE DECLINED.

Boston and John Winthrop

In 1930 I witnessed the much-publicized reenactment of the entry into Salem Harbor of Governor Winthrop's flagship, the *Arbella*, on June 12, 1630.

Soon after the *Arbella* dropped anchor, the passengers, for the most part Salem folk dressed in Puritan costumes, scurried ashore to join in the conviviality of Salem's tercentenary.

The modern full-size model of the *Arbella* served its dramatic role, but she was not seaworthy. Her superstructure was superimposed upon an old hulk — a weird-looking apparition out of the past surrounded by curious yachtsmen getting a close look at her lofty poop, the great cabin, high forecastle and lateen-rigged mizzen. The *Arbella* drove home the hazards and discomforts of sea travel in the seventeenth century to everyone who saw her, if nothing more.

At the close of the celebrations the *Arbella* was moved to the edge of Pioneers' Village in Forest River Park where she was permanently moored, and where for more than three decades she withstood northeasters and hurricanes; but she was scorned by sailors, and reduced to a disintegrating curiosity.

Winthrop and eleven venturous members of the Massachusetts Bay Company on August 26, 1629, signed an agreement in Cambridge, England, to emigrate to the Plantation of the Massachusetts Bay Company if the powers of government and the Royal patent remained in their custody. The Company voted to grant these concessions and two months later Winthrop was elected by a unanimous vote to the office of Governor, in which he was to serve as the guiding spirit of the new colony. He had education, breeding and understanding — indispensable qualities for the role of leadership.

Four of the twelve ships fitted out for the expedition sailed April 8, 1630. As companions, Winthrop selected a distinguished group of Puritans; among those aboard the *Arbella* (named for Lady Arbella, daughter of the Earl of Lincoln and wife of Isaac Johnson) were Lady Arbella and her husband; Sir Richard Saltonstall, William Coddington, the first Governor of Rhode Island; and Simon Bradstreet, the youngest assistant of the Massachusetts Bay Company. They were to transplant to New England from Old England the traditions of the land from which they were parting, not as separatists from the Church of England as the Pilgrims had been nearly ten years before, but with a charter leaving their religious affairs and ecclesiastical drives free.

On June 12, 1630, after a rough crossing of seventy days, four ships, the *Arbella,* the *Ambrose,* the *Jewel* and the *Talbot* overshot their mark for a landfall in the vicinity of Boston and sailed into Salem Harbor.

John Endicott, the acting Governor under the Massachusetts Bay Company, had been head of the settlement at Salem which had 300 people. At Plymouth the Pilgrims rose to three hundred souls during the nine years preceding Winthrop's arrival, and with those aboard Winthrop's four ships and the settlers who soon followed him, the original contingent amounted to eight hundred, which ultimately increased to two thousand.

Winthrop's sudden arrival at Salem with so many unannounced kinfolk, related or not, must have caught them with unmade beds, a situation which Governor Winthrop attempted to rectify without delay; so with genteel farewells he moved his company closer to their original point of entry and settled at Charlestown, across the river from Shawmut. The excessive heat of summer, and illness among the settlers, brought a rash of deaths among the group already too exhausted from the voyage to withstand further hardships.

Parson William Blackstone extended an invitation to Governor Winthrop to join him on his peninsula, where more favorable conditions existed, and the changeover was effected without incident by simply crossing the Charles River; and they lost no time digging in for the winter — it was then September, 1630.

A three-pronged hill across the river interested the settlers; called Trimountaine, it survives today as Beacon Hill. The first legislative body of the Colony voted soon after departing from Charlestown, that Trimountaine should henceforth be called Boston, after Boston in old England.

Governor Winthrop kept a journal for nineteen years in which he made entries pertaining to the crossing and later on covering the affairs of the Colony in great detail — a moving account of the rules by which the Colonists conducted their lives.

The Old Testament served as the guide for dealing with sins and sinners; and villages were required to have stocks on their greens for punitive purposes and so small an item as an overcharge on a bill would be sufficient cause to clamp one in that device!

The fundamental laws of the colony were inspired by the Book of Leviticus, which the Reverend John Cotton (who arrived in 1633 from Boston, England) consulted with other men of the cloth when they were asked to cooperate with the judiciary in effecting laws for civil affairs.

The church and the courts were interdependent and many colonists were deprived of their right to vote on civil matters when, soon after the founding of Boston, the General Court passed an order giving the vote to church members only. By 1676 such a vast number of disenfranchised men were unable to take part in the decisions of government that the situation had become intolerable.

The crusade to rectify matters was due to arrive; after a serious review of existing conditions, bold and rebellious groups made their feelings known with verbal bombasts and rhetoric such as the clergy and the judiciary never anticipated or cared to condone.

Mrs. Anne Hutchinson, whose house stood where the modified "Old Corner Bookstore" building stands today at the corner of School and Washington Streets, became the fiery and outspoken proponent of radical changes. She came to Boston shortly after the arrival of the Reverend John Cotton, whose personality and preaching she had admired in Lincolnshire. She continued to praise Cotton's abilities highly at the expense of the other clergy in the colony and openly made unkind remarks about their shortcomings.

In due time Anne Hutchinson became a marked woman for her brazenness, but she had an enormous appeal to her women followers and a more formidable association of crusaders couldn't have been organized. People went from one church to another or wherever the most peppery condemnations against Anne Hutchinson were anticipated. To the clergy she was evil and troublesome; still, no one dared touch her!

Governor Winthrop and the Reverend John Wilson saw eye to eye as friends in the entire affair of church versus Anne Hutchinson. She countered with the able support of Sir Harry Vane, a brilliant but tempestuous personality who managed within a year of his coming to Boston in 1635 to be elected Governor at the age of twenty-four. Vane's presence in that office became an enigma to many, but Anne Hutchinson admired him and made use of his office to further her own schemes; and since Vane made his position known in support of the new element, she took comfort in his protection.

Winthrop's stature grew with the passing of time; Vane's lessened due to some serious indiscretions perpetrated while he was in office, and Vane was voted out. This left the way wide open for the enemies of Anne Hutchinson to immobilize her tongue and to threaten her with bodily harm.

After a disgraceful performance of a trial the verdict was one of expected severity — the state ordered her banished. In addition, an ecclesiastical court, at which Anne Hutchinson's archenemy, the Reverend John Wilson, presided, pronounced a verdict of excommunication.

The sentences meant her immediate removal from the Massachusetts Bay Colony, and Anne Hutchinson went to Rhode Island and later to Manhattan Island, where the final chapter of her life was written by the Indians with her blood. Subsequently most of her family suffered a similar fate.

Louisburg Square
BOSTON

Charming Louisburg Square, and much that is known as Beacon Hill, has been declared a "Historic District," and is assured legal protection against alteration in a rapidly changing world. The Square is flanked by brick houses built around 1840, at which time the Square was enlarged and made into the bow-ended rectangular shape it still has. It is surrounded by an iron fence within which there are shrubs and trees, tastefully arranged, including two statues — Aristides at one end and Columbus at the other.

The proprietors of Louisburg Square, whose dignified red brick Greek Revival homes with pedimented doorways rise sharply out of brick sidewalks, are solely responsible for the general appearance. From time to time exceptionally famous personalities have been associated with the Square: Jenny Lind, the Swedish singer, visited and was married there; and Louisa May Alcott and William D. Howells lived here.

Christmas Eve in Louisburg Square has traditional significance, and attracts hundreds of people who mill around the Square while carol singers mingle with the crowds. It is the time when this exclusive community thaws its seclusion, throws back the old shutters and illuminates the windows with soft candlelight. But this friendly gesture by the proprietors is neither year-round nor to be

PHILIP KAPPEL

Louisburg Square and the statue of Columbus

construed as a carte blanche invitation to further intimacies — or to park cars in the cobblestoned square.

When the bells toll in the Charles Street Meeting House which Asher Benjamin designed, situated at the foot of Mt. Vernon Street, the square resembles one in London, rather than in the heart of a great American city.

Some people insist that Louisburg Square was named for the Battle of Louisburg, Nova Scotia, when the French were defeated in 1748 by the English; many Bostonians participated in the drive to get the French out and thereby secure the Atlantic seaboard.

A legend prevails that within the area of Beacon Hill and Louisburg Square, the first white settler of Boston lived in a makeshift house as a hermit on his farm. He was the Reverend William Blackstone, a nonconformist who came over with the Robert Gorges's expedition in 1623 and remained after the others returned to England. He learned about the plight of Governor Winthrop and his small colony at Charlestown, where there was a drastic shortage of fresh water; he invited them to his area where there was a gushing spring on his land and they came. It was late in the fall, and they built hastily to face the rigors of winter. To this day, Blackstone's spring asserts the right to emerge from hidden sources under parts of Beacon Hill, in spite of concrete and asphalt surfacing.

The General Court purchased from Blackstone, in 1634, that portion of his landholdings which is now Boston Common. They set it aside for common pasturage and militia training, after the manner of the English villages. The city fathers paid Blackstone about one hundred and fifty dollars and struck the best bargain in Boston's history.

The Reverend Blackstone found the newcomers rather unendurable — in the vernacular of our time, he felt that he was being "squeezed out" of his domain, whereupon he sold the rest of his landholdings, except a few acres, professed his love for the society of the Indians to that of the Puritans, and moved to a place, identified merely as being near Pawtucket, Rhode Island, where he married and had one son. He continued to live as a recluse from white society and associated with the Indians exclusively. History has handed down little more to further clarify his mysterious behavior, but he made one major contribution — he planted the first orchards in Massachusetts.

Acorn Street

BOSTON

Acorn Street might be a motorist's dilemma but it is the sentimentalist's delight. It is truly a one-way street through which a narrow automobile might squeeze through for the privilege of getting thoroughly shaken up by the original cobble-

Acorn Street on Beacon Hill

stones, removed from the beaches and laid hit or miss. The sidewalks are brick, proportionately narrow, and slant towards the road, at night the shadows are barely dispelled by the few feeble public street lamps, though these are an improvement over the earlier whale-oil lamps of the late eighteenth century.

Acorn Street is reminiscent of the rapid growth of the early Federal development of Boston, when the city gradually acquired its classic red-brick buildings and fashionable residential areas. New houses were frequently built between older buildings and seldom faced the street; every available plot of land formerly used for gardens or orchards was requisitioned with little thought given to accessibility.

An Artist's Paradise

BOSTON

Wherever fancy overtakes the artist, there he sets up his easel and goes to work, unaware of traffic, passersby and the hecklers who offer unsolicited criticism.

For decades, seaports like Rockport, Gloucester and Provincetown have attracted serious artists, the amateur, or just those who seek the bonhomie of the artistic set. In the main the artistic mavericks pause awhile and then move on to other centers, but the serious workers return to the same communities where they maintain their studios. Collectors frequent the exhibitions and sometimes discover talent of exceptional caliber; in fact an art colony gives the artist a chance to be discovered.

There are other artists who avoid art colonies altogether, and work in self-imposed isolation, like the lady in this drawing caught in the act of sketching the lambent light in Louisburg Square, before darkness overtook the Square. She had no fancy paraphernalia, just a shopping cart she used to carry her supplies in, which also served as an easel. Dressed properly for the cold, she wore a quilted jacket and gloves.

Art is an unfathomable ecstasy. It may be felt, but seldom understood; it is a speculation dependent on moods, and the passing scene is seldom seen in the same way by two different people — it's an interpretation, an idealism, the essence of an inspiration culminated, a thought that acquired form and a symbol.

PHILIP KAPPEL

Sketching Louisburg Square

T Wharf

When I first saw T Wharf a few years back I just wanted to sit in contemplation and try to pierce the pithy silence, disturbed now and then by scolding gulls. Not even the slapping harbor waters broke the ghostly quiet, where once proud vessels sought the security of its pilings, or withdrew from the wharf to reenter the harbor currents, either to depart for the mystical bazaars of foreign places, or simply ply between our coastal ports. There was something about the wharf that generated sympathy for its prophetic and dispirited decline.

The modern wharves of Boston are located in South and East Boston, but to most of us the old wharves speak more eloquently of what we associate with Boston. The new maps of Boston Harbor do not superimpose upon the old, since so much of Paul Revere's town has drastically changed. The waterfront to a large extent is filled-in marshland and mud flats once covered by high tides.

An old engraving by Paul Revere which he made in 1768 shows the embryonic Minot's T Wharf as an offshoot of Long Wharf — stubby in appearance and looking like something put there as an afterthought. When Atlantic Avenue was filled in and laid out, the crossing of the T was covered by fill and the wharf appeared as an independent segment jutting out into the harbor. Then in 1917, on the filled-in land near Atlantic Avenue, the Quincy Cold Storage Warehouse was built at the head of the wharf. Between 1883 and 1914, T Wharf was one of the world's greatest fish piers.

Long Wharf and T Wharf extend equidistantly into the harbor, but Long Wharf is much older. It was from Long Wharf that the expedition against Louisbourg sailed in 1745. Long Wharf was at the time Boston's most important pier. Here the British disembarked during the Revolution and from Long Wharf they departed. Boston's lucrative trade with the West Indies was carried on from here.

The waterfront changed constantly. In 1806 India Wharf was built, and along about 1823 Central Wharf appeared and Commercial Street was made ready to be included in the newer maps of Boston. The Faneuil Hall Market (Quincy Market) dates from 1826, and between 1835 and 1847 the Custom House was built (the tower was added in 1914).

The approximate place where the Boston Tea Party took place appears on an old map made in 1835, near the foot of Pearl Street, between Liverpool and Russia Wharves.

Before Atlantic Avenue was built the clipper ships of Donald McKay would tie up at Central and India Wharves; and the Maine Packets and the Way-Down-

The mordancy of neglect — T Wharf, Boston

East Steamers used T Wharf. The boats for Philadelphia, New York and the Southern ports left from Long Wharf.

In 1860 a few fish houses appeared on T Wharf, and the famous grindstones used throughout New England continued to be sold there. The stone came from the area of the Bay of Fundy in New Brunswick and was fashioned into grindstones and gristmills after leaving the holds of the boats that sailed for Maine points and Halifax from T Wharf. By 1880 T Wharf had become predominantly a fish pier. The buildings shown in this sketch were built around 1882. T Wharf is truly a ghost wharf. The bell tower over the former Fish Exchange no longer announces when a boat load of fish is to be auctioned. Since 1914 the bell has been frozen in silence; and, adding insult to injury, the hurricane of 1938 blew away the fish weathervane.

Within walking distance some of the most famous Colonial shrines still uphold the old traditions: Faneuil Hall; the Old North Church; St. Stephen's Church, which Bulfinch designed in 1804; and the old State House built in 1748.

Prior to World War II many of the buildings on the wharf were occupied as studios, or as living quarters. Life must have been rather colorful, but it terminated almost as fast as the Bohemians appeared.

34 Beacon Street

BOSTON

Architecturally, greater Boston is gaining a new look, like the rest of New England; however, nowhere is traditional consciousness more consolidated and less moved by trends than Beacon Hill. A short walk into other areas will reveal mammoth demolition projects, to accommodate the expansion of Boston; when one returns to Beacon Hill it is with a sigh of relief. Beacon Hill is in a sense a safety isle in the midst of old Boston with its one-way streets, untouched by parkways with their relentless traffic.

The grim reality is that what interests and serves one generation seldom survives to please the second. Our chrome and brash neon-light era has too often sacrificed many buildings that should have been spared, preserved or modified to function for us; the historically conscious American discovers too late that much falls prey to that hackneyed exhortation, "Let's build for modern living."

Little, Brown and Company purchased in 1909 the building it still occupies on the corner of Joy and Beacon Streets, facing Boston Common. It formerly was the family residence of Susan B. Cabot of Salem, Massachusetts. The façade, with its cast-iron balcony, is more reminiscent of New Orleans than New England and combines the charm of both. It was built in 1825.

34 Beacon Street, Boston

The interior was altered discreetly to accommodate Little, Brown and Company's business requirements without sacrificing the elegance of the building — a credit to this firm, which has been publishing the literary works of many of America's most noted authors for over one hundred and twenty-five years.

A short distance east of the building stands Charles Bulfinch's masterpiece, a red brick building with a gold dome, known to everyone as the State House, that set the standard for capitol architecture. Bulfinch also designed the State House at Hartford, Connecticut, and the one at Augusta, Maine; and he spent twelve years in Washington, D.C., where he worked on the national Capitol.

The east and west wings of the Boston State House were added much later. The corner stone was laid with public ceremonies July 4, 1795, by His Excellency Samuel Adams, Governor, assisted by the Most Worshipful Paul Revere, Grand Master, and other brethren of the Grand Lodge of Masons. The State House was completed in 1798; in 1802 the dome was sheathed in copper by Paul Revere and Son. The copper was removed in 1831 and gilded, but gold leaf was applied in 1874 and since that time it has been regilded six times.

The historic codfish carving, originally in the Old State House, now hangs opposite the Speaker's chair in the House of Representatives.

One of our most valuable historic treasures, the manuscript "Of Plymouth Plantation" by Governor Bradford — also known as "the log of the *Mayflower*" — is displayed in the state library. On view in the wall safe in the Archives division is the charter granted by Charles I, entitled "The Governor and Company of the Massachusetts Bay in New England" — the document which founded Massachusetts as a self-governing Commonwealth.

Union Oyster House
BOSTON

Visitors to Boston for decades have dined at the Union Oyster House which has been in continuous business since 1826. The same old stalls and oyster bar are in their original position. Wherever the eye wanders, a medley of commercial signs peer down upon this ancient mellow brick building, which has worn its age well.

Prior to 1826, Thomas Capen's store was located where the Union Oyster House is situated. It was a rendezvous for customers interested in imported silks and fancy dress goods. Thomas Capen succeeded his father, Hopestill Capen, with whom in 1769 Benjamin Thompson, of Woburn, afterwards Count Rumford, served as an apprenticed clerk. At the same time Thomas Parkman, who later became a distinguished Boston merchant, learned his trade under Hopeswell Capen.

From 1771 to the start of hostilities between the Colonies and England, the upper part of the building was the headquarters of Isaiah Thomas, who published

The old Union Oyster House, Boston, near Faneuil Hall

the *Massachusetts Spy*. Other occupants of the building from time to time included Ebenezer Hancock, a Continental Army paymaster, who maintained his headquarters here for a brief period, and Louis Philippe, afterward King of France, who tutored prominent Bostonians in French, on the second floor.

The Union Oyster House is a stone's throw from Faneuil Hall, with its distinctive gilded grasshopper weathervane made from a sheet of copper in 1742 by "Deacon" Shem Drowne. The original Hall was built in 1742 by Peter Faneuil as a gift to the town of Boston; it burned in 1762 and was rebuilt in 1763. Charles Bulfinch enlarged the structure in 1805. The famous hall is incorporated in the present building as we see it today.

Before and after the American Revolution, patriotic meetings were held in the Hall. British officers used the Hall as a playhouse during the siege. After the war President George Washington was officially banqueted here by the city of Boston.

Paul Revere's house, the oldest frame building in Boston, is located on North Square, a short walk from Faneuil Hall. The house was built in 1676, right after the disastrous fire of Boston, on the site of Increase Mather's house, which had burned to the ground. The Revere house is low-studded, two stories high with the second story projecting beyond the first, and has a pitched roof with a huge chimney crushed against an adjoining building; the windows have leaded diamond panes. The house is owned by the Paul Revere Memorial Association and held as an Historic Shrine. It is furnished in period appointments, some of which were actually owned by Paul Revere.

Old South Meeting House
BOSTON

This place of worship participated deeply in our country's history, and within its quiet confines today the imaginer of vital actions is able to recreate the deeds and spirit of the Founding Fathers of our nation.

Possibly not everyone who passes the Old South and sets his watch by the clock in the tower realizes that the clock was ticking away the hours when President Washington was welcomed by Boston.

Reverend Thomas Prince had his study in the "Steeple Chamber" where, it is said, he spent many hours with his book collection. Among the treasures in his "New England Collection" was the "History of Plimoth Plantation" by Governor Bradford. This valuable document in some mysterious manner disappeared. It turned up later in the palace of the Bishop of London, at Fulham, of all places. It was returned to this country and is now safe in the State House on Beacon Street, where anyone may see its browned pages.

The Old South was erected in 1729 and dedicated in 1730. It replaced the

The Old South Meeting House, Boston

"Cedar" meeting house, the first home of the third Congregational church gathered in Boston. The membership was dedicated to freedom of worship and political equality, therefore when Faneuil Hall proved inadequate to hold all the Patriots at town meetings they habitually gathered in Old South. It was in this meeting house that Governor Andros forced upon the Congregational membership the reading of the Episcopal service.

When Benjamin Franklin was only three hours old he was taken by his father, Josiah Franklin, on January 17, 1706, to the "Old House" to be baptized, while a blizzard raged outside.

The Old South Meeting House ranks in importance with Philadelphia's Independence Hall as a Revolutionary landmark. In Old South in 1770, a capacity crowd waited throughout the night until Governor Hutchinson agreed to withdraw the British regiments after the Boston Massacre. Five thousand citizens on November 29, 1773, voiced their determination to thwart the landing of tea in Boston Harbor; later, several thousand gathered here on December 16, 1773, and waited for word from Governor Hutchinson at Milton, to whom messengers were dispatched to request a stay in the landing of tea. When Governor Hutchinson refused to move the tea from Boston, Samuel Adams, who was waiting for this cue, stood up in the pulpit and announced, "This Meeting can do nothing to save the country." Immediately, as if this were the signal to move into action, the "Indians" rushed to Griffin's Wharf for the most famous tea party ever held.

Commemorative orations on the Boston Massacre were delivered in the Old South from 1771 to 1775 by Church, John Hancock, Lovell and Warren. Several months before General Joseph Warren met his death at Bunker Hill he delivered his second oration; British soldiers and officers blocked the aisles, thus forcing Warren to climb through a window into the church to reach the pulpit.

The pews and pulpits were destroyed by the British in 1775 and used for firewood. Then the floor was covered with dirt. General Burgoyne used the church as a riding school for British troops. When Washington triumphantly entered Boston in March 1776, he looked down from the eastern gallery of the church upon a scene of revolting vandalism.

Before King's Chapel was built, no Congregational meeting house would permit the Church of England service to be read within its doors. But within four months of his arrival in Boston as the first commissioned royal governor of the Province, Sir Edmund Andros had in his possession the keys of the Old South Church, and for nearly two years the parishioners had to wait outside until the Anglican service was concluded.

To further complicate matters, when Governor Andros tried to buy land upon which to build a church, the Congregationalists refused to sell, and no Anglican owned land to offer him! Andros finally succeeded in building a wooden structure, on one corner of the burying ground where King's Chapel stands now, and this church was first used on June 30, 1689. The granite walls of the present King's

Chapel were built around the wooden structure; and at the end of five years when the stonework was completed, the wooden chapel was torn down and thrown through the windows into the street.

The bell in the tower is the one Paul Revere and Son recast in 1816. The crown and two bishop's mitres are still in their original places above the organ, which was brought to this country from England in 1756. A tradition mentions that Handel selected the organ. Of great interest is the furnished Governor's, or Royal Pew. Pew number 102 belonged to Oliver Wendell Holmes.

King's Chapel is known as the first Episcopal Church in New England and is often spoken of as the first American Unitarian Church.

Soon after Boston was settled, the King's Chapel burying ground was established, in 1630. Governor Winthrop's interment in 1649 is the earliest recorded. The land was owned originally by Sir Isaac Johnson who ventured to Boston with Governor Winthrop in the ship *Arbella*. Sir Isaac was buried here on September 30, 1630, carrying out a wish made known on his deathbed.

When Governor Andros took the corner of the burying ground for the site of the first Episcopal chapel in 1688, the remains from the early graves were placed in tombs beneath the chapel, where in 1710 additional space was provided for the deceased.

The gravestones throughout the burying ground read like pages of history. One marker bears the name of William Dawes, Jr., who made the midnight ride in 1775 with Paul Revere. Another marks the grave of Captain Robert Keayne, the founder and first commander of the Ancient and Honorable Artillery Company, the oldest military organization in our country, which maintains a museum and armory on the third floor of Faneuil Hall. Mary Chilton, who is buried here, was the first white woman to live in Boston; furthermore, she was the first Pilgrim to step on Plymouth Rock.

The prominent citizens who are buried in this ancient burying place include illustrious ministers and early governors; but among those who are assured a lasting place in history, one grave is marked for perpetual interest for no reason other than as the resting place of the heroine of Hawthorne's *The Scarlet Letter*.

The Bulfinch-Otis Houses
BOSTON

John Singleton Copley, the Colonial portrait painter, lived on a farm on Beacon Hill, Boston. The Somerset Club, which occupies the site of Copley's house, is a massive Greek-Revival granite bow-front building built for David Sears in 1819 from designs made by Alexander Parris. A succession of new homes appeared on the Hill, but the main drive to develop the area was vested in a group of influential and prosperous Bostonians with vision, among whom were Charles Bulfinch, the architect, and Harrison Gray Otis, a lawyer of great wealth. They formed a syndicate called the Mount Vernon Proprietors and purchased the Copley farm in 1795 after the painter moved to England.

The syndicate developed the southwest slope of Beacon Street into a fine residential area. The land that formed part of the Copley farm no longer harbored blueberry bushes and pasture privileges; instead fifteen houses sprang up and destroyed the bucolic atmosphere between the years 1806 and 1812.

The first mansion by Bulfinch for Harrison Gray Otis was built in 1797, at the corner of Cambridge and Lynde Streets. It is now the Headquarters of the Society for the Preservation of New England Antiquities. The second mansion designed for Otis by Bulfinch was built in 1802 on Mount Vernon Street — a superb brick building with white classic trim, set back from the street about thirty feet with a cobblestone carriageway into the yard. Bulfinch gave all the windows stone lintels and slat blinds and ornamented the two upper stories with white wooden pilasters. The four long sash windows on the front open on to wrought-iron balconies of fretwork design, the motif of which shows Chinese influence.

On the roof there is a chamfered cupola, and also a roof rail above the cornice. This handsome and unusual architectural touch became a common adoption among sea captains and merchants who watched their sailing vessels leave port, and return, from their rooftop observation posts.

The third, and last, magnificent mansion designed for Otis by Bulfinch is illustrated here. It was built in 1806 on Beacon Street, facing the Common. Otis occupied the mansion for forty years until his death in 1848. Otis entertained lavishly at 45 Beacon Street and received many prominent people. President Monroe had Thanksgiving dinner here in 1817.

The original stable is still in the yard, reached by a cobblestone driveway; there are trees also which cast their cool shadows across the fine arched doors of the stable, designed with a flair, giving unexpected emphasis to small details. In the mansion, Bulfinch ordered stone lintels over the windows on the upper floors, and cornices of wood above the long sash windows of the drawing room on the second. The windows open onto wrought-iron balconies with fret details similar to those installed in the second Otis mansion, differing in one respect — the same motif is repeated in the railings along the street and above the entrance-porch roof.

The American Meteorological Society occupies the mansion today. The exterior is basically the same in appearance as the day the mansion was built except for the absence of the bow-end on the east side, removed in 1831 when Otis built a house for his daughter on the garden plot just east of the mansion. The interior of the building, however, has been altered severely, thereby losing much of the original design and charm.

Bulfinch's third mansion for Harrison Gray Otis — 45 Beacon Street, Boston

Old North Church

BOSTON

Christ Church, better known as the "Old North Church," was designed after the manner of Sir Christopher Wren. It is the oldest church building in Boston, a simplified American interpretation of the English Georgian style built by James Varney and Ebenezer Clough, masons, in 1723. The congregation was organized when King's Chapel was unable to accommodate all those who desired to worship in the Church of England.

The signal lanterns of Paul Revere, displayed from the steeple on April 18, 1775, warned the country that the British troops were on the march to Lexington and Concord.

The Old North Church has survived an incredibly weird series of attempts by the elements to remove it from the roster of our great Colonial shrines. In 1804 the steeple above the lantern windows was blown down; it was rebuilt in 1806 to a height of 175 feet. Further repairs were made in 1834, but thirteen years later the wooden sector was lowered away and replaced on a brick tower.

The Old North Church was to be further plagued when fire damaged the steeple in 1853. The descendants of Paul Revere restored the steeple in 1912. When Hurricane Carol swept across Boston August 31, 1954, the entire wooden steeple of the church was toppled. A new steeple was erected the following year to its original height of 190 feet.

Paul Revere, at the age of fifteen, assisted in organizing a guild to ring the eight bells which were cast in Gloucester, England, and hung in the church in 1744. They were the first bells cast for the British Empire in North America, and still peal before Sunday morning services.

Paul Revere's eldest son owned Pew 54, and in all probability it was also used by Paul Revere. General Thomas Gage, Governor of Massachusetts Bay Colony, occupied Pew 62 and it is said that he witnessed the Battle of Bunker Hill from the church steeple.

The "Vinegar Bible" and the Prayer Book, both of which were printed in 1717, and the communion service which included two flagons, chalice, paten and alms basin, were given to the church by King George II in 1733.

Over one thousand people are buried in tombs under the church, among them the first rector of Christ Church, the Reverend Timothy Cutler, D.D., and Commodore Samuel Nicholson, the first commander of the U.S. Frigate *Constitution*.

In a niche, framed by the window through which sexton Robert Newman made his escape after displaying the lanterns as directed by Paul Revere, there is a bust of George Washington modeled from a plaster bust made by Christian Gulliver

The Old North Church, Boston, from Revere Mall

29

in 1790. When General Lafayette visited the church in 1824 he remarked that the likeness of General Washington was "more like him than any other portrait."

Copp's Hill is a short distance from Old North Church, commanding a sweeping view of the harbor and the Bunker Hill Monument on Breed's Hill, Charlestown, where the so-called Battle of Bunker Hill was fought on June 17, 1775. Copp's Hill was named after William Copp, a shoemaker from Stratford-on-Avon, England, who had his house on the hill. Copp's Hill was sometimes called Mill Field because of the windmill erected there in 1634, the first mill in Boston used for grinding corn.

As early as 1631 the Charlestown ferry carried the colonists across the Charles River from the foot of Copp's Hill. Paul Revere rowed from here to Charlestown to begin his famous ride.

Hull Street, which runs beside Copp's Hill, was named for John Hull, the Colonial silversmith, who with Robert Sanderson made the Pine Tree Shillings in 1652 — the first silver coins authorized in New England by the General Court. The dies were designed by Joseph Jenks, of Lynn, New England's first ironfounder.

For the most part, Copp's Hill is cloaked in solemnity. There are more than 225 tombs in this ancient burial ground, the first of which were built in 1717; and the earliest interment recorded was about 1660. The Reverend Doctors Increase, Cotton, and Samuel Mather are buried in one tomb; others here are Robert Newman, sexton of Christ Church, who displayed the lanterns at Revere's orders, and Daniel Malcolm, patriot, who wished to be buried ten feet deep to be safe from British musketballs. Six years after he died British soldiers used his tombstone for a target. The bullet marks plainly show; they have not been erased by the erosion of time and weather.

The British placed heavy guns on Copp's Hill and it is said that these guns started the devastating fire in Charlestown. Generals Clinton and Burgoyne watched the Battle of Bunker Hill from Copp's Hill, from which they directed the fire of the battery.

Near the location of Hartt's Shipyard, where the U.S. Frigate *Constitution* was launched October 21, 1797, she now lies docked at the United States Navy Yard — a living symbol of our young nation's protector during one of its most critical periods. "Old Ironsides" helped clear our coast and the West Indies of French privateers in 1798. During the War of 1812 she sunk the frigates *Guerrière* and *Java* and captured the corvette *Cyane* and the sloop *Levante*. Between 1803 and 1805, "Old Ironsides" brought the Barbary States to terms by softening up the forts at Tripoli, thereby forcing them to accept a dictated peace without tribute.

When "Old Ironsides" was condemned to be broken up in 1830, Oliver Wendell Holmes wrote "Old Ironsides," which aroused such indignation that money was appropriated in 1833 for the rebuilding of the frigate. In recent times the frigate underwent another overhauling and refitting; about fifteen per cent of her original timbers still remain in the ship. Paul Revere made the copper bolts and fittings; the heavier part of the battery came from Maryland and Connecticut. The sails were made in the Old Granary where the Park Street Church now stands on Brimstone Corner. (The sobriquet Brimstone Corner remains from the War of 1812, when gunpowder was stored in the church basement.)

The Granary Burying Ground, beside the Park Street Church, was once part of Boston Common. Under a very conspicuous monument lie the bodies of Benjamin Franklin's parents. Paul Revere is also buried here. Other graves contain the remains of General Joseph Ware, Peter Faneuil, John Hancock, James Otis, Samuel Adams, Elisha Brown and John Phillips, Boston's first mayor. The victims of the Boston Massacre are not far from the graves of Chief Justice Samuel Sewall and Mint Master John Hull. Mary Goose, wife of Isaac Goose, reposes here too; it is said that she wrote the nursery rhymes for her grandchildren.

In the Park Street Church, "America" was first publicly sung at a children's celebration on July 4, 1831. On another July Fourth, in 1829, William Lloyd Garrison gave his first impassioned address in Boston against slavery.

Harvard College

CAMBRIDGE

My acquaintance with Harvard University is purely peripheral; for many years I passed Harvard on my way to a loft building on Brattle Street where I printed my intaglio etching plates.

I made a habit of going to Cambridge from Boston by subway. The ride underground is brief, and for a short time the train rolls along above ground in the sunshine, while crossing the Charles River, then plunges back into the tunnel before coming to a halt under Harvard Square — the station name in white tile on a large oblong of crimson tile simply reads HARVARD, without fanfare or further publicity.

The short walk from the subway kiosk to Brattle Street is never devoid of fascination; habitually, I always take a last fleeting glance back toward Harvard in the distance.

Harvard Square is not really a square, but a misshapen triangle. The longest side of the triangle is formed by Massachusetts Avenue, which for some distance curves along the western contour of the Yard — the oldest part of Harvard, surrounded by a brick wall. The other two sides contain a strange assortment of small stores, eating places, Harvard offices and specialty shops; collectively they serve the needs of the public in the commingling communities of Cambridge and Harvard, but row after row of ugly nondescript buildings in a Colonial town should have been more conforming and architecturally tasteful.

Students streaming across the streets from the yard mercilessly hold up traffic until all have crossed the Square where boys and girls from Harvard and Radcliffe are joined by students from two nearby high schools, but the motorcars and students on bicycles are such a formidable avalanche that the lone pedestrian has little desire to step off the curb when the light is against him.

It is hard to believe that Cambridge was ever quiet — that there was a time when Lowell, Holmes and Longfellow found the shaded streets of Cambridge conducive for a leisurely stroll and scholars talked shop wherever they chanced to meet, threatened by nothing more dangerous than a runaway horse — until one enters the Yard.

Harvard Yard is the antithesis of Harvard Square. The tree-studded yard is shaded, quiet and idyllic in atmosphere and filled with old buildings and many Victorian examples. Widener Library, Memorial Church and all the other buildings within the Yard are reached by walks that cross and recross in severe geometrical patterns, traversed by students, professors and visitors — including a generous quota of young brides pushing their progeny before them in carriages, or heading for the steps of various buildings just to sit or chat in the flickering shadows.

I selected University Hall, the ivy-covered administration building in the center of the Yard, as my choice to represent Harvard in this book. It is a superb example of Charles Bulfinch's genius — the only building in the Yard by this famous son of Boston. Its charms outweigh those of the Victorian and other buildings, whose presence in the Yard couldn't have been the result of serious concern for architectural conformity.

The bronze statue of John Harvard by Daniel Chester French is a splendid imaginative work — a fabricated likeness of a seventeenth-century young man, since no authentic portrait exists.

Across the Old Yard is Massachusetts Hall, built in 1720, which now houses the offices of the President and Fellows of the University. The first building in the yard, now gone, was erected in 1637, and there the first Commencement took place in 1642.

The college was a courageous undertaking for so small a colony. Sir Harry Vane, Governor of the Colony, in October 28, 1636, announced that the General Court of the Colony agreed to give £400 towards a school or college — "£200 shall be paid the following year and an equal amount when the work was completed." The unanimous choice for the location of the college was at Newtowne, later renamed Cambridge.

John Harvard (1607–1638) was an obscure scholar but left an imperishable legacy by bequeathing the College half of his estate (which amounted to £780) and a library of 320 volumes. John Harvard was born in Southwark, England and received his M.A. from Emmanuel College, Cambridge, England, 1635. He

University Hall, Harvard, with Daniel Chester French's statue of John Harvard

migrated to Charlestown, Massachusetts, in 1637 to become a teaching elder and an assistant to the pastor of the First Church. The General Court in 1638 acknowledged Harvard's gift by appropriately naming the College at Cambridge after him.

Harvard has operated longer than any other institution of higher learning in the United States. The College of William and Mary, founded at Williamsburg, Virginia, in 1693, is second oldest, and Yale University, established in 1701, is third.

The graduates of Harvard in its early years were mostly ministers, but many infiltrated other fields with their skills — some became royal governors, merchant princes and members of Parliament.

General Gage of the American Revolution assailed Harvard College as a "nest of sedition." He couldn't have been more correct. The honored gentlemen who wore the label of Gage's allegations with pride included James Otis, Samuel Adams, John Adams, and John Hancock. Cambridge, on the other hand, was also the seat of the leading Tories.

A succession of heated debates over Revolutionary matters eventually created a resolution setting forth the desires of Cambridge's Patriot townsmen at a town meeting in 1773 to join at short notice with Boston and other towns. That chance arrived quickly. On September 2, 1774, several thousand men gathered on Cambridge Common and proceeded in an orderly manner up Brattle Street to the house of the Lieutenant Governor of the Province, Thomas Oliver, to force the resignation of two of His Majesty's privy councilors, and also to receive the resignation of Oliver himself. Outside waited the thousands of inspired Patriots whose presence hastened his signature, but it was not given without disgruntled protestations.

The first and second of the Provincial Congresses met in Cambridge.

The running battle of April 19, 1775, swept from Concord through the borders of Cambridge, and the patriots who followed the British on their retreat spent the evening of April 19 resting with their arms on Cambridge Common.

For almost a year after the Concord skirmish, Cambridge was a fortified camp. The College buildings, Christ Church and the larger homes were requisitioned as barracks.

General Ward occupied the house that later became the birthplace of Oliver Wendell Holmes. Ward made it his headquarters, where on the lawn, Prescott's men were drawn up before marching to Bunker Hill to receive the blessings of President Langdon of the College, in cap and gown, who prayed for their success.

George Washington reached the camp two weeks later, July 3, and standing under the "Washington Elm," today marked by a plaque, at the western end of the Common, took command of the Continental Army. Washington lived in President Langdon's house for a time and subsequently made his headquarters in the Vassal mansion, later the home of Longfellow.

With the evacuation of Boston by the British after March 1776, Cambridge ceased to be involved in military events of the Revolution with the exception of a massive influx in 1777 of prisoners from Burgoyne's vanquished army. They were quartered in the Harvard buildings, where they swung in their hammocks while Burgoyne lived in style in Cambridge Town.

Lexington Green

If they want war, let it begin here. These words, attributed to Captain John Parker, are inscribed on a marker on Lexington Green. They were spoken early in the morning of April 19, 1775, to a little band in homespuns and poorly disciplined — a ragged company of seventy men drawn up on the green and wheeled into line in the path of the smartly dressed British Regulars, of whose coming they had been warned. Captain Parker ordered each man to load his piece with powder and ball, and impressed on each, "Don't fire, unless fired upon; but if they want war, let it begin here."

In face of the approaching Regulars, a few Americans spoke of dropping out, whereupon Captain Parker replied, "I will order the first man shot dead that leaves his place."

The English commander cried out, "Disperse, you rebels! Lay down your arms and disperse!" Not a man stirred. The command was repeated, still the men did not stir. Then Major Pitcairn ordered the vanguard to fire over the heads of the Patriots, whereupon the whole main body leveled their pieces and fired. A few Patriots returned the shots; from somewhere behind a fence a shot hit Pitcairn's horse, throwing the major to the ground. The ruffled British fired back and the "battle" of Lexington was over in less than a half-hour. On the green lay seven Patriots killed and nine wounded — almost a quarter of those who stood in arms early that morning under the eyes of John Hancock and Samuel Adams.

Samuel Adams, who agitated consistently for the Revolution, said of what happened on Lexington green, "Oh! What a glorious morning is this!" At long last his mission was accomplished. A short distance from the green stands the Hancock-Clark House where John Hancock and Samuel Adams slept on the night of the eighteenth of April until awakened by Paul Revere.

It is interesting, by the way, to note how many of the Munro clan, captured by Cromwell more than a century before and exiled for their loyalty to the Stuarts, turned up as Lexington farmer-patriots to face the hirelings of the House of Hanover. Ensign Roberts, one of the Munro clan, was first to be killed by Pitcairn's volley. He had been color-bearer in the capture of Louisbourg in 1745. Two of Roberts's sons and two sons-in-law were on Lexington Green facing the British.

In all, eleven of the Munro clan stood there in arms that morning after convening with the other patriots at the Buckman Tavern (which is still standing).

The Jonathan Harrington house with its Georgian doorway, overlooking the Green, appears today much as it did that April morning of 1775 when Harrington dragged himself across the Green to his home and died at his wife's feet from his wounds.

During the winter that preceded the fateful spring of 1775, a considerable store of arms and ammunition had been gathered at Concord by the patriots, only seventeen miles outside of Boston. Only a few men were entrusted with the secret, but someone betrayed the Patriots, for word of it was carried to General Gage.

It is relatively certain now that his informant was Dr. Benjamin Church, who, while holding a position of trust in the confidence of the patriots, was also playing the role of informant for the British.

Gage laid his plans with great pains just before the fourteenth of April, and only two people beside Gage knew of them: Lord Percy and his wife. Colonel Smith was to command the raiding party, with Major Pitcairn as second-in-command, both of whom were unaware of the objective until almost the moment of their departure from Boston.

Colonel Smith with 800 men embarked in transport boats from the Back Bay at the foot of Boston Common, crossed over to Cambridge before dawn, and marched immediately to Lexington.

For the time being, Lord Percy was to remain in Boston with the reserves to await orders and be ready to march by way of Roxbury Neck, taking a route which in a roundabout way passed through Cambridge, if his support was necessary.

The Patriots acquired, in some manner, information that betrayed Gage's closely guarded plans. Legend has it that Lady Percy, an American, was the informer; but it is worth noting that this story was circulated by those under the command of Percy, for whom his men had sparse admiration. Dr. Joseph Warren, chief of the Liberty Boys in Boston, had heard early in April that Gage intended to send an expedition to capture the stores at Concord and arrest Hancock and Adams.

When Gage's plans were readied for execution, Dr. Warren sent William Dawes off on horseback over the back roads to Lexington to give the alarm throughout the countryside and to warn Hancock and Adams, then he sent Paul Revere on the same mission to make sure someone would get through. Revere was captured after warning Hancock and Adams, but later he was released.

The bronze statue of the minuteman at the head of Lexington green speaks eloquently for itself. Sculptor Henry Hudson Kitson's use of stones from the walls found along the country roads is appropriate and fitting for the base of this spirited work.

PHILIP KAPPEL

The Lexington Minuteman

Concord Bridge

CONCORD

Here once the embattled farmers stood,
And fired the shot heard round the world.
— RALPH WALDO EMERSON

A Puritan minister, the Rev. Peter Bulkeley from Bedfordshire, England, and Simon Willard, a tradesman from Kent, England, received from Winthrop and his legislature, in September 1635, the grant to found Concord.

Twelve other families joined them in the grant, and the Rev. John Jones brought a number of families across the sea to Concord a month later. Rev. Peter Bulkeley (an ancestor of Concord's most illustrious citizen, Ralph Waldo Emerson) left the lovely Bedfordshire countryside when he was fifty-two, rather late in life to face the unforeseen in a new land, but the ecclesiastical tyranny of William Laud and his bishops he could no longer tolerate and he decided to establish in the new world a true church of God. His efforts met with exasperating problems from the start. When he attempted to organize his church at Cambridge in July 1636 he expected the presence of Sir Henry Vane and John Winthrop at his ordination (Vane was governor that year, and Winthrop the deputy governor); both boycotted him on grounds of his oversight of minor details in procedure and prior notification of his intentions.

A second rebuff to Bulkeley came the following year. Winthrop's explanations broadly hinted that Bulkeley's principle brought back the ghosts of Wheelwright and Mrs. Hutchinson; nothing could have been more condemning to Bulkeley. Nevertheless he was finally ordained at the height of the controversy between John Cotton and his former supporters, Wheelwright and Vane, who came close to breaking up the little colony.

It is in Concord, and indeed all New England, that history reminds us that democracy was brought about through Calvinism in spite of all the reactionary ministers and recalcitrants who were blind to man's ultimate emergence into his new role and legacy.

Concord braced itself in 1774 for the consequences of the Boston Tea Party, and Parliament's passage of the Boston Port Bill — everyone felt the mordancy of the inevitable clash with England. They banded together but the situation was further provoked by Colonial resistance to the importation of British goods.

In their hearts the Patriots hoped for and strove for legal solutions even as the dark clouds of war were gathering. The Second Provincial Congress of 1775 met

Concord Bridge — across the river is the monument to the British dead

in Concord for four weeks with high purpose during March and April; it had adjourned only four days before the British marched on Lexington from Boston under cover of night to trap John Hancock and Samuel Adams and then go on to Concord to destroy the Colonial military supplies.

"The fate of a nation was riding that night," wrote Longfellow of Paul Revere's ride. Paul Revere's part in the episode became one of America's best-known legends, though his fellow riders, Dawes and Prescott, became lost in obscurity. Revere was one of the leaders of the Boston Tea Party, but one of his earliest military acts of the Revolution, about which little is circulated, occurred in December of 1774, when as official courier of the Massachusetts Assembly he persuaded the patriots of Portsmouth, New Hampshire, to seize the British military supplies in the town.

Samuel Adams and John Hancock, who attended the Provincial Congress in Concord, were in Lexington sleeping in the parsonage of the Rev. Mr. Clark, a relation of Hancock, and were almost caught by the British soldiers.

The Redcoats, led by Pitcairn, spent a brief half-hour at Lexington, then were on their way to Concord. As they neared the town they heard the church bells ringing out the alarm. From all the small towns lying along the Concord and Merrimack rivers the patriots were pouring into the approaches to Concord Bridge, well in advance of Pitcairn's arrival.

In that morning battle, 273 men and officers were lost by the British, more than at Quebec where Wolfe died in the midst of triumph, and the minutemen lost 91 in the British rout that ushered in the Revolution.

Concord Bridge became a symbol of the American Revolution, but Concord acquired another image, one of a cultural character. Sixty years after the British flight from Concord a fraternal renascence in literature replaced the horrors of war.

Emerson in 1836 brought out his first philosophical work which was written at the Old Manse, now a historic shrine. Emerson's residence in Concord was fixed by ancestry, but Thoreau, Hawthorne, Alcott, and Channing were in Concord because of personal choice or as friends of Emerson.

Intellectuals, moralists, nonconformists and those who believed they had solved the riddle of life itself became linked with the literary complex in Concord. If our political growth was fostered by such men as Franklin, the Adamses, Jefferson and Washington, it is reasonably certain that the literary folk of Concord proclaimed and founded American literary maturity.

Early Puritan thinking was not a favorable climate for intellectual fortitude or experimentation. The Puritans and Pilgrims were too involved with making a foothold on a new continent to think of much besides church and survival. Life was narrowed and confined by rigid church laws, heresy-seeking eavesdropping and for a time even witchcraft, public punishment and dozens of restrictions to prevent the releasing of the full flowering of thought and imaginative literary thinking.

Bronson Alcott's mystic brilliance was too intense to sit mired down in complacency without the freedom to exercise his intellectual gifts and philosophies. When he was eighty he made his divine experiment — transcendentalism — at the Concord School of Philosophy, which brought into its fold disciples many of whom had already brought to Concord literary fame of the first magnitude.

At "Fruitlands," Clara Endicott Sears has restored the early eighteenth-century farmhouse on Prospect Hill at Harvard, Massachusetts, where Bronson Alcott tried to establish in 1843 a community under a new social order known as the Consociate Family, as a museum of the Transcendentalist Movement. It contains memorabilia of the leaders of the movement — Alcott, Emerson, Thoreau, Margaret Fuller and others — and furnishings and possessions of the Alcott family, including Louisa May Alcott. The restored colonial kitchen indicates the manner of living in the early period of the house.

Walden Pond, celebrated by Henry David Thoreau, is one and a half miles south of the village of Concord. Near Monument Square stands the Colonial Inn, where Thoreau once lived. *Little Women* was written by Louisa Alcott at Orchard House. And nothing matches the appeal of the purple Concord grape, originated at the vineyard of Ephraim Bull, the horticulturist, in 1849.

But when evening closes in with its chilling mists on the Concord River, the famed replica of Concord Bridge, and the bronze minuteman facing the simple monument on the far shore where the British stood and challenged the men in homespuns, all this becomes a shrouded symbol returned to the night — haunting, though, with all the latitude of the imagination and the fulfillment of pride that momentarily goes to rest.

Gore Place

WALTHAM

Christopher Gore, lawyer, diplomat and Governor of Massachusetts in 1809 and 1810, was born in 1758; he graduated from Harvard at seventeen in 1776, he later prepared for the legal profession and in 1789 became the first United States Attorney for Massachusetts — he also served in the commission under Jay's Treaty to settle claims from 1796 to 1804, and acted as chargé d'affaires for the American

Embassy at the Court of St. James's from 1802 to 1803. During his stay in London he traveled extensively on the Continent where he was accepted in the best circles. He returned to Boston in 1804 to resume his law practice. In his office Daniel Webster was once a clerk.

After his term as governor, Gore returned to Waltham to enjoy private life. In 1813 he reentered public service to fill a vacancy in the United States Senate for three years, retired again — this time in poor health — and died in 1827. He is buried in the Granary Burying Ground, next to the Park Street Church.

Gore was a gentleman of taste and a scholar, and he came by the amenities naturally. His leanings toward sophisticated society were matched by his tremendous wealth, and his predilection for good living on the grand scale resulted in the building of a princely country mansion in Waltham, on forty acres acquired in 1786.

Gore's holdings eventually grew to four hundred acres, more or less, part of which he farmed; the property extended south to the Charles River. The original mansion, built of wood, burned in 1799; and the present brick mansion was planned while the Gores were in Europe. With the assistance of Monsieur Legrand, a French architect, construction of the mansion was begun in 1805. Gore was influenced by English landscaping and employed the services of Humphry Repton, the leading and most popular English landscape architect of the day. Repton stressed the importance of open rolling fields, large trees in masses and reflecting ponds, while other landscape architects remained adherents of the classical treatment and formal gardens which Repton disdained. Gore faithfully confined his landscaping to the original forty acres around the mansion, and evidence of the master plan is visible today.

In style, scale and scope, Gore Place is unmistakably in the Regency, or Adam, manner, which is consistent throughout in the furnishings and the rooms used for entertaining, but the family rooms are delightfully intimate.

Gore Place is one of the most impressive restorations in New England. The circular staircase leading up from the marble-floored entrance hall is the finest I have seen, with the exception of the staircase in Houmas House at Burnside, Louisiana. Another noteworthy item in Gore Place is the elaborate chandelier in the state dining room, which came from the later law offices of orator Daniel Webster.

Gore Place, Waltham

Lyman House

WALTHAM

Beyond Gore Place, off to the right, is the Lyman House, or The Vale, a sizable, handsome white house, impressively reflected in a body of water nearby. The imposing grace of this sylvan setting has been with us since 1795.

One should never undervalue the importance of the surroundings of a fine house, which a good designer ideally always incorporates in his general plan. The Lymans knew what they wanted, and they secured the services of the celebrated Samuel McIntire, who was never known to work so far from Salem. His work in the Lyman House is superb and equal to the best. Of particular merit is Mc-Intire's carving in the ballroom. Also of special interest is the bow parlor, which contains some very rare McIntire furniture, lending authentic dignity to the room. McIntire must have been carried away with his assignment to have so painstakingly wedded the furnishings and the house into one harmonious whole.

There is much more to the Lyman House than the house itself; there is also a McIntire stable and charming greenhouses. The old trees are gnarled and their sprawling roots trip the unwary; everything is oversize with age. The delightful old brick wall, with its unusual summer porch, delicate columns, and door that allows convenient access to the woods, is truly handsome.

The gentleman in the drawing is Alexander Williams, without whose assistance and acquaintanceship with the area, I might have never seen the Lyman House. Alex told me that the greenhouses were the first of their kind in North America. Also, the first rare varieties of grapes were grown here and persevered through the years, and a limited quantity of grapes is still sold each year to a waiting list of purchasers.

The greenhouses have their original oven-like niches in the basements where wood was burned to maintain the proper temperature during the cold months. Row after row of the "ovens" must have kept the men busy stoking them — a delicate task before the coming of thermostats.

In its entirety, the Lyman House is eminently suited to a scale of living which our generation seldom finds necessary — or possible — to emulate.

The old garden wall at Lyman House, Waltham

The Witch House

SALEM

Sometimes a myth is more persistent than the truth. At least this happens to be so in the case of those who, they say, were burned as witches in Salem in the seventeenth century, for the truth is that the witches were never burned at the stake — they were hanged on Gallows Hill after being tried and convicted according to the regular court procedure of the time. Over 150 persons were arrested and charged with witchcraft up to and including 1692.

Witchcraft in the seventeenth century was treated as an offense as serious as treason, a crime whose punishment was prescribed in the Bible — "Thou shalt not suffer a witch to live" (Exodus 22:18) — and the Colonists accepted the Bible verbatim. To deny the existence of witchcraft and sorcery was tantamount to contradicting the word of God.

The first execution for witchcraft in the Colonies took place in Boston in 1646, and in 1648 two persons were executed in Connecticut. But the more tolerant Legislature of Rhode Island voted in 1647 to outlaw witchcraft trials, and the Pilgrims in the Plymouth Plantation never executed anyone for witchcraft.

Due to pressure from enlightened people the belief in witchcraft began to wane by 1693 in Salem. Nathaniel Saltonstall, who was one of the original Salem judges at the witch trials, resigned from the bench on this account. So fantastic were the accusations against the victims — and equally preposterous were the rules of evidence applied — that the Massachusetts General Court designated January 14, 1697, as a fast day to expiate the senseless travesty of justice. On that day Judge Sewall stood up in the Old South Meeting House in Boston while the pastor read his confession of guilt and error.

In 1711, as a consolation, 479 pounds was paid out by Massachusetts to the heirs of those condemned and the rights of citizenship restored, if requested. The British Parliament on March 24, 1734, repealed the statutes against witchcraft and the American Colonies gradually followed suit.

In 1948 the city of Salem acquired the Witch House property, removed the commercial additions and restored the building completely, and then leased it to an association called Historic Salem, Inc., which presently operates it as a museum to which the public is admitted for a fee.

The preliminary witchcraft trials are said to have been held in the Witch House, which was built before 1675. Jonathan Corwin, one of the judges of the witchcraft court, lived in the house; among the Corwin papers in possession of the Essex Institute is the original contract for finishing the house in 1674-1675,

PHILIP KAPPEL

The Witch House, Salem

at which time the chimneys were taken down and the building was remodeled. The building still retains the overhanging second story, and within is the great chimney which measures twelve by eight feet on the first floor.

Near the Witch House is the First Church Meeting House, and a small portion of its tower shows above a clump of trees in the drawing. This church was dedicated in 1836 and was built of the famous Quincy granite in the Early English Gothic style. It is the fifth place of worship of the First Church — the first four were located at the southeast corner of Washington and Essex Streets (they were built in 1634, 1672, 1718 and 1826, respectively).

The First Congregational Society gathered on August 6, 1629 — first of the order in America to gather formally. The Reverend Francis Higginson and the Reverend Samuel Skelton were ordained as Teacher and Pastor on July 20, 1629. Governor Endicott and the ministers greeted Governor Bradford and Dr. Fuller, who arrived in Salem from Plymouth late in the day to give the "Right Hand of Fellowship," an ancient Biblical phrase used to the present time in welcoming new members.

Shortly after Roger Williams arrived in Boston on February 1631, he accepted the position of Teacher after Mr. Higginson's death. Williams later left for Plymouth, returning to Salem in 1633. After Mr. Skelton's death he was installed as minister in the spring of 1635, but Williams was too caustic to gain friends. His extreme separation and intemperate attacks on the churches and government, finally led to his banishment from the colony by the General Court in September 1635. He escaped arrest by the magistrates in Boston by fleeing from Salem in January 1636 into the winter wilderness in Rhode Island, where he cooled off and became more tolerant, liberal and understanding.

The First Church united with the North Church in Salem in 1923; the North Society gave up its organization and the First Society moved into the building of the North Society on Essex Street near the Witch House, which united two of the oldest churches of Salem. The First Church, which was originally Trinitarian Congregational, is now Unitarian.

The Ropes Memorial
SALEM

The story of Salem isn't entirely told in words. More absorbing than words are the surviving old homes that are inextricably tied in with the history of Salem, thereby becoming an integral part of the history of New England, and America itself.

The Ropes mansion on Essex Street, just west of the old Witch House and the gray stone First Church, is among many notable houses in the area. The

The Ropes Memorial, Salem

49

Ropes mansion is especially impressive as it stands back from the street behind an elaborate wooden fence flanking a brick walk.

The Ropes Memorial is maintained by a Trust under the will of the last of the Ropes owners, which made available to the public one of the most outstanding homes in Salem — an example of the home of a well-to-do family in the eighteenth century. The house and gardens are open to the public on designated days.

The house was built about 1719 and purchased by Judge Nathaniel Ropes in 1768, and it remained in possession of the Ropes family in direct line until 1907. Judge Ropes was a staunch Loyalist, which prompted a mob of patriots on March 17, 1774, to attack his home.

The contents of the house as we see them today were owned by the Judge and his descendants; they include family portraits, old china, documents, costumes and an abundance of furniture of about 1750–1840, all of which are preserved in their original setting. One of the most noteworthy items in the Ropes mansion is the double set of choice tableware and beautiful glass imported in 1816 for the wedding outfit of Sally Ropes, who married her cousin Joseph Orne, a member of one of Salem's distinguished merchant families.

The garden in the rear of the mansion is laid out in the old formal manner, with shrubs around the borders and clumps of brilliant flowers in the central beds. The lawns at each side are shaded by old trees. Botanical lectures are given during the months of January and February by prominent instructors, a service maintained by a special fund under the terms of the will.

The Custom House

SALEM

The name Salem has a romantic ring. It conjures up a picture of moored sailing vessels, sea captains and merchant princes; of hogsheads of foreign goods on wharves and capacious warehouses pungent with strange smells and the more commonplace odors of spices, molasses, rum and hemp.

There are few American cities in which it is so easy to feel the influence of the past — you are surrounded by it wherever you roam in Salem, justly called "the museum city." In a quiet way Salem is strangely reminiscent of both her romantic golden era of commerce and her Calvinistic background and ideals; the ruggedness of her founders and their dreams.

Other cities along the Atlantic seaboard also have imposing brick Federal mansions, and wooden houses built in the seventeenth century, but Salem is overwhelmingly blessed with houses containing their original furnishings and decora-

The old Custom House on Derby Street, Salem

tions, imported by sea captains and wealthy merchant princes during the heyday of Yankee shipping. Furthermore, Salem has a monopoly of Samuel McIntire's work.

Samuel McIntire was born in Salem in 1757, the son of a carpenter and joiner in whose workshop Samuel learned his trade step by step. At the age of twenty-five the young McIntire achieved one of his greatest works, the Peirce-Nichols House — the finest wooden house in New England, without question. For a period of thirty years afterward his genius dominated Salem architecture.

The demand for McIntire's work was largely instigated by the flow of wealth into Salem from the sailing vessels whose cargoes were unloaded within sight of the Custom House which looks down upon Derby Wharf. The cacophony of haggling sailors, working winches, and boisterous inquisitive boys collecting on the wharf, transformed the area into picturesque turmoil with the arrival of every ship. Added to all that were scurrying shipowners and captains going to and from the custom house, attending to the serious business of clearing ships in whose holds foreign goods had lain for months, sometimes for years.

The customary Salem method of making a trading voyage was to start off with an assorted cargo, assembled from Southern ports, the West Indies, the Baltic and New England, then peddle it off at the Cape of Good Hope, Mauritius and ports in the East Indies. Putting aboard freight when the occasion arose and picking up oddments and purchasing bills of exchange on Amsterdam or London, making as many as three or four turnovers before embarking for home, a ship clearing from Salem around 1790 was likely to have aboard salt fish, soap, gin, ale, hams, flints, whale oil, lard, flour, and tobacco, also saddles and bridles, desks and chairs — all disposed of by shipmasters with full discretionary liberty to deal with them.

The old Custom House was erected in 1819. Here Nathaniel Hawthorne worked as Surveyor of the Port of Salem from 1846 to 1849. Today, the Custom House is part of the Salem Maritime National Historic Site, founded in 1938. Upon this site formerly stood the home of George Crowninshield, father of Benjamin Crowninshield, member of Congress and Secretary of the Navy, and Jacob Crowninshield, who became a member of Congress but declined the offer of the Navy portfolio.

Hawthorne occupied the southwestern front room on the lower floor. His desk is here, and the stencil with which he marked the goods he inspected with "N Hawthorne." In the introduction of The Scarlet Letter many of the characters and scenes associated with the Custom House became living realities and are still frequently inquired for. He had a way of using local names to fit his characters and often purloined names on gravestones — that of Dr. Swinnerton is on a stone in the Charter Street burial ground; the names of Judge Pyncheon and Jervase Helwyse he plucked from the branches of his own family tree.

The room in the rear of the collector's private office on the second floor, where

Hawthorne says the scarlet letter was found, was in his time a vacant room filled with sundry old papers. The pre-Revolutionary records are missing, mysteriously destroyed — possibly in the fire of October 6, 1774, which burned down the building formerly used as the custom house elsewhere in Salem.

Dr. Nathaniel Bowditch, whose name is closely associated with the Custom House, rose to international fame as a mathematician. *The American Practical Navigator,* first published by him in 1802, is still the standard work in navigation. For many years Bowditch was an official of the East India Marine Society, which founded a museum in 1799, later endowed by George Peabody in 1867, and named for him. After the death of Bowditch in 1838, the Museum inherited his valuable personal material.

At the head of the inlet between Central and Derby wharves, facing the harbor, stands a large ivy-covered brick house which formerly was the residence of Benjamin Crowninshield; it was built from designs made by McIntire, in 1811. It is situated just west of the Custom House on Derby Street.

General James Miller, the hero of Lundy's Lane, lived here at one time. William C. Endicott, Secretary of War under Cleveland, was born in the house. President Monroe was entertained here in 1817 by Benjamin Crowninshield. Today, the old mansion serves as a home for elderly ladies.

The Hawkes House, attractively situated on a plot just east of the Custom House, was designed by McIntire for Elias Derby. For some reason, this frame house, for which the ground was broken in 1780, remained unfinished until it was purchased in 1801 by Captain Benjamin Hawkes, shipbuilder and merchant.

Next door to the Hawkes House is Salem's oldest brick building. Captain Richard Derby had it built in 1761–1762 for his son, Elias Hasket Derby, who moved into the house after his marriage in 1761. After the Revolution it was occupied by Captain Henry Prince, a master in the Derby Fleet who made the first recorded voyage in an American vessel to Manila, in 1796.

The Derby House contains rare furnishings and other items of the eighteenth century, notably pewter, superb china and furniture from many sources which enhance the extensive restorations. The entrance is crowned by an unusual classic doorway. Throughout the interior superb paneling of quality rivals the intricate and painstaking turning of the stairway balusters, designed in several patterns which disclose the splendor of eighteenth-century Salem craftsmanship.

The Derby House was formerly owned by the Society for the Preservation of New England Antiquities. It was turned over to the Salem Maritime National Historic Site in 1938.

It was Captain John Derby who took the news of Lexington to London in advance of the government in 1775 and at the close of the Revolution brought home from Paris in his ship, *Astrea,* the first news of peace.

Elias Hasket Derby, one of the greatest figures in the development of American foreign trade, prospered from privateering during the Revolution and became one of the first American millionaires. His brig *Grand Turk,* an 18-gunner, took thirty-one English prizes during the War of 1812. Derby sent ships wherever he could find trade — to India, China, Java, Mauritius and the Philippines. His ships were small but suitable for the kind of cargo they carried — tea, spices, silks, ebony, coffee and ivory — which fetched handsome prices at the time our nation was emerging.

The old Custom House, a focal point during all this maritime traffic, still looks down on the long dark wharf named after Elias Hasket Derby, but the bristling masts are gone. The carved eagle on the parapet rail of the Custom House, is still there as the sole witness of those frantically busy years when Salem was a great seaport.

The House of the Seven Gables
SALEM

An object of great tourist attraction in Salem is the House of the Seven Gables on Turner Street, located at the water's edge four streets east of Derby Wharf and the Custom House.

John Turner, a prosperous merchant, built the house in 1668, which to this day wears its historic distinction with graciousness, but it was Nathaniel Hawthorne who immortalized the House of the Seven Gables with his romantic novel of 1852.

The House of the Seven Gables is unquestionably the best documented house in Salem and decidedly the most elastic. Every addition and alteration is easily traced. As various families prospered or fell from grace, the house grew with them or suffered dismemberment. The present rambling austere mansion started in the seventeenth century with four rooms and as many gables, increasing over the years to fourteen rooms and eight gables. In time the house gradually shrank — all its removable gables disappeared, also the lean-to, the overhang and the original central chimney. At the time restoration began in the spring of 1909, the house had only three gables.

When John Turner died in 1679 at the height of his success he was only thirty-six, leaving behind five children and his wife, Elizabeth. She remarried in 1687 but died a short time later. Captain Charles Redford, the widower, about to make a sea voyage, made his last will and testament on April 29, 1691; as his will was probated October 20, 1691, Redford's fears about sea-travel were justified. Redford left four-fifths of his property to the children of John and Elizabeth Turner. Meanwhile John Turner's only son turned twenty-one in 1692 and was made administrator of his father's estate and guardian of his youngest sister, Abial.

The House of the Seven Gables, Salem

He managed his father's business and the estate ably, but the times were darkening — 1692 happened to be Salem's tragic year of the witchcraft delusion.

One theory advanced to explain the secret stairway Turner installed within the original chimney, is that he was anxious for the safety of his sisters and had made the supreme effort to provide a hideout from witch hunters.

In 1701 Turner married Mary Kitchen — the "belle of the village." He left Salem in 1703 to play an aggresive part in the French and Indian War, returned home as a colonel, and became a very successful merchant during Salem's era of prosperity.

Around 1720, John Turner bowed to fashion and ordered numerous changes made to the House of Seven Gables. The removal of the leaded diamond panes of glass, beautifully marked with jeweled irregularities, was a mistake. They were replaced with double hung windows, with square panes separated by wooden mullions, which still adorn the house.

John Turner's death in 1742 and that of his wife in 1769 came at the time when the Turner landholdings were at their maximum. The land around the House of Seven Gables was bounded by Derby, Turner and Hardy streets, exclusive of one small lot. The property across Turner Street consisted of approximately five acres, all of which was inherited by Colonel Turner, the third, a prominent citizen of Salem who had distinguished himself during the Revolution.

In 1782, misfortune overtook Colonel Turner, forcing him to dispose of all his properties, including the House of the Seven Gables. When he died in 1786 he left a hollow inheritance to his son, Edward Kitchen Turner, except the good and honorable name. Edward left no male heirs, and the Turner name, like his father's fortune, became extinct.

The old house changed hands again and fell to Captain Samuel Ingersoll, a prosperous merchant who occasionally sailed his own ships. Most of his great wealth came to him through his wife, Susannah Hawthorne, who was the great-granddaughter of Philip and Mary English. Madam English also lived in the House of Seven Gables; she was frequently visited by the Reverend Dr. Bentley, to whom she related many stories about the hardships suffered during the witchcraft delusion which Bentley carefully entered in his diary — a reliable source of information about the times and the Ingersoll family.

Captain Ingersoll died in 1804 while at sea and the property was left to his wife. After her death in 1811 the estate went to Susannah, their only surviving child. She lived in the House of the Seven Gables all her life as a tragic recluse following an unfortunate love affair with a naval officer who disappeared. Henceforth she closed her doors to all men, except her kinsman, Nathaniel Hawthorne, who was twenty-one years her junior.

Hawthorne continued to visit Miss Ingersoll until she died in 1858, and later saw her "adopted" son, Horace Conolly, inherit the house, upon which he spent a great deal of money, making improvements and apparently matching Miss Ingersoll's attachment for the place. But Horace violated her great secret — his illegitimacy. Unworthy of Miss Ingersoll's deep affection and loyalty, he openly told his friends that he was her son and took the name of Ingersoll, which he thoroughly discredited by embarking on a course of dissipation and getting into deep debt. Finally, he was forced to sell the House of the Seven Gables to pay his debts in 1879, and thereafter he lived by his wits and the charity of friends, eventually dying ignobly in the Salem Almshouse.

In 1883, Henry Upton purchased the house and rescued it from becoming a tenement house. In the process of rebuilding the great chimney — a fire hazard, because it was constructed with clay instead of mortar — workmen discovered the secret stairway, which Upton descended. He came out, to his amazement, in the dining room closet proudly holding a pine tree sixpence and a prayer book he had found. Miss Caroline O. Emmerton visited the house soon after Upton acquired it and on numerous occasions she was permitted to show the house to her friends, never suspecting that in 1908, by a quirk of fate, she would become its proud possessor.

Hawthorne once stated that he had no definite house in mind when he wrote *The House of the Seven Gables,* but his descriptive passages in the novel fit the house exactly, and he spent so much time there that few are willing to accept his denial.

Thanks to the inspired efforts of Miss Emmerton, whose interest in settlement work equaled her love for the preservation of old houses, the House of the Seven Gables was restored half a century ago. She believed that people would gladly pay a small fee to see it once it was restored and filled with period antiques as Hawthorne described it in his novel. Miss Emmerton's civic-minded efforts to make the house pay for itself as an old landmark, and at the same time contribute towards the support of her settlement work, exceeded all expectations.

In the informal courtyard behind the house a group of ancient houses enrich the grounds with their own testimony. The Hathaway House was formerly known as the "Old Bakery" before it was moved from its site on Washington Street where it was built in 1682. Salemites, years ago, carried their beans and brown bread to the bakery, and stopped for them Saturday night or early Sunday morning, ready to eat as soon as they reached home.

The Retire Beckett House was built in 1655 and once stood a quarter of a mile east of the House of Seven Gables. Six generations of Becketts lived in this house, five of them carried on their shipbuilding activities in Salem. Retire Beckett built the first yacht here for George Crowninshield — the brig *Cleopatra's Barge,* in which Crowninshield proposed to sail to St. Helena to rescue Napoleon and bring him to America.

The Beckett shipyards launched ten ships, seven brigs, two brigantines and five schooners besides *Cleopatra's Barge.* The largest of the ships was the *America,* which held the record of never having been outsailed.

The more recent addition to the cluster of seventeenth-century buildings is the gambrel-roofed house in which Nathaniel Hawthorne was born on July 4, 1804, when it stood on Union Street. The house was built prior to the time of the witchcraft delusion; it came into the possession of Hawthorne's grandfather in 1772.

Chestnut Street
SALEM

More than a half-century ago, on June 25, 1914, a disastrous fire started at midday from exploding chemicals in a leather factory in the "Blubber Hollow" district of Salem, near Gallows Hill. The fire cut a swath of destruction two miles long and about three-quarters of a mile in width, until it could go no further before a fickle wind blowing toward the harbor, where the fire died at the water's edge.

If the wind had come from any other quarter the fire would have embossed its seal of doom on most of Salem's priceless areas. Even so, during the height of the fire embers threatened such remote historic places of interest as Derby Wharf, the old Custom House, the Grimshawe House on Charter Street and Nathaniel Hawthorne's birthplace on Union Street. A house at the upper end of Chestnut Street had its roof set afire by flying embers; fortunately, volunteers were able to extinguish the blaze before it got out of hand, and save historic Chestnut Street with its Federalist-style brick houses built at the height of Salem's great era of trade with the Orient.

Chestnut Street was laid out in 1796. Many of its mansions were designed by Samuel McIntire for retired sea captains and merchants. Architecturally, Chestnut Street is, without reservation, one of the most attractive streets in America.

During the seventeenth and eighteenth centuries, Salem turned to the sea and developed a profitable salt fish trade with the West Indies and the Mediterranean before the American Revolution; after the Revolution trade accelerated with Sumatra, India and China. Astronomical fortunes were made in a short time, and beautiful mansions appeared on Washington Square, Essex and Federal Streets about the same time Chestnut Street was developed.

Sentimentally, I am committed to 10 Chestnut Street; this square brick house built in 1804 was where Philip and Lucretia Little lived over fifty years, and to them I am enormously indebted for the introduction to the maritime climate which determined the course of my life's work.

One summer early in the 1920's, I first met Philip Little at Boothbay Harbor, Maine, to which place he made weekly shopping trips by launch from his summer

Spring comes to Chestnut Street, Salem

home on MacMahan Island, eight miles away. He accidentally came upon my small exhibition of drawings hung in the centrally located Chamber of Commerce building. Only the price *tags* were large — the prices were low to effect a quick sale; I was broke.

Philip Little's reputation as a marine painter and etcher was impressive to another artist trying to gain a foothold, and, when I received a note from Philip Little saying how much he liked my work and wanted to meet me, I was ebullient. Subsequently arrangements were made to meet at the town pier, after my teaching assignment terminated at East Boothbay Harbor, for a visit with the Littles.

The Littles were unsympathetic with my teaching arrangements in Maine and offered me the use of their studio on Daniels Street Court in Salem during the summertime, which became my seasonal workshop and home for a score of years.

Next door to 10 Chestnut Street lived Frank Benson, another noted artist, with whom Philip Little conspired to teach me, by association, the "tricks" of their art. Their interest proved to be beyond estimation, and has never gone unappreciated.

Daniels Street Court is hard by Salem Harbor, in the heart of the area which made Salem a great seaport in its heyday. Inspired by its moods and reveling in its historic past, I never worked harder or produced more work. Every summer passed too quickly.

Byron Fellows arrived at the studio frequently. Fellows ran away from home as a boy to go to sea in the days when square-riggers were still vainly trying to compete with steam. He became my mentor in all matters pertaining to the sea and the ships that sailed upon it, and I submitted my work after each voyage to him for final approval. No one cut a deeper path of understanding or earned greater esteem from those whose lives he touched.

On the corner of Chestnut Street and Cambridge, diagonally across the way from the Little House is Hamilton Hall — a portion of the portico is shown in the drawing. Hamilton Hall was designed by Samuel McIntire and built in 1805. It has been the center of much of Salem's social activity, the scene of many assemblies and celebrations. Pickering was entertained at dinner in Hamilton Hall in 1908, Bainbridge in 1813 and Lafayette on August 31, 1824.

Many years ago Philip Little took me on a tour through Hamilton Hall. As we were descending the long flight of stairs that led from the second floor to the first, I noticed a series of large white circles painted on the top step, and a similar treatment accorded the last step. (I have since learned that the circles have been removed.) When I asked the purpose of this unusual feature, Philip Little forthrightly informed me that the circles served as warning signals for those who might have "sipped too long and too much at the punchbowl," alerting them to the impending dangers of a fall when taking the first step into space, the circles on the last step signifying that all was well; a successful landing had been effected.

10 Chestnut Street, Salem — the Little House seen from Hamilton Hall

61

Derby Wharf

SALEM

One of my vividest memories of Salem's waterfront is Derby Wharf, a granite finger jutting out into Salem Harbor straight as an arrow for a distance of 2000 feet, which once beckoned home the great sailing ships belonging to Elias Hasket Derby, in the eighteenth and nineteenth centuries. At the end of the wharf stands a white square tower — rebuilt in 1871 — with a light 25 feet above the water which guides barges and small craft through the silted channel.

In the early 1920's Joseph Hergesheimer's novel *Java Head* was filmed here. Well in advance of the actors and cameras, workmen arrived to transform the wharf into a realistic replica of its greater days, with its warehouses and maritime appurtenances. A sailing ship was towed to Salem and warped to Derby Wharf for added realism and color. When the filming was completed the wharf was returned to its austere nakedness with its surface pockmarked by potholes that filled with water after summer showers. Small boys habitually swarmed over the wharf to daydream or fish. And on very warm days they would capriciously dive into the harbor when someone suddenly shouted, "Last one in is a stinker," and churn the harbor to froth with lashing legs and arms.

Above all, Derby Wharf is for those of us who love its ghosts — the characters who make up the saga of its past, with whom we sail in imagination as supercargo aboard tall ships to trade in strange ports, overpowered by the appeal of those vibrant days long past!

Strange though it may seem, the sailing vessels that nestled close to Derby Wharf were of shallow draft, and after 1850 Salem's ocean commerce declined because larger sailing ships and steamers were unable to navigate the silted shallow channels of the harbor. The wharf area has recently been declared the Salem Maritime National Historic Site; for all time, Uncle Sam assumes the responsibility of keeping a watchful eye on our inheritance.

Just west of Derby Wharf is Central Wharf, which runs parallel to Derby Wharf but is only one-third as long. It was built in 1791–1792 by Simon Forrester, captain of a Derby privateer in the Revolution and a prominent merchant.

The daring menfolk of Salem, during the Revolution, played a major role in the conflict with the British on the high seas; they also fitted out the privateers and furnished them with supplies at Derby Wharf — Salem has the distinction of being the only American continental port of importance that did not fall into British hands during the Revolution!

Derby Wharf Light, Salem

A tablet at Salem's North Bridge indicates where the first incident of resistance to the British actually happened, prior to that which took place at Lexington. British troops who sought to seize the cannon belonging to the local minutemen in February 1775, only a few months before the battle of Lexington and Concord, were held off by the men of Salem on a bitter cold Sunday afternoon when General Gage dispatched Colonel Leslie with the Sixty-Fourth Regiment to carry out orders to seize the ammunition in North Salem.

Colonel Leslie waited until the people were at the afternoon church service, then marched rapidly from Marblehead, but he was observed by several people who spread the alarm. The Reverend Thomas Barnard, Jr., stopped his service at the new North Meeting House and rushed out with his congregation to meet Colonel Leslie at the North Bridge, where they hoisted the drawbridge.

Barnard and Captain Felt made an agreement with Colonel Leslie to allow his men to march across the bridge to the far side of the river if they turned around immediately without molesting anything, then marched back to Marblehead.

The English press claimed that this incident was the first encounter of the Revolution but was settled through persuasion and negotiation. However, when hostilities began in earnest, Salem merchants tipped the scales by sending out armed merchant vessels in lieu of the navy, which was nonexistent, to take on the mighty British men-of-war; they captured about 445 enemy ships and their vitally needed cargoes!

A short walk from Derby Wharf will take you to historic Washington Square with its elegant brick houses designed by Samuel McIntire, where you will see a superb statue of Roger Conant by Henry H. Kitson. Salem was founded in 1626 by Roger Conant, first as Naumkeag; two years later it became the first town of the Colony of Massachusetts Bay. I have always been able to interpret in the statue the character of Conant, who led the first settlers through the wilderness to Naumkeag, bringing with them the Sheffield patent authorizing the settling of the North Shore of Massachusetts Bay. The Sheffield patent may be seen today in the Essex Institute.

When Governor Endicott arrived in 1628 with his group of courageous settlers, Conant and Endicott were not in complete accord concerning property rights and community regulations. Bitter wrangling broke out to cloud the peace, but eventually their differences were "adjusted." The name of Naumkeag was changed to Salem, taken from the Hebrew word "Sholom," meaning peace. However, peace was significantly brief and at the height of renewed quarreling, Conant and his followers, no longer able to tolerate the situation, packed up and abandoned the homes and gardens which had taken them nine years to develop, and moved to the other side of North River.

Salem grew with astounding speed but somehow along the way a noticeable swing towards religious laxity manifested itself in the settlement — which Calvinism was disinclined to ignore. With one sweeping effort hellfire broke loose from the pulpit; but this proved to be ineffectual. Scapegoats had to be found, so the harmless Quakers were subjected to shameful persecution.

Pioneer Village
SALEM

In observance of the three hundredth anniversary of the founding of Massachusetts and the arrival of Governor Winthrop in 1630 with the charter of the Massachusetts Bay Company, Pioneer Village was established in 1930 as Salem's contribution to its observance.

On a plot of three acres in Forest River Park, representing a sector of the wilderness the settlers cleared, the visitor can see how they built their homes four years after Roger Conant and the Old Planters had established themselves in 1626, and two years after the arrival of John Endicott, Governor and agent of the English Syndicate which purchased the land from the Plymouth Company.

Here among the numerous buildings are dugouts of palisaded logs with sod roofs, and "English" wigwams that preceded the more permanent thatch-roofed pine cottages with their catted chimneys of logs and clay with deep fireplaces, typical of the homes the settlers left behind in England. There is also a replica of the "Governor's fayre house" with its large central chimney and wide fireplaces representing the last word in New England housing at the time.

On the Village square are twelve buildings faithfully reproduced, including the pillory and stocks which were required by law in Massachusetts settlements. The weathered pillory in Pioneer Village, into which wrongdoers were once clamped and exposed to public ridicule, is today the focal point of interest for camera fans who take photographs of their "victims" amid lusty merriment and buffoonery!

The Puritan village erected in Salem, and the Plimoth Plantation of the Pilgrims at Plymouth are not dissimilar. Both emphasize the severity and simplicity of the furnishings, the gardens kept for their usefulness in cooking or for their medicinal value instead of for aesthetic value. Very much in evidence are the apparatus for making salt from seawater, the pit for sawing logs, the forge and a brick kiln.

At Salem the replica of Governor Winthrop's flagship, the *Arbella*, which sailed into Salem Harbor in 1630 has been moored at the edge of the Village since 1930. Lady Arbella Johnson, for whom the *Arbella* was named, is probably buried in Salem's oldest burial ground on Charter Street, directly in back of the Peabody

Museum fronting on Essex Street. No stone exists to mark her grave or those of Governor Endicott's first wife and Mrs. George Phillips, who also came with Winthrop's fleet.

A stroll through the Charter Street Burial Ground is akin to walking straight into the historic past of America. Here is buried Captain Richard More, who crossed the Atlantic on the *Mayflower;* the younger brother of Cotton Mather, Nathaniel Mather, is also buried here, as well as the Reverend John Higginson, Chief Justice Lynde and Judge Hathorne of the witchcraft court. The stone slab marking Governor Bradstreet's grave is illegible, its Latin inscription effaced by the weather, but the grave is marked by a monument erected by the Province.

Those Incomparable Marbleheaders
MARBLEHEAD

Marblehead, Massachusetts, is as snug and beautiful a harbor as you will discover anywhere along the coast, and one of the best-loved of our New England fishing villages, bewitched by legend and sea-history. The first settlers arrived from Cornwall in 1629, settling in Marblehead to fish.

The following three centuries credited the inhabitants of Marblehead with fanatical acts of patriotism and adventure, and they were admired by other colonists for their brusque independence and fortitude. The jumble of fascinating small but practical houses built along the rock-rimmed harbor, on crooked streets and narrow lanes, attest to the Marbleheader's individualistic leanings and taste; large trees, hollyhocks and small gardens growing in improbable places, enliven the scene with patches of contrasting color.

Not every house in Marblehead is possessed by modest taste — there are today many opulent mansions in good repair that were built during the great pre-Revolutionary shipping period of prosperity, standing near small houses, fishing shanties and boatyards.

Marblehead's favorable situation and climate have made it the yachting center of the Eastern seaboard. In August, during Race Week, the commodious harbor is thick with visiting sailing craft — it is almost possible to cross from one side of the harbor to the other by jumping from deck to deck.

Colonel John Glover marched out of Marblehead in June 1775, at the head of a daring company of Marblehead fishermen. His "Amphibian Regiment" was chosen by Washington to row him and his troops across the Delaware River the following year and to lead the advance at the Battle of Trenton. Glover and his men also ferried Washington's army across the East River after the Battle of Long Island, saving it from surrender.

"Try this for size" — the stocks at Pioneer Village, Salem

The Olde Town House, built in 1727 in Market Square, is known as Marblehead's "Cradle of Liberty" and antedates Boston's Faneuil Hall. Old Town Hall was the scene of many turbulent demonstrations of Marblehead patriots.

Marbleheaders were in the thick of the Battle of Bunker Hill; in the War of 1812 they made up a large part of the crew aboard the frigate *Constitution*, and Marbleheaders manned a fleet of privateers during the Revolution that scored victories in many a sea-fight. They also answered the call to arms during the Civil War and a thousand strong left Marblehead to help save the Union.

After a meeting of the Province Committee of Safety and Supplies, at great risk to their lives, Colonel Jeremiah Lee, Colonel Orne and Elbridge Gerry barely made their escape from the British by hiding in a cornfield behind Wetherby's Black Horse Tavern.

In 1744, Elbridge Gerry was born in the house on Washington Street to which Marblehead points with pride. This eloquent man distinguished himself as one of her illustrious citizens and patriots; he was a signer of the Declaration of Independence, Governor of Massachusetts and later became Vice President of the United States.

Colonel Jeremiah Lee's mansion, near Abbot Hall, is one of the finest examples of Georgian architecture in New England. It was built in 1768 by Lee, a distinguished patriot, shipowner and merchant prince, who imported most of the material for his mansion from abroad in his own ships. The mansion has three "rusticated" stories with a cupola flanked by two massive chimneys. Colonel Lee entertained lavishly and owned many slaves, who looked after the comforts of his guests and unloaded his ships in the harbor. Among the recorded guests at the Lee mansion appear Presidents Washington, Monroe and Jackson and General Lafayette. Lafayette came to Marblehead in 1784 to receive the toast of the townfolk, returning again in 1824.

Another mansion of distinction belonged to Robert Hooper, called "King" because of his integrity and fair treatment of his sailors, and for his generosity to the town. His mansion on Hooper Street is imposing and strikingly elegant inside and out. After serving as a home for King Hooper, who built it in 1745, it suffered the indignity of being used as a dry-goods shop, an antique shop, and as the local YMCA. John Hooper occupied the mansion after his father died in 1790, and later traded it away to one Jason Chamberlain for a schooner. Presently the mansion is owned by the Marblehead Arts Association. Art exhibitions are held in the banquet hall on the third floor, which has a graceful vaulted ceiling, delicate chandeliers and two fireplaces.

Abbot Hall towers above Washington Square and is seen for miles around. It was built of brick in 1877 without a thought given to its incongruity with old Marblehead. Abbot Hall houses the library and is also the seat of the town government. For whatever purpose you may visit Abbot Hall, don't miss the famous life-size painting of *The Spirit of '76* in the reading room. It is "holy" to Marble-

Circle Street, Marblehead

headers, and is generally considered to be one of the important patriotic paintings in America. The artist painted it in 1876, but there are many copies extant from the brushes of Archibald M. Willard, who sold the painting in Abbot Hall to General John Devereux, whose son was the model for the drummer boy. The General presented the painting to Marblehead in 1880, the home of the Devereux ancestors.

In the same room you may see the original deed to Marblehead from the Nanepashemet Indians, dated 1684.

Fort Sewall, situated at the entrance of Marblehead Harbor, was built in 1742 and served during three wars; today the fort is a park. It was named after Chief Justice Sewall, a Marblehead citizen who distinguished himself as chief justice of Massachusetts.

The famous frigate *Constitution* once sought shelter under the fort's guns when chased by H.M.S. *Tenedos* and *Endymion,* in 1814.

The Old Powder House, a small brick magazine located on Green Street, was built in 1755 and used as an ammunition storehouse during the French and Indian War, the American Revolution and the War of 1812.

A short distance from the fort once stood the Fountain Inn, where Sir Harry Frankland, His Majesty's Collector for the Port of Boston, resided while supervising the building of Fort Sewall. He met barefooted Agnes Surriage, a poor fisherman's daughter who later became Lady Frankland. The well is all that remains to identify the site of the inn where one of the most controversial eighteenth-century romances began.

The Old Burial Hill overlooking Fort Sewall was the site of the first meetinghouse in 1684. Here six hundred Revolutionary War dead are buried, among them General John Glover.

A white obelisk commemorates the tragic loss of sixty-five Marblehead fishermen who perished in a gale, in 1846, when ten fishing boats foundered.

The intrepid James Mugford, Jr., is buried here. He was the commander of the schooner *Franklin* that captured the British transport *Hope,* laden with guns and ammunition, and took her into Boston Harbor as a prize. Mugford set out to sea again in his spunky schooner, hailed as a credit to the newly created American navy, only to meet with the misfortune of running aground. In her predicament she was attacked by two hundred sailors dispatched in boats from the British fleet lying nearby; the sailors were beaten off by the crew with cutlasses and guns, inflicting a loss to the British of seventy men. The only American killed was the gallant commander of the *Franklin,* whose body was aboard the schooner when she sailed into Marblehead Harbor one day in May 1776.

Historic St. Michael's Church, on Summer Street, was built in 1714 with

PHILIP KAPPEL

The Old Powder House, Marblehead

timbers brought over from England. This almost square building is believed to be the oldest church of the Episcopal denomination in New England.

Marbleheaders seldom do things halfway. When the news reached the town of the Declaration of Independence, a frenzied crowd broke into the church and removed the coat of arms of George I, and then rang the old English bell so violently that it cracked. Throughout the Revolution it remained silent until Paul Revere recast it.

The Reverend David Mossom, the second rector of St. Michael's Church, afterward settled in Virginia where he officiated at the wedding of George Washington and the widow Custis.

Cape Ann

I remember Essex as if I had been there yesterday, and the Essex River winding through the marshes, and especially the celebrated clams that were sold fried or raw beside the roadside. Nowhere else does seafood taste better. Here you may feast and at the same time watch the ribs of a ship being jockeyed into place, just as it has been done for over three hundred years.

Essex is pervaded by the sea, salt marshes and a great peace. Nearby are the dunes of Ipswich and Annisquam — this is truly the unspoiled area of Cape Ann, which juts out into the Atlantic Ocean north of Boston. In 1614, Captain John Smith named the place Cape Anna, and in 1623 some fishermen settled in Gloucester.

Not far from Gloucester is Rockport; its tiny harbor and narrow streets attract artists from many states who form the art colony on Bearskin Neck. Its counterpart in Gloucester is equally famous, since Gloucester is one of the most fascinating fishing ports in New England.

The charm of Cape Ann has many facets — the small towns are worthy of individual mention, but Ipswich, five miles from Essex, deserves especially close examination, for it has more seventeenth-century houses than any other town in the United States.

Within a generation of the settling of Agawam (later renamed Ipswich), shipbuilding became a profitable industry there and vessels bound for the West Indies or Europe sailed down the Ipswich River.

In 1668 the center of shipbuilding moved five miles away to Chebacco Parish, now the town of Essex. In that year Essex was granted an acre of land "for a yard to build vessels in," and the descendants of the seventeenth-century builders of ships still work at the family's old trade.

Shipbuilding at Essex

Castle Hill in Ipswich received its name long before any castle stood on it. The Crane family, of plumbing fame, once owned Castle Hill — all of its 350 acres — upon which they built a huge house and terraced gardens. The woodlands were there, and the magnificent views in every direction of the ocean, the Rowley marshes and Plum Island; on fair days you can see the Isles of Shoals. In the opposite direction, beyond the Ipswich Beach, lie Cape Ann's outcropping rocks and the vast moors. Castle Hill is administered by the Trustees of Reservations and by the Castle Hill Foundation, a nonprofit corporation which arranges cultural activities for the benefit of the public.

Backtracking towards Gloucester, your nose will tell you when you are approaching the outskirts of Gloucester by the pungent odors of drying cod in the open, or by its many fish-slick docks. Perhaps you will identify your location by the ringing carillon in the Sailors' Church of Our Lady of Good Voyage, and catch the spirit of the Portuguese-descended fishermen who exhibit their faith unabashed.

The sea has claimed hundreds of Gloucester fishermen over the years and Gloucester remembers them every summer on a certain Sunday afternoon when the tide begins to ebb, at which time a brief but colorful ceremony is held at Leonard Craske's famous statue of a fisherman at the wheel, facing Gloucester Harbor. At a given moment the people standing along the canal cast flowers into the water and the ebbing tide swiftly carries the flowers out to sea.

Gloucestermen don't take chances — they demand sturdily built vessels and they have them built the way they want them at the Essex shipyards, from which over three thousand vessels have gone to sea since the yards began operations three centuries ago. Only wooden ships are built in Essex — all by hand. The timbers are fitted without mechanical assistance and lifted into place without power cranes. The whining power saw and the electric drill are the only modern aids; but children for generations were lulled to sleep by workmen dubbing the ship's planks with adzes and the dull tapping sounds of caulking mallets driving oakum into place.

The average vessel used by Gloucester fishermen requires ten months to complete, and before it goes to work on the high seas it is blessed by a priest, after which the crew is joined by merrymakers aboard the vessel to celebrate the occasion.

Essex shipbuilders are traditionally modest and accept their heritage without self-praise. Whenever queried about the boats they have built they simply admit that they have built quite a few since 1630. For diversion they may take time out searching for clams; in flat-bottomed dories they may run out with the tide through the marshes to the beaches. But they seldom stray far from the shipyards, where the abstract patterns and shadows cast by the "trunnels," or wooden pegs, driven into the ship's planks bind legend, workmen and tradition into one inseparable blend of freedom and work the New England way.

Mending nets at Gloucester

The cupola

Laissez-Faire and Timothy Dexter
NEWBURYPORT

Timothy Dexter moved to High Street before 1800, in the proud prosperous days of Newburyport, where he established himself as "Lord" Timothy Dexter — a title which hatched in his own fertile and eccentric mind. Dexter was, however, no fool, as everyone soon found out. He accumulated a fortune right under the noses of his eighteenth-century contemporaries by brazen exploitation in many fields and markets. The greater the risks involved, the more successful his ventures proved to be, as Newburyport stood by aghast but fascinated by Dexter's barefaced gaudiness and numerous improprieties.

Dexter became a legendary figure beyond the borders of Newburyport, with serious aspects of immortality, in whom the late John Marquand became interested. One day in 1959, he led me to the cupola which graced Dexter's house, where this drawing was made, showing the yard and the vast salt marshes in the distance which filled and drained with the tides.

The square white Dexter House, set back from the street, is a shadow of its former self. The cupola is as it was in Dexter's day, surrounded by the balustrades on the roof, and the gilded eagle still glares down upon Newburyport from its perch on top of the cupola where Dexter ordered it placed.

The salt marshes, from the cupola of the Timothy Dexter House, Newburyport

Dexter's bursts of uncontrolled temper and eccentric behavior were not evident during his childhood in Malden, where he was born in 1747. His very poor parents committed him to early apprenticeship so that he might be equipped with a trade and pay his way in life, but Dexter abandoned the trade of tanner soon after he arrived in Newburyport, sometime around 1770. He had grandiose ideas about getting rich quick, and his schemes and hunches paid off well. He made a fortune buying up depreciated Continental currency, which was afterwards redeemed at full value.

Dexter wrote *A Pickle for the Knowing Ones* in 1802 — a remarkable book, of individual spelling and totally without punctuation. When he was chided for the lack of punctuation he published a second edition and added a page of "stops" so that readers could insert the proper punctuation themselves, or "pepper and salt" it as they pleased.

Dexter's ability to draw attention to himself and his originality were fathomless. Newburyport expected anything to happen on staid old High Street. Dexter ordered wooden statues of famous men mounted on columns and placed around the garden. They were painted with buff waistcoats, blue coats and brass buttons. Because Dexter admired George Washington he had him placed over the arched entrance to his home; on Washington's right stood Adams, and on his left, Jefferson. From time to time other figures were added until the number reached forty. When a character bored Dexter he turned him into someone else — this is what happened to a certain American general, who was changed into Napoleon, whom Dexter admired enormously. Dexter included a statue of himself among his notables. He was shown holding a scroll upon which were the words: "I am the first in the East; first in the West; and the greatest Philosopher in the known world."

Dexter had his own poet laureate — a former fish peddler by the name of Jonathan Plummer, whom Dexter dressed in black, with a cocked hat and silver-buckled shoes. Plummer wrote odes of praise about his "Lordship" which naturally pleased Dexter. Plummer strikes one as having been New England's first public relations man.

None of Dexter's obsessions quite equaled the lunacy of ordering his own mock funeral. He went so far as to send out invitations and ordered mourning for his family. A minister went along with the scheme and the procession followed the empty coffin in obsequious silence past the statues in the garden to the vault someplace in the rear of the house, while Dexter watched his own funeral from an upper window. After it was over he began beating his wife mercilessly for not making a better showing of grief.

When Dexter actually died in 1806, he was laid to rest in the Old Hill Burial Ground near Bartlett Mall; the Newburyport Board of Health frowned upon Dexter's desire to be buried in his own back yard.

The array of statues in Dexter's garden disappeared soon after his death; no one is around to tell us how or why. Only one complete figure, that of William Pitt, survives; it may be seen in the Smithsonian Institution in Washington.

Requiem: The Dreadnought
NEWBURYPORT

Many sailing vessels slipped down the ways of the shipyards along the Merrimack, but only one was destined to rise to real fame; the ship *Dreadnought*. She was built in Newburyport by Currier and Townsend for a group of well-known merchants, among whom was Edwin D. Morgan, later Governor of New York.

Captain Samuel Samuels, who commanded the *Dreadnought* for ten years, watched the laying of the keel in June 1853, and after months of supervision, was on hand for the launching on October 6 the same year. He knew how well the *Dreadnought* was built, and he was aware of her ability to stand hard driving. He earned for his ship the title of "The Wild Ship of the Atlantic," bestowed on her by the crews of other ships, who saw her on the high seas plunging through the spray flung high over her crosstrees. She was never hove to in foul weather but stormed ahead under close-reefed topsails and furled mainsail — the smallest amount of canvas that the *Dreadnought* was brought under by her master.

The *Dreadnought* was a semi-clipper, or packet, built to carry an enormous amount of canvas and at the same time more cargo at less displacement than the extreme clippers. In 1855 the *Dreadnought* beat the *Lightning* in a race side by side. In 1859 she made the phenomenally fast passage of 13 days and 8 hours from New York to Liverpool. Her staterooms were generally engaged a year in advance.

The *Dreadnought* was a beautiful vessel. She had a fine bow, a clean run fore and aft, noble bearings, well-formed sides, a round stern and an unusually long curving overhang to the stem. She was 200 feet long between perpendiculars, 217 feet on deck with a beam of 39 feet at load line; she was registered as being of 1413 72/95 tons, old measure. Under Captain Samuels's command the *Dreadnought* carried royals, stun'sails and single topsails. She had a winged dragon figurehead in gold which surmounted the stem; the tail of the dragon curled gracefully and ran down along the stem to the waterline. The stern had a gold spread eagle with "DREADNOUGHT, N.Y." underneath it. The house-flag insignia of the Red Cross Line was painted on the foretopsail; an American shield in colors was painted on the ends of the catheads. The only running light was white, placed on the end of the bowsprit under the jib boom.

The *Dreadnought's* skipper and the men who manned her have made their last voyage, and the great era of sail has died with them never to return, but the ships and the fortitude of courageous men are indelibly recorded. Whenever we tire of mundane things which saturate our lives, the image of those great white-winged ships returns to haunt us — the far horizons, billowing canvas and the voices of sailormen and their chanteys.

All that and considerably more is what I see in the rotting pile ends along the waterfront of Newburyport, Massachusetts.

The Dalton House

NEWBURYPORT

If one had to content himself with just one example of a New England city once renowned as a glittering seaport, now shorn of its former maritime greatness, Newburyport would be an admirable choice.

The Merrimack River still flows swiftly past the banks of this modern city but the colorful shipping is gone. Today it's questionable whether a square-rigger could cross the bar at the mouth of the river, which over the years has been building up, sealing off Newburyport from the sea, save for the sporting shallow-draft boats one sees straining at their hooks anchored deep in the Merrimack's muddy bottom.

In the summer of 1925, John Marquand and I walked down to the banks of the Merrimack; I can still remember the pride he felt for his native city — how he reconstructed for me the historic lore and fame of the few remaining ware-houses of the old seaport still standing on the waterfront, and bade me look at the charming Federal mansions scattered about town. Of special interest to him was the house of Timothy Dexter, about whom he wrote a book which I illustrated that same year. I can also recall Marquand's concern over the city's languid interest in its old landmarks. When I returned to Newburyport in 1959 as Marquand's guest and illustrator of his book *Timothy Dexter Revisited* to reexamine the local scene, his fears of 1925 proved well founded — nothing remained on the banks of the Merrimack that sustained a relationship with the ethos of Newburyport's great past. Dexter's house was still around, but High Street looked a bit seedy, and Dexter's house had been converted into an antique shop — which bothered Marquand no end. He pointed out the Custom House, which was used as a depository for junk offered for sale, indecorously displayed and nearly flowing onto the sidewalk!

We purchased the one and only product reminiscent of the days of sail, which happens to be nearly as good today as that which flowed from the rum vats in the old days.

Waterfront Decay — Newburyport

One of the high points of my visit to Newburyport was the Dalton House, illustrated here. A charming mansion which was once in a bucolic setting, it is presently in the heart of Newburyport. The building is owned by the Dalton Club. The name is derived from the family that lived in it for many years. John Marquand is shown about to enter the Club, and our mutual friend Alexander Williams is not far behind. Little did any of us expect, that happy day, that shortly thereafter, one of the greatest storytellers of our time would casually retire one night and slip into permanent sleep on July 16, 1960. Whatever sentimentality I had for Newburyport — especially Kent's Island, Marquand's house almost surrounded by salt marshes swollen with deep blue water during flood tides — would cease to entice me that way again.

Michael Dalton was born February 22, 1709. He was a great-grandson of Philemon Dalton, who came to New England in 1635. Michael Dalton went to Newbury to engage in a seafaring life when quite young and became a master mariner with several successful voyages to his credit, but switched later to agriculture. Still later, he became a very successful merchant. Michael Dalton purchased in May 1746 the land the club house now occupies and soon thereafter he built the magnificent mansion facing State Street which he deeded to his son Tristram a few years before his death.

Tristram Dalton was born on May 28, 1738, and graduated from Harvard in the class of 1755, a classmate of John Adams. Dalton studied law at Salem, and married in 1758 the daughter of Robert Hooper, a wealthy Marblehead merchant. Dalton became interested in the affairs of town, state and the nation. He was a delegate to the Provincial Congress, also a representative to the General Court, a member of the State Senate. As a delegate to the Constitutional Convention of 1788 he was a zealous advocate of the adoption of the Constitution. He was one of the two first senators to represent Massachusetts in the national senate. During his residence in Newburyport he entertained many persons of national and world fame. George Washington had breakfast in the Dalton House on October 31, 1789.

In 1792 Tristram Dalton deeded the house to Moses Brown, a noted Newburyport merchant, who owned the property until his death in 1827. A succession of owners followed, and in 1897 the property was deeded to the Dalton Club by Timothy and John A. Remick and has since that time remained in the club's hands.

Stored in the Old Armory at Spanish Town, on the island of Jamaica, is an extraordinary cache of eighteenth- and early nineteenth-century naval documents — hundreds of semi-decayed bundles of ships' papers, logs and personal letters that belonged to captured crews taken by the Royal Naval vessels patrolling the Caribbean and adjacent areas during the Revolutionary War. Many American ships were captured by the British trying to run the blockade, especially in the vicinity of Turks Island, where Americans loaded their ships with precious salt

John Marquand walking into the Dalton House, Newburyport

83

needed by the Colonists for salting down meats and fish. Others were intercepted plying the shipping lanes between the French West Indian islands and France, carrying cargoes to exchange for coffee, cotton, molasses and other vitally needed items. In spite of the tremendous risks, the high wages seamen demanded and soaring insurance rates, the profits earned by the successful runs netted the American shipowners fortunes, and those already rich became richer.

Among the papers at Spanish Town are those taken from Tristram Dalton's ship *Antelope,* which was captured by the British. The letter written by Dalton to the commander of his ship was dated 1782, giving instructions and the particulars and suppositions of risks.

It was customary for captured vessels to be escorted to Kingston, Jamaica, where their cargoes were condemned and sold at auction at Port Royal. The letters sent to the sailors from home were, by and large, confiscated for intelligence purposes. The fragmentary stories contained in those personal letters ran from bitterness of separation, love and human misery to the movement of troops through the towns at home, but many of the letters from the shipowners to their commanders responsible for their vessels revealed the callousness and the customary harsh treatment toward the seamen — for example, turning off some of the crew as an economy measure, thus stranding them in faroff places.

The Bethel on Johnny Cake Hill
NEW BEDFORD

The aura of New Bedford's past still clings to this onetime whaling capital of the world. Within a few remaining buildings on Johnny Cake Hill the traditions of the sea are kept alive — where in the background hovers the immortal drama of those deepwatermen whose lives were spent at sea, enamored of its somber might, its temptations and mystery.

New Bedford is *Moby Dick* country and the home port of Herman Melville. The ship *Acushnet,* on which Melville sailed, became the living background for *Moby Dick.* The *Acushnet* was fitted out for the trip at Kelley's Boatyard. Much of the area has in recent times remained inactive, but Merrill's Wharf, the Sail Loft, the Candleworks and the Counting House, which are referred to by Melville, actually existed and a few structures still remain to prove it.

In the Whaling Museum on Johnny Cake Hill it is possible to see and board the world's largest ship model — the half-size replica of the whaling bark *Lagoda,* once owned by the Bourne family. She was called the "greasiest" whaler on the high seas and engaged in whaling from 1841 to 1860, making tremendous profits for her owners. The museum has a fully equipped 30-foot whaleboat once manned

RATES FOR DOCKAGE

VESSELS UNDER 50 TONS BURDEN 50 cts. PER CALENDAR DAY.

Over 50 To 100 Tons		$1.00
" 100 .. 150		1.25
" 150 .. 200		1.50
" 200 .. 250		1.75
" 250 .. 300		2.00
" 300 .. 400		2.50
" 400 .. 500		3.00
" 500 .. 600		3.50
" 600 .. 700		4.00
" 700 .. 800		4.50
" 800 .. 900		5.00
" 900 .. 1000		5.50
" 1000 .. 1100		6.00
" 1100 .. 1200		6.50
Coal .. Scows		50 cts.

For vessels moored or lying at another
wharf but with line made fast to this
wharf fifty per cent discount from
the above rates if dues are paid before
vessel leaves this port

J.C STANLEY OWNER
.... DE WHARFINGER

PHILIP KAPPEL

Old dockage rate sign, Newburyport

by six men — it was from the platform of this boat that the actual harpooning of a whale took place. Throughout the museum there are numerous shops that show how the barrelmakers, the sailmakers, the blacksmiths and various artisans performed their trades.

When sailors were not reducing whale blubber to valuable oil, they often occupied their time by converting whalebone into pieces of "scrimshaw," which are highly prized today for their winsome shapes and pictures of ships. A large collection of this skilled artistry may be seen at the museum.

The Bethel, opposite the Whaling Museum, was built in 1828. It is an exalting experience to leave the busy streets of New Bedford and sit quietly in this simple church. The pulpit is in the form of a ship's prow; presumably, sailors felt more at home in such a church, where the minister used to ascend the pulpit by a rope ladder. The walls are lined with commemorative tablets. At the height of New Bedford's whaling industry, around five thousand seamen were employed out of this port. My drawing of the interior of the chapel was made from the pew in which Melville attended worship in 1841.

Next to the Bethel is the Old Mariner's Home, which was built in 1787 and is still a haven for sailors who have retired from the sea. The house was moved to Johnny Cake Hill and presented to the New Bedford Port Society. Prior to this there are no records to indicate that any care was given to shipwrecked sailors.

Around the corner is the Old Customs House. Another place of interest is the Old Dartmouth Historical Society where additional displays of whaling interest may be inspected. New Bedford's waterfront today bears scant resemblance to the sailing activity of yesteryear — instead, power-driven fishing vessels drag for scallops or fish off the Grand Banks.

Nantucket

When I had the time many years ago, I had not the money to explore the out-of-the-way places in New England and later I had not the time. Recently, while visiting friends living on the Cape, I expressed a desire to revisit Nantucket. Many years ago, on a yachting trip down the coast, not nearly enough time was available for me to evoke anything but a superficial acquaintance with the island. Therefore when my friends suggested that we fly from nearby Hyannis to the island the invitation was accepted.

The trip will always remain as an unforgettable experience — the pattern of Nantucket as it lay sprawling beneath an opening in the morning fog, surrounded by deep blue water flooded by spears of sunshine. Nantucket's situation,

Interior of the Bethel, New Bedford

thirty miles from the Massachusetts coast, and its isolation enables it to maintain its delightful charm, but too, Nantucket is inherently conservative and eminently proud. It welcomes your approval of what there is to offer, but the visitor is held at arm's length at all times — on probation, so to speak.

The island's charm lies in unpretentiousness and restraint, where even the flora seems to fit the island. There are few full-size trees and fewer stands of pines, but the vastness of the springy heath that covers much of Nantucket is breathtaking.

Nantucket's great whaling days began by chance in 1712 when one Christopher Hussey was blown out to sea by a northerly gale, sighted a sperm whale, killed it, and started an industry. Nantucket's whaling fleet in 1830 consisted of seventy ships seeking whales as far away as Hawaii and Japan. Whaling has long since passed from the scene but the portraits of the old-time whaling men grace the halls of the museum. The great days of whaling really belonged to them — the Gardners, the Starbucks, the Coffins and the others.

An old brick building erected in 1772 stands at one end of the cobbled Main Street square and is reserved as a club for the exclusive use of descendants of whalers who sailed the Pacific. It was built by William Rotch and Sons, the famous shipowners and leading whaling merchants. This was also the home office of the three whaleships that participated in the famous "Boston Tea Party" in 1773. The *Dartmouth, Beaver* and the *Eleanor,* after discharging cargoes of oil in London, were chartered by the East India Company to carry the famous tea to Boston.

The sketch shows part of the famous "Three Bricks" on upper Main Street. Joseph Starbuck, owner of whaling ships, built for each of his three sons a brick house identical in appearance — by far the most impressive architectural delights in the residential area since 1837.

In contrast with the large houses, you will find on the other side of Nantucket, at Siasconset, a select community of rose-covered small houses, situated between cranberry bogs and the bluffs, looking like a toy village exposed to the open sea. Winter storms make 'Sconset untenable after November, but seldom do they inflict more serious damage than blowing away some weathered shingles from the charming diminutive cottages.

Superimposed upon Nantucket's simple grandeur is a spiritual essence that is predominantly Quaker, but the most outstanding and conspicuous architectural landmark is the Unitarian Church. Its gilded dome catches the first light of morning and the setting sun, proclaiming the start of a new day or its subtle closing for rest. Everywhere there is present a proportionate balance, since Nantucket is neither anxious to be overwhelmingly modern or behind the times too far, as is apparent the moment you enter Main Street where cars rumble over the rough cobble-

Upper Main Street, Nantucket

stones; where there are many fashionable shops, thriving art galleries and fine antique stores, and good hotels.

But Nantucket never lets you forget her whaling heritage, preserved in the extraordinary Whaling Museum. This old brick building where long ago candles were made from sperm whale oil, contains one of the finest collections of navigating instruments, sea chests, log books and every known relic of the old whaling days — nothing particularly spectacular, monumental or elegant, simply the tools that once belonged to men who went down to the sea in ships. They are the spectral manifestations of thrumming shrouds in storms, creaking winches, sharp lances cutting into the carcasses of whales and the ghostly voices of men — their commands and castigations. They bring to mind blubber boiling on the decks beneath billowing sails and barrels of oil securely stowed away beneath decks, homeward bound — the end of the sea-hunt and the last "Nantucket sleighride!"

Sankaty Head

NANTUCKET

The ladies at the rail fence had "done all the sights" within the time allotted by steamer or air flight schedules to and from the mainland. They had listened to a guide whose gibberish was memorized and run off like a record — who, when interrupted by queries, had to start over again. His story resembled a rerun on a tape machine. Besides, he was unable to sense what his charges really wanted to see after all. The time had come to pause and reflect.

At the edge of Sankaty Head, just beyond the lighthouse, there is a rail fence warning the public of danger beyond — the bluff drops at this point 110 feet to the ocean below. Here it is possible to lean comfortably on the fence, look into space and renounce the world; here, where land goes no further, you are suspended between sky and ocean. The nearest land to the east is Spain and Portugal, at a distance of 3188 miles; to the south lie the West Indies, 1463 miles away.

If lighthouses have personality, and I believe they have, Sankaty Head Lighthouse has a better than average appeal. On the eastern shore of Nantucket, one and one-half miles north of Siasconset, Sankaty Head light is farther at sea than any of our Atlantic coast lighthouses.

It was built in 1849 and was first lighted February 1, 1850. The tower is 70 feet in height, white at the top and bottom with a broad band of red around the middle. The light stands near the highest point on the island — 110 feet elevation

The pause that refreshes

— which puts the light 180 feet above the water and makes it visible at a distance of 18 miles. In spite of every precautionary measure taken to protect the sea lanes off Nantucket, accidents still happen. Fog makes open mockery of lighthouses, bell buoys — or floodlights installed on airfields. Even radar failed to avert one of the most tragic disasters in our time on July 25, 1956, when the Italian liner *Andrea Doria,* traveling toward New York on a fog-enshrouded sea off Nantucket, was rammed and sunk by the Swedish liner *Stockholm,* with a loss of fifty lives.

Brant Point Light, guarding Nantucket Harbor, is the oldest lighthouse site in America still in use. It was built in 1746. The first lighthouse was installed on Great Brewster Island, Boston Harbor, in 1716, and abandoned in 1754 — a light was then built on Lighthouse Island. The third lighthouse was built at New London, Connecticut, about twenty years later.

The Brant Point light was not government-controlled until 1795. The present white lighthouse was built in 1901.

Another lighthouse of importance is on Great Point, on the site of a wooden structure, built in 1784, which was destroyed by fire in 1816. The present lighthouse was built of stone and painted white in 1818. Its light, 70 feet above the water, is visible for 11 miles. Treacherous Handkerchief Shoal is a little west of north, and about seven miles from the lighthouse. The light is fixed white of 12,000 candlepower, with a red sector covering Cross Rip and Tuckernuck shoals. Only ten miles of open water separates Great Point from Monomoy Island, extending southward ten miles from Chatham on the southeastern end of Cape Cod — waters notorious for shipwrecks.

Cape Cod

Seventy miles into the Atlantic Ocean extends what Henry David Thoreau called "the bare and bended arm of Massachusetts." It is said that you can never get farther away from salt water than six miles on Cape Cod — this paradox of shifting dunes and lush meadows, towering trees and dwarfed pines with a heady scent, "salt-box" houses of simple dimensions and mansions of considerable size, and countless ponds, large and small, of fresh water surrounded by the sea. Cape Cod is a haven for the vacationer; there are miles of sandy beaches, and the sea which merges into a sharp blue edge across the breadth of the sky.

Bending before the wind, sailboats may be seen rounding a buoy in an afternoon Yacht Club regatta. The Cape is also the home of the hard-working fisherman whose boat heads into the open sea past the yachts in the harbor which toss

Sankaty Head Light

Ascending the Great Dune at Race Point near the Coast Guard Station

Provincetown

and creak at their anchors long before the sun rises. The Cape is a favorite haunt of the amateur artist and the professional, the art colonies and their strange mixture of serious workers and many who are spurious.

In the main, the Cape means something to almost everyone. It's a melting pot of taste and interests, of faddists, intellectuals and the well-bred. And there are areas taken over by the tourists that resemble small-scale Coney Islands — distasteful to those who love the Cape but who can only stand by helplessly and see it violated. When summertime comes to a close, the Cape returns to a sensible pace. The native collects his thoughts and plans ahead for the next season, counts his profits, and battens down for the winter.

The 17-mile Cape Cod Canal severs the Cape from the mainland and joins Cape Cod Bay with Buzzards Bay. East of the Sagamore Bridge, on the north shore is one of the Cape's earliest towns, Sandwich, settled in 1637. Antique collectors know it for its Sandwich glass — pressed or lace, which was the first in the United States — made in Sandwich a hundred years ago.

Barnstable Harbor, on Cape Cod Bay, was once a busy whaling port and the home of many deepwater sailors. Other towns along the north shore blend into each other, and everywhere the beauty of the spired churches and the Greek Revival houses speak of riches brought to the towns by those who followed the sea. At Barnstable the first library in the country was established.

Further east are Yarmouth and the Dennises — East, South, West and Dennis Port. In the 1850's a fleet of eighty-five coastal vessels and a fishing fleet of forty-eight employed twelve hundred men and boys who made their homes in Dennis. Fishing is still an important part of the Cape's economy, but the picturesque fishing boats with billowing sails are gone, as is the coastal shipping. The Cape now depends largely on the cranberry bogs, the vacationers and the summer residents.

In the heyday of sail, Brewster had the largest number of deep-water sea captains, many of whom amassed great fortunes.

Captain Asa Eldridge, who made his home in Yarmouthport, became one of the Cape's most celebrated sea captains. He was daring, a man of outstanding skill. As master of the *Red Jacket,* an extreme clipper ship, he and the ship became legend. The *Red Jacket* put out of New York on January 11, 1854, and reached Liverpool in 13 days and one hour, dock to dock, logging 413 miles a day. The ship was sold by her owners in England. Two years later Captain Eldridge took command of the *Pacific,* a Collins liner. He tried to double back on his record run; but neither he nor his ship was ever heard from again.

Cape Cod on a map looks indeed like a giant flexed arm, with the biceps extending to Orleans, where the elbow bends, and Provincetown located in the fist. Race Point and the Coast Guard Station are on the tip, where the shifting dunes and the spikes of beach grass wage an endless battle. Walking along or climbing the dunes will soon fill your shoes with sand and the sun-glared water will torment you, but adventuring beside the sea, seventy miles from the mainland, has many rewards. At low tide it's amusing to watch the sandpipers with jerky, springy bursts of movement, trying to evade the spent breakers which carry with them the loose sand and vegetation. Nothing here is static — there is a special beauty and enchantment in the changing dunes. The stillness is pronounced, but suddenly the distinctive call of "bobwhite" fills the air somewhere in the brush, far behind the shore.

Near the wrist lies Truro. We are now in the land where the Pilgrims roamed while the *Mayflower* lay at anchor in Provincetown Harbor for five weeks to make repairs and to permit the exhausted passengers to evaluate the land to which they came before crossing Cape Cod Bay to Plymouth. Near Truro, sixteen Pilgrims led by Myles Standish discovered a cache of Indian corn on a hill overlooking the bay. The hill is still called Corn Hill.

On the ocean side of Truro, now a part of the National Seashore, stands Highland Light, one of the most powerful beacons on the Atlantic Coast. Highland Light was Cape Cod's first lighthouse. The original one was erected in 1797–1798 after much agitation by the Reverend Levi Whitman of Wellfleet in 1794. The present structure was built in 1857. Nearby are the Peaked Hill Bars, where more ships have come to grief than any place on the Eastern seaboard. The Chatham Light warns shipping of the hazards that forced the Pilgrims to turn north, round the tip of the Cape and anchor in the calm water of Provincetown Harbor, after a voyage of sixty-seven grueling days. To commemorate the landing of the Pilgrims at Provincetown, a 255-foot granite monument, copied from the Torre del Manglia in Siena, Italy, was erected on a hill one hundred feet high in honor of the 102 men, women and children who, according to Governor Bradford's chronicles, "fell upon their knees and blessed the God of Heaven who had brought them over the vast and furious ocean, and delivered them from all the perils and miseries thereof, again to set their feet upon firm and stable earth, their proper element."

Near Orleans there is an historic spot named the First Encounter. This was the place where Myles Standish and his colleagues were first attacked by the Indians on December 8, 1620. The battle was merely a skirmish but the settlers considered it of great importance. A plaque on a stone a short distance from the beach at Bayshore, Eastham, tells the story. With Myles Standish when the attack occurred were William Bradford, Edward Winslow, Edward Tilley and eight other Pilgrims, including a master mate, master gunner and three sailors. It is said that this attack was in revenge for the abduction of several Indians whom Captain Thomas Hunt made slaves in 1614.

Whaling was for many years the main industry of Provincetown. When it collapsed the economic void was filled by the summer visitors, theater, the art colony and the symphony orchestra. Of the seventy-five wharves that flourished only a few still remain. Commercial fishermen unload their hauls at the wharf named for Provincetown's Arctic explorer, Donald B. MacMillan. The draggers, the trawlers and the scallopers are manned by Portuguese-descended fishermen

After the regatta, Bass River

River mist, Bass River

who each year, late in June, participate in a colorful religious rite — the Blessing of the Fleet, which signals the start of another season.

Author Joseph C. Lincoln lived for many years at Chatham during the summertime, in a house which overlooked the sea. The fame of Cape Cod, as one of the foremost playgrounds, rose simultaneously with the popularity of Lincoln's books about colorful Cape Cod characters.

The north shore and the south shore differ from each other conspicuously. The large trees and the abundance of growing plants on the north shore reflect the calm of the Bay, free of the persistent winds right off the ocean to which the south shore is subjected. There the ravages of storms, hot summer days plus a preponderance of sandy soil have reduced the oaks and the pines to misshapen dwarfs.

The south shore from Chatham westward evokes a different mood; more congestion is noticeable in such towns as Harwich, South Yarmouth, Bass River and Hyannis on Nantucket Sound. Further along are Oyster Harbor, Wianno and Osterville — summer settlements of large estates.

Woods Hole is in the southwest corner of the Cape; by and large it's a working community, where the Government Station and the research laboratories of the United States Fish and Wildlife Service are located.

Falmouth is north of Woods Hole. The oldest house in the town dates from 1685, and a steepled meetinghouse from 1796. Queen Awashonks, who ruled the Narragansetts, used to spend her summers in Falmouth.

The bell in the First Congregational Church was cast by Paul Revere and bears an inscription which reads: "The living to the church I call/And to the grave I summon all." In the War of 1812 the bell sounded the alarm when British warships appeared off the town's shores. Captain Weston Jenkins, commander of the Falmouth Artillery Company, which consisted of two field pieces, used them effectively whenever enemy ships appeared.

When the Falmouth citizenry detained a Nantucket packet sloop because the crew was suspected of collaborating with the British — a suspicion that proved correct — the captain of the British brig *Nimrod* demanded the return of the packet and the surrender of the field pieces. In reply to the British demand, Captain Jenkins said, "If you want the pieces, come and get them." The British captain warned the civilian population to leave town, go to high ground out of range of his cannon, and see their town wiped off the map. The British blazed away for several hours, but inflicted slight damage.

Frolicking wildfowl at low tide, Falmouth Harbor

Weekend Sailors

CAPE COD

This scene could be anywhere in New England on any of its rivers and lakes, but the sketch happens to have been made at Bass River, Cape Cod. Interest in boating has risen in recent times to an all-time high; it is a commonplace sight today to see a boat lashed to a trailer being hauled by the family car to some campsite by lake, or sea or river. Bass River, with its huge boatyard and resident interest in boats, makes it one of the most active yachting areas on the Cape. Up and down the river, as far as the South Yarmouth bridge, pass sloops, knockabouts, catboats and a myriad of motor boats used for pleasure or business. The tremendous breakwater thrown nearly across the mouth of the river was partially destroyed during one of the hurricanes but has since been repaired to keep the channel open and protected.

Bass River is the best known of the Cape's creeks. Along its shores are attractive cottages and year-round homes of quality, an old windmill and antique houses that have survived the sweeping change that has come to all seaside places.

Many years before the building of the Cape Cod Canal, Bass River was a potential aid to those seeking a shortcut across the waist of the Cape without having to go around the tip of Race Point. Bass River terminates at Weir Village and gets lost in a group of ponds which nearly connect White's Brook and Yarmouth. Possibly here, as was the case with Scusset Creek and Monomet River, the slight carryover between the respective streams may have been used to avoid going around the Cape. It is said that the Pilgrims used this route crossing from one side of the Cape to the other in the seventeenth century, but it was Myles Sandish who saw the possibilities of a Cape Cod canal precisely where it was later developed.

There is possible evidence that the Norsemen probed Bass River and left traces of their presence.

The habits of Bass River are baffling — believe it or not, the river flows two ways. On the flow tide it slides to the northwest, and on the ebb tide to the southwest. Rowing across the river, counter tide or ebb tide would certainly test anyone's prowess.

A weekend sailor at Bass River

Old Brewster Mill Site

CAPE COD

Brewsterites admire Thoreau with some reservation, notwithstanding the rating his book on Cape Cod enjoys as a classic. Thoreau must have passed through Brewster in 1849 with his eyes closed, otherwise how could he have made such curt allusions to the town? Other writers discovered the inner sanctum of Brewster and its hall-marks, its spired meetinghouse on a knoll, an array of old trees and well cared-for white houses with gardens in bloom. In the old cemetery lie the adventurous ancestors of those who still reside in the community.

Brewster also has the distinction of having been the home of more deepwater captains than any other community of equal size. There are many houses in Brewster that reflect the resourcefulness of the shipmasters, who were remarkable traders as well as being good sailors.

As many as fifty and sixty Brewster shipmasters sailed the high seas at one time, many of whom figured in episodes of astounding audacity. Captain Jeremiah Mayo, whose ship *Sally* lay in the port of Havre, prepared to take Napoleon out of France if he lost at Waterloo, by a prearranged scheme with representatives, but the British were too alert.

Seafaring days were over when Joseph C. Lincoln was born in Brewster in 1870, but he kept a rendezvous with shipmasters who had retired from the sea.

Not far from where Lincoln was born there are some landmarks, not generally known, which establish the existence on the Cape of a tribe of redskins. In West Brewster, squaws ground corn on a mill rock on the western shore of Lower Mill Pond. Another landmark is the Prayer Rock which is about fifteen feet high, flat on top, and faces a hollow of land, forming a natural amphitheater in the center of which the rock served as a pulpit, around which the Wampanoags gathered for their religious exercises. This rock is located on the eastern shore of the Lower Mill Pond; not easily located due to undergrowth.

All that happened a long time before Stony Brook was harnessed for waterpower. The restored mill with its overshot water wheel is the site of the first woolen mill in America (1680) and also the site of one of the first four water-driven gristmills in the country (1660).

The Indian appellation of Setucket was first given to West Brewster. Around 1660, Thomas Prince, Governor of the Plymouth Colony, established a gristmill on Stony Brook. Between 1775 and 1875 this place was an active manufacturing center due to available waterpower.

A walk at low tide to Wings Island through the marsh grass will be well rewarded. It is just off West Brewster beyond reach of automobiles and tourists.

The restored Brewster mill

Here, extensive salt works were established that almost covered the entire island; in its heyday it must have been a picturesque place with its windmills pumping sea water into the evaporation vats. The salt works were spared from destruction by the British man-o'-war *Spencer* in 1814, and Brewster paid $4000 as her part of the bargain. Today nothing remains of the salt works. The few visitors to the island go there in the late summer to pick the beach plums which are sold to the tourists as jam.

The Herring Are Running!

CAPE COD

It was a biting cold day early in April when I first witnessed the "herring run" in Stony Brook, which courses over the dam and goes under Setucket Road. The herring fall easy prey to visitors and fishermen who sluice them into batches and take them by hand, net or spear. The drama of the herring run, one of nature's unsolved riddles, is awe-inspiring as the alewives dash upstream, a determined mass of silver bodies trying to reach a group of fresh-water ponds above the old gristmill to spawn, after leaving Cape Cod Bay.

The colonists spoke of alewives coming up the streams in tremendous numbers, and William Bradford's *Of Plymouth Plantation* confirms the importance of the alewives to the Pilgrims that first year after the *Mayflower* departed for England. It was Squanto who told them about the migration of the alewives in mid-April and how the fish would arrive in large numbers in the brook that still runs through the town of Plymouth. The Pilgrims were thankful for so bountiful a supply of fish close at hand which offset starvation, with enough left over to use as fertilizer.

When they began to decline in numbers strict laws were enacted as early as 1709 to prevent the obstruction of the natural passage of the alewives. Industrial expansion along the streams, and dams raised for water power across the runs, together with wastes dumped into the water made many streams unfit for migration.

Since the fish ladders were built at Brewster in 1945 the fish have increased, but the alewife population is estimated at a third of what it was fifty years ago. Therefore, controls were effected to keep the herring runs safe from molestation during the spawning season, and to see that no individual takes more than his legal allotment of fish. The town of Brewster sells its annual rights for fishing to the highest bidder each year, permitting the taking of fish four days each week — on other days the alewives are allowed to fulfill their mission. It is estimated that over five hundred barrels of alewives are taken annually from Stony Brook.

The fishways were designed to permit the fish to reach the fresh water ponds on higher ground. The resting pools are deep enough to check the velocity of the

Fish ladder at Brewster

water and also permit the fish to wait before leaping to the next pool. At Stony Brook there are ten pools of various sizes, extending a considerable distance downstream north of the road. The Brook is the outlet to Cape Cod Bay for three interconnected ponds — Lower Mill Pond, Upper Mill Pond and Walker's Pond — covering a distance of two and a quarter miles. The largest of the three is Upper Mill Pond, which is one and a half miles long by a quarter mile in width.

A single female alewife may deposit as many as a hundred thousand eggs, in shallow water, that adhere to stones, sticks, gravel, or anything they happen to settle on. The male immediately covers the eggs with milt which he scatters by violently thrashing his tail. The eggs hatch in about six days at a water temperature of 60 degrees, and within three at 72. Thousands of eggs are eaten by the omnipresent suckers who follow the spawning alewives, but nature counted on such casualties and provided an inexhaustible supply.

In July, or thereabouts, the silver fry instinctively leave the ponds where they were hatched, by way of the herring run, and enter Cape Cod Bay, completing the first stage of a complicated cycle of life.

Cranberry Time
CAPE COD

The cranberry is associated particularly with Cape Cod, where it was originally discovered growing wild in its sandy acid soil and bogs. Cranberries are also found in Wisconsin and southern New Jersey where soil conditions match those of Cape Cod, but I never heard a Cape Codder admit it. New England is blessed with weather conditions most favorable to cranberry culture; Cape Cod, and its immediate environment, produce more than half the cranberries grown in the entire world.

Throughout the Cape, beside the roads, you may see the cranberry bogs looking like smooth sunken dark green carpets of tiny glossy leaves, a number of feet below the level of the scrubby landscape that surrounds them. The drainage ditches and the nearby water storage reservoirs are necessary to maintain water level in the bogs at least twelve inches from the surface. A new bog will produce its first crop of moderate yield in its fourth year and will thereafter continue to yield cranberries for a hundred years, with proper care.

Should frost threaten in the spring when the delicate flower buds appear, or in the autumn before the berries are harvested, a wild dash is made to reach the floodgates of the reservoirs to flood the bogs. After danger has passed the water is drained to its proper level. During the wintertime cranberry bogs are kept flooded to prevent the evergreen vines from being winter-killed. The orthodox way to harvest cranberries is by hand, "raking." The power harvester has made its appearance but has not replaced the seasonal Portuguese pickers.

A cranberry bog at harvest time

At first the red berries were considered "too sour to eat" and were abandoned to the herons and the cranes — possibly the "crane-berry" got its name from the birds that ate them — but in 1677 the Massachusetts subjects of Charles II sent him a gift of ten barrels of cranberries. No account exists of the king's reaction to this gift of fruit.

Fishing off the banks and whaling around the world were the chief interests of Cape Codders until economic reverses arrived. In 1845 began the commercial production of cranberries; at the same time white sugar also made it possible to tame the sour cranberry, henceforth the traditional associate of the Thanksgiving and Christmas dinner. Cranberry growing is a multimillion-dollar business today.

This sketch of a bog was made near Harwich, where cranberries were first launched commercially.

Wellfleet

CAPE COD

The First Congregational Church, topped by a robin's-egg blue cupola, dominates the town of Wellfleet and the harbor from the hill upon which it stands. The church has the only town clock in the world which strikes ship's time.

Wellfleet reaches across the Cape, separated from the mainland by sixty miles on one side and buffeted on the other by the winds of the open Atlantic. There are no trees of any stature here and the apparent barrenness is composed of plant life which has learned to hang on against winds and shifting sand.

The town of Wellfleet divorced itself from Eastham and was established as an independent district in 1763. The early settlers and the Indians lived very well on the rich yields of the sea all around them. Wellfleet acquired its name from the Wellfleet oysters culled or tonged from Blackwater Bay in England. The oyster industry preceded whaling, but whaling was Wellfleet's mainstay from which fortunes were made. Isaac Rich amassed a fortune in the oyster business and founded Boston University. Another native who became very rich was Frank Crowell, who invented a paper bag with a square bottom. Captain L. D. Baker, who startled the world with the introduction of the banana to the north, was born in Wellfleet in 1840. At ten he was already at sea, and when he became twenty-one he was master of a ship. On his ship, *Telegraph*, he brought back a deckful of Jamaican bananas. Their success here was immediate and he returned the next year with a cargo of bananas to Long Wharf, Boston, where a plaque states that this was the first shipload of bananas brought to the United States. From this humble start the great United Fruit Company was born. Another first for the area was Marconi's experimental wireless message sent out from the towers installed at South Wellfleet in 1903.

Sunday morning at the First Congregational Church, Wellfleet

Nauset Beach

CAPE COD

Nauset Light was built in 1839 and rebuilt in 1923. The upper part is red and the lower part white, and it stands on a high bluff 114 feet above the Atlantic. Many ships have come to grief on Cape Cod's bars in fog and gale, and their disintegrating skeletons lie in the shifting sands of the beaches where they periodically appear and disappear. The schooner *Montclair,* driven aground in 1927 with a loss of six lives, lies deep in the sand of Nauset Beach with her timbers exposed.

In 1849, Henry David Thoreau and a companion walked from Nauset Beach Lights — there were three at the time — to Provincetown. Thoreau would be delighted to see Nauset Beach made part of the Great Outer Beach which has recently been authorized as the Cape Cod National Seashore. The naturalist, obsessed with isolation and the wild life of Cape Cod, wrote soon after his visit to the Cape: "The time will come when this coast will be a place of resort for those New Englanders who really wish to visit the seaside. At present it is wholly unknown to the fashionable world, and probably it will never be agreeable to them." The Cape became too agreeable and in places it was horribly exploited. The blight threatened to overrun it, but here future generations will have a wild untamed region spared from the bulldozer and the conniving developer.

North of Nauset Harbor a modest frame house sits among the dunes. It is owned by the Massachusetts Audubon Society and naturalists spend their summers there, but its greater claim to fame lies in Henry Beston's Cape Cod classic, *Outermost House.*

A short distance inland, the pines and black oaks are never quite able to evade the storm-driven sands that determine their sometimes grotesque shapes. In the more protected areas the impoverished soil mixed with sand supports the beach plum, sweet fern, blueberry and cranberry plants.

The Cape Cod National Seashore includes, in addition to the Great Outer Beach on the Atlantic, a stretch of beach in Truro and Wellfleet Townships, making a total of 27,000 acres — nearly one-tenth of the Cape's entire area. Monomoy Island, a small spit jutting south from the elbow of Cape Cod, is already under the guardianship of the United States Fish and Wildlife Service as a refuge for thousands of duck, geese and shore birds.

Nauset Light, Cape Cod

The Mission House
STOCKBRIDGE

John Sergeant, missionary to the Housatonic Indians, had this house built for him in 1739. Known today as the Mission House, it is one of those architectural gems that might have been lost to us. Fortunately, Miss Mabel Choate bought it in 1928 and restored it to its charming weathered simplicity. It was a courageous undertaking, since the house was in very poor condition. Miss Choate ordered the building taken down piece by piece and numbered, and reconstructed on the site it now occupies on the village street.

Ephraim Williams, Sergeant's father-in-law, built his house on Prospect Hill overlooking the makeshift village street below, where John lived among the Indians prior to his marriage to Abigail Williams in 1739, two years after she came to the frontier village of Stockbridge. There was one condition to their marriage — John would have to live on the Hill near the stockaded house of her parents, and this he did, but his resources were strained when he was obliged to build a new house. John's income from his missionary work never exceeded four hundred pounds and at the time of his death in 1749 he was in debt. Abigail continued to live in her house on the Hill. Three years after the death of her husband she married Colonel Joseph Dwight, a widower with five children. The combined broods of both families made a merry but crowded existence, and at the end of four years they moved to Great Barrington where a larger dwelling was constructed, containing many of the features found in the Mission House. I was informed that the house is still standing.

The striking "Connecticut doorway," according to legend, was brought by ox-team to Stockbridge from Westfield, where it was made. This type of doorway is indigenous to the Connecticut Valley — one example is preserved in the Boston Art Museum, another in the Metropolitan Art Museum.

Jonathan Edwards, the noted divine, moved to Stockbridge in 1751 after his dismissal from his pastorate of twenty-three years in Northampton, forty miles away. Edwards remained in Stockbridge for six years, until the death of his son-in-law, the Reverend Aaron Burr, and became president of the College of New Jersey (now Princeton), a post he held for three months before his death.

Stockbridge is also noted for another resident — Daniel Chester French (1850–1931). When French was only twenty-two, and before he made a statue of any importance, he was invited to make the Concord Minuteman which Ralph Waldo Emerson unveiled on the nineteenth of April, 1875. It brought immediate fame to this youthful sculptor. Fifty years later he was present at the dedication of his seated Lincoln in the Lincoln Memorial.

Weathered elegance — the Mission House, Stockbridge

115

At his studio at Chesterwood, the original plaster casts of his monumental pieces may be seen. Here are the three-foot bronze of the Minuteman; the small sketch of John Harvard from which he made the statue in Harvard Yard; the model for the standing Lincoln in front of the State House in Lincoln, Nebraska, the War Memorial for St. Paul's School, and a pair of the bronze doors for the Boston Public Library.

The Church on the Hill

LENOX

This Congregational church is just north of the village center on Route 7, impressively situated on high ground. Lenox established a church right after the settlers returned in 1762; they had fled in 1750, after a brief stay in the area, out of fear of Indian raids. When they resettled in sufficient numbers, they purchased one of the ten lots in Western Massachusetts put up for auction by the financially embarrassed General Court.

The settlers met at the home of Israel Dewey on March 11, 1767, to discuss church matters and ways and means of supporting a minister. All went harmoniously and a site for the church was selected. At the next meeting it was rescinded, for a free site loomed ahead. Land for a church was presented to the town by the heirs of the Reverend Peter Reynolds of Somers, Connecticut, one of the seven men to whom most of the 4000 acres of forest lands lying north of Stockbridge had been granted, including most of the village of Lenox. To Mr. Reynolds came the part including the hill which his descendants conveyed to the town. It contained three acres lying on the east end of the mountain for a meetinghouse and a graveyard. The new site was immediately decided upon by the committee, and the church was begun in 1770 and completed five years later, a little southwest of the present church.

Samuel Munson of New Haven, a graduate of Yale, was ordained the first pastor, at a salary of 45 pounds a year. The bitterness of war and many disagreeable factors made the relationship between the pastor and the church members anything but pleasant; Shays's Rebellion added further fuel to the emotional fires. For seven years public worship was discontinued. Eventually, the pastor's position was intolerable and the displeased members of the church were glad to see him leave in 1793.

When the Reverend Samuel Shepard succeeded Munson, he was twenty-two and just out of Yale. The church and Lenox grew side by side and before long Mr. Shepard felt the need of additional room. By 1803 Lenox had become a village of over a thousand inhabitants and membership in the church had increased to over

The Congregational Church, Lenox

117

a hundred and it was decided to build a new meetinghouse. Benjamin D. Goodrich, living in Richmond, was entrusted with the construction of the church. The architect is unknown, but he may have been influenced by the work of Bulfinch. The fine proportions and symmetry were not accidental and embrace the best elements of architectural grace. One hundred and fifty years ago the interior of the church was prosaic and oversimplified. It was drastically changed later to its present completeness and dignity.

The town held its meetings in the old church until it was sold by public auction in 1806 for $205.51. Many of the old beams and siding went into the construction of homes and barns in the area.

The present church was dedicated on January 1, 1806, with Mr. Shepard officiating. He served the church and the town of Lenox for fifty years, and on April 30, 1845, preached his own semicentennial sermon. He died in 1846.

The one hundred and seventy-fifth anniversary of the church was celebrated on July 25, 1944, attended by neighboring clergy and friends. Dr. Serge Koussevitsky of the Tanglewood Music Center was among those present and he sponsored a short concert by the Tanglewood String Quintet. Koussevitsky is buried in the cemetery. At his request, each year on a July Sunday a musical service is held in his memory.

The Library

LENOX

The Lenox Library Association is the outcome of the Lenox Academy, which was incorporated in 1803. The Lenox Academy was not a public library, but the property of fifty-eight proprietors, and served but one-fourth of the town's population.

The opening of the free library in 1855 in the old Town Hall, now the Werner Block, was a good start but still inadequate. To assure its proper growth and usefulness a town meeting was held to enact by-laws and appoint trustees. Among the early benefactors of the library was Henry Ward Beecher, who donated the proceeds of his lectures to the library.

On October 18, 1856, it was incorporated as the Lenox Library Association and in 1873 negotiations were started to move from the Town Hall into new quarters in the Court House — since 1787 Lenox had been the county seat. In 1815–1816 the handsome brick building which housed the county courts was built and designed by Captain Isaac Damon of Northampton. Later, when Pittsfield became the county seat, the Lenox Court House was left unoccupied.

Around 1848 Lenox began to attract fashionable summer visitors, among them Mrs. Adeline Schemerhorn, who built a home on Walker Street. During the

The library, Lenox

winter of 1871 while she was in Rome she received word that the Court House was going to be auctioned. She commissioned Judge Julius Rockwell to acquire the building, "to make therein a public library and reading room free to all visitors and inhabitants of Lenox." The deed was prepared and sent to her in Florence but she died on June 8, 1873. Her children carried out her wishes and conveyed the Court House property to the trustees she had previously named, and the building was dedicated to the memory of "one of Lenox's most useful and beloved townsmen," Charles Sedgwick, who had been Clerk of the Courts for thirty-five years.

When Tanglewood was presented to the Boston Symphony Orchestra as a Summer Music Center, the library expanded its list of books on music. Serge Koussevitsky presented to the library a complete set of summer concert recordings, and after his death his wife gave his entire library of miniature scores.

In recent years the library has added the vocal score collections of Geraldine Farrar and Florence Easton. The library also acquired from Miss Ellen Bullard the endowed art collection she formed in memory of her cousin, Francis Bullard.

Williams College
WILLIAMSTOWN

Williams College is located in Williamstown, in the northwest part of Massachusetts, with the Green Mountains of Vermont to the north, the Hoosick range to the East, the Berkshires to the South and the Taconic range to the West. These mountains were well known to a British soldier, Colonel Ephraim Williams, who was killed in the French and Indian War. His will provided for the establishment of a "free school" in the Hoosac River valley in Western Massachusetts, and Williams was founded as such a school in 1791. Two years later it developed into a college.

The tomb of Colonel Williams is in the Thompson Memorial Chapel on the campus.

The oldest building on the campus is West College, constructed in 1790. Fire gutted the dormitory in December 1950, but it proved possible to construct the new building within the standing walls of the old, and the traditional appearance of the building is unaltered. Among the other notable buildings at Williams, Griffin Hall and the Hopkins Observatory command attention.

Hopkins is the oldest astronomical observatory in the United States, over 125 years old. The building was recently moved to its present location overlooking Main Street, the third time the building has been moved.

Astronomy has been taught at Williams for over 167 years; it was a required subject for nearly a century until 1893. It became increasingly important under

PHILIP KAPPEL

Hopkins Observatory, Williams College

121

Albert Hopkins, professor of mathematics and natural philosophy in 1829, who was the younger brother of Mark Hopkins, president of the college from 1836 to 1872. The alumni contributed $4000 for the purchase of astronomical instruments. In 1834, Albert Hopkins went to Europe to get them and within a year of his return he began the construction of the observatory. Still mounted in the dome, and fully operative, is the 7-inch refractor installed in 1852.

In its new location the reactivated Hopkins Observatory will continue as a planetarium and astronomical museum. The old transit and the sidereal clock are to be remounted in the East Wing. Here too will be showcases to display early instruments used in astronomy, navigation and surveying. The West Wing will have modern exhibits designed to explain graphically the latest knowledge of the universe.

Nearby, the Sterling and Francine Clark Art Institute of Williamstown is one of the finest and newest of the nation's smaller museums. Its classical exterior is built of Danby Imperial Marble from Vermont. This museum is a valuable "classroom" in the arts for Williams College, but the general public comes by the thousands each year and to date over a quarter-million visitors have passed through the museum doors.

Valor to Share

GREAT BARRINGTON

This roadside marker is placed just off Route 7 on the outskirts of Great Barrington. Henry Knox received orders to get the desperately needed artillery taken at Fort Ticonderoga and Crown Point by Ethan Allen, Benedict Arnold and Seth Warner. He accomplished his mission under trying circumstances and delivered fifty-five mortars, howitzers and cannon on sledges drawn by oxen over almost impassable roads, over frozen ponds and lakes and deep snow from Lake Champlain to Boston, where George Washington immediately placed the cannon on Dorchester Heights. This strategy won for the Americans their first heartening victory over the British.

Knox became George Washington's confidant and military adviser, a loyal friend and constant companion. He was made a colonel and placed in command of the American artillery in most of the Revolutionary battles.

Knox was made a major general in December 1783. In 1789, President Washington appointed him his first Secretary of War; while Secretary he established the United States Military Academy at West Point. General Knox died at the age of fifty-six, completely ruined financially by speculations that failed. It is ironic that Fort Knox, Kentucky, should have been named after him.

The monument text reads:

THROUGH THIS PLACE PASSED
GENERAL HENRY KNOX
IN THE WINTER OF
1775 — 1776
TO DELIVER TO
GENERAL GEORGE WASHINGTON
AT CAMBRIDGE
THE TRAIN OF ARTILLERY
FROM FORT TICONDEROGA USED
TO FORCE THE BRITISH ARMY
TO EVACUATE BOSTON
ERECTED BY THE COMMONWEALTH
OF MASSACHUSETTS 1927

Monument commemorating the feat of General Knox

Pioneer Valley

HADLEY

One July day I crossed the Connecticut River east of Northampton, Massachusetts, in search of a covered bridge I heard was somewhere in the vicinity. The bridge which I was seeking had burned several weeks before, but I continued to explore the area. That was how I accidentally discovered Hadley — a delightful village with old trees and cooling shade.

This characteristic New England village was among the first to be settled in New England. A group of English pioneers followed the Connecticut River upstream from Windsor, Connecticut, in 1659 in search of a permanent settlement. They were tired of wandering, having first gone to Dorchester on Massachusetts Bay, and later to Windsor. They made one more try and found the ideal place after thirty tiresome years and settled at Hadley on a stretch of fertile plain excellent for tillage.

I admired the orderly farms, with their radiating rows of asparagus, potatoes and onions, for which Hadley is noted. For centuries the alluvial deposits of the Connecticut River produced loam that is rich, deep and very productive. Throughout the valley on both sides of the Connecticut River, weathered barns for curing tobacco leaf rise amid stretches of white-tented acres.

Hadley Center has a fine Congregational meetinghouse with a Christopher Wren spire, atop which is a 200-year-old weathervane imported from England for another meetinghouse and later transferred to the present structure in 1808. Behind the church is the gleaming white Farm Museum with its pigeon tenants and a great well-sweep. The Farm Museum had been the barn built at Forty Acres in 1783. Henry Johnson in 1929 moved it to its present location to hold his rare collection of household and farm implements.

Forty Acres, also known as the Porter-Phelps-Huntington House, is two miles north of the center, near the east bank of the Connecticut River. The house was one of the first to be built outside the stockade. This three-story gambrel-roofed mansion was built by Moses Porter, who moved into it in 1752. The present generation is the tenth to occupy the land, and the sixth in the house.

Recently incorporated, it will be a valuable source for the study of the Colonial era in American history. This property with important family furnishings, together with valuable documents of national interest dating back to 1697, has remained unchanged except for simple improvements made in 1799.

The Sessions farm, Hadley

125

Moses Porter was a captain in the regiment commanded by Colonel Ephraim Williams, which was ambushed in 1755 while on a scouting mission near
Lake George. None of the officers survived, and few of the men. Captain Porter's
body servant returned to Hadley and knocked on the window where Mrs. Porter
was putting her child to bed. Apprehensively she pushed back the heavy shutter
and received her husband's sword through the window, the significance of which
she recognized at once. Today the sword may be seen in the room where Mrs. Porter received it.

The only child of Moses and Elizabeth Porter married Charles Phelps when
she was twenty-two. He was an astute businessman trained for the legal profession.
The landholdings were increased, the house was improved and the planting was
perfected until the plantation reached the perfection we see today.

To Charles and Elizabeth Phelps were born a son and a daughter. When his
father died in 1814, this son gave up a law office in Boston and returned to Hadley.
In 1817 he built the large house across the road which, since 1929, has been known
as the John A. Sessions place. The great barns on the Sessions farm are illustrated
here, with their luminous shadows and the cows clustered in the yard, emphasizing
the rural aspect of New England.

One year after Charles Phelps built the house, his mother died at Forty Acres;
the estate was divided between the two heirs. Into Forty Acres moved the sister of
Charles Phelps, who returned to Hadley with her husband, the Reverend Dan
Huntington, and their six sons and three daughters. Here, they had two more children, a daughter and a seventh son, Frederic.

In 1847 Frederic's mother died; he decided to buy all the outstanding shares
of Forty Acres in the hands of his brothers and sisters. It took seventeen years to
accomplish this and by 1864 he became the sole owner of Forty Acres, including
the furnishings and the documents intact. Forty Acres was Frederic's summer home
while he was rector of Emmanuel Church in Boston and, after 1869, Bishop of
Central New York. On his death in 1904, Forty Acres was left to the six surviving
children and remained undivided for twenty years until Dr. James Lincoln Huntington purchased the estate from his brothers and sister.

In 1955 Dr. Huntington received the Award of Merit of the American Association of State and Local History, for his "valiant and intelligent fight to save Forty
Acres." Forty Acres is made available for the study of Colonial history to students
of Smith, Mount Holyoke and Amherst, and to historians at large.

Dangerously close did the priceless collections at Forty Acres come to destruction by the rampaging waters of the Connecticut during the worst flood that the
valley ever witnessed, in March 1936. Foreseeing the danger that threatened
Hadley, in the absence of Dr. Lincoln Huntington, his cousins across the road,
John and Daheny Sessions, hurried over to the house and removed, in the nick of
time, most of the contents from the lower to the upper floors.

Deerfield

Deerfield's mile-long village street makes a striking bucolic picture, with numerous seventeenth-century houses beneath ancient trees. It appears more like a theatrical setting; but Deerfield is not imagery — her story is real.

By May 1673 there were sufficient settlers in Deerfield to be granted "Liberty of Township" by the General Court, which remained Deerfield's only "Act of Incorporation." And by 1674, the charming village street had been planned and house lots apportioned, and the settlement named.

The open meadows required no clearing of trees or rocks preliminary to planting; all that was needed was to plow the rich alluvial soil, drop the seeds and watch them grow. Stock roamed at will in the lush grass outside the fenced area for crops. The settlers were at ease, and with their Indian neighbors they enjoyed years of harmony.

The situation changed as soon as King Philip's War spread to western Massachusetts and soldiers arrived with orders to defend the river towns.

Henceforth a succession of tragic events followed. On September 18, 1675, Captain Lothrop and a company of men arrived from Essex to escort a wagon train of wheat for the troops at Hadley. The wild grapes growing on vines along the way were too tempting to be ignored by the band, and everything ground to a halt near a small stream where the teamsters and the troops threw their weapons to the ground to free their hands for grape-picking. Without warning a thousand Indians appeared out of ambush and cut into the disarmed men. In memory of the sixty-four teamsters and soldiers who perished, the stream was named Bloody Brook.

Following this disaster the settlers abandoned Deerfield and the Indians gathered in the neighboring woods to wait for the venturesome to return to their homes. A few did so in 1677 and were promptly killed. And others later were captured and carried off to Canada, the first of many captives to follow the same long trail northward. Thereafter, the General Court passed an act governing the resettlement of abandoned villages. By virtue of this act the orderly resettlement of Deerfield began in the spring of 1682, at which time new settlers appeared to pick up new land grants. The plantation of Deerfield was reborn sufficiently to have sixty proprietors by 1686.

The village developed on the mile-long plateau high above the surrounding meadows. Every precaution was taken against surprise attacks by Indians. Everywhere, even in church, men carried their guns; Deerfield was virtually an armed camp in constant fear of Indians.

At the start of Queen Anne's War in 1702, Deerfield had 300 souls; the following year Lord Cornbury, Governor of New York, informed Captain Wells, commander of the fortifications on Meeting House Hill, that he had learned from his informers that an expedition was being fitted out against Deerfield; a similar warning was forwarded to Reverend John Williams by Major Peter Schuyler.

When the eastern Indians attacked the settlements in Maine in July, twenty soldiers arrived at Deerfield to reinforce the home guard. Sixteen more arrived on October 8, after two men were captured and taken to Canada. The frequent alarms completely demoralized Deerfield. The settlers herded together in the fort for their safety and left their chores undone. When winter came everyone breathed a sigh of relief — the danger from Indian attacks had moderated, it seemed.

But early in the morning of February 29, 1704, an army of French troops and Indians under the command of Hertel de Rouville crossed the frozen Deerfield River and stole towards the village unnoticed over the encrusted snow. When the northwest corner of the stockade was reached some of the Indians scaled the fourteen-foot palisades, with the aid of deep snow drifts, and quietly dropped into the enclosure. The sentinel was overpowered before he could give the alarm. The Indians opened the north gate for their comrades and, uttering war-whoops, ferociously set upon the inhabitants with tomahawks and guns. Thanks to the stubborn resistance at the Benoni Stebbins House, the enemy was held engaged until reinforcements arrived from the towns south of Deerfield. They pursued the enemy into the North Meadows, but were ambushed and forced to return to the stockade.

In the meantime Hertel de Rouville and his warriors, flushed with success, marched to their camp across the river, where they collected their 112 Deerfield captives and set out on the 300-mile trek to Canada. Twenty people were murdered or starved to death on the journey; most of the captives who survived the hardships were later redeemed. Others who preferred to remain in Canada married into French or Indian families.

Property losses ran high in the village — about half of the houses and barns had been looted and burned; more than half of the inhabitants were tomahawked, shot or taken captive, and the village was reduced to an isolated military outpost.

Two years later — 1706 — many of the survivors returned to rebuild their homes, notwithstanding the threats of further Indian raids. In 1735, Governor Jonathan Belcher of the Province of Massachusetts met with emissaries from six Iroquois Indian nations at Deerfield, where they concluded pledges of permanent friendship which proved effective and lasting.

Deerfield was no longer a frontier village; it became a manufacturing and trade center, and its numerous inns could accommodate all so engaged. In 1775, Colonel Benedict Arnold came to the Barnard Tavern — Frary House — to arrange for the purchase of beef to be sent to Ticonderoga.

Main Street, Deerfield

Three months before the Battle of Lexington, General Gage sent a representative to Deerfield to inform the Tories that it would be safer for them to be in Boston when the dissidents were forced to lay down their arms. The agent was treated to some fitting abuse by the patriots, who continued to assemble ammunition and arms. Shortly thereafter, while the patriots were holding one of their meetings, a messenger brought the news of Lexington and Concord. Before midnight fifty men, under the command of Captain James Locke, Lieutenant Thomas Bardwell and Lieutenant Joseph Stebbins, were marching towards Cambridge. Stebbins took part in the construction of the redoubt on Bunker Hill with General Putnam, and participated in the battle. Bardwell and Stebbins marched to Bennington to meet Burgoyne's invasion forces in 1777, but the battle of Walloomsac was over and the meetinghouse was packed with Hessian prisoners. The job of rounding up Burgoyne's stragglers was left to Bardwell and Stebbins.

The town records prove, by an entry made on June 25, that Deerfield declared her desire for independence from Great Britain before the famous Declaration of Independence of July 4, 1776.

The eighteenth-century houses on Deerfield's village street are part of a restoration program similar to that of Williamsburg but on a lesser scale. The restoration of Deerfield owes its success to the generosity and vision of the Henry N. Flynt family. Individually and collectively, the various architectural gems have been authentically restored and their backgrounds accurately recreated.

The Little Brown House

DEERFIELD

Albany Road runs west off the old village street, past the Deerfield Academy buildings. When the road was originally part of the main highway to Albany, it forded the Deerfield River. About midway between the Old Fort Well and the Old Burying Ground is the Little Brown House (1760), on the grounds of the Academy, a charming building partially smothered by shrubs.

Whenever I discover a suitable subject for a drawing I habitually ask one of the local people to pose for me. This frequently adds a touch of human interest — and effusive information. But the man in the rocker disqualified himself right from the start — his well of knowledge ran dry and he froze in a pose and peered into space; he was still posing long after I left the scene.

Diagonally across the street from the Little Brown House is the Reverend John Williams House, which was moved from its original site on the Common. The present house was built in 1707 to replace the one which was destroyed by Hertel

Lilac time — the Little Brown House, Deerfield

de Rouville. The building, now used by the Academy, has an exquisite scroll pedimented doorway and a finely carved side doorway and window pediments.

In 1797 the Legislature of Massachusetts granted a charter to a group of trustees to form Deerfield Academy, a college preparatory school with a present accounting of four hundred boarding and approximately sixty-five day students and one of the outstanding schools in America.

Further west, past the Academy, is the Old Burying Ground. Near the south side of the burial ground is the common grave of forty-eight men, women and children who perished at the hands of the French and Indian invaders during the Massacre of 1704. In the center of the cemetery, beneath a group of evergreens, are the graves of Reverend John Williams and his wife, Eunice. The epitaphs of the cemetery are well worth anyone's attention. The oldest stone in the graveyard marks the resting place of Deerfield's first Town Clerk, Joseph Barnard, who was killed by Indians in 1695.

The Dwight-Barnard House, Deerfield

The statue of Roger Williams looks across to the Capitol Building, Providence

Rhode Island

Rhode Island and Roger Williams

The first English colony in New England to grant religious freedom through legal recognition was officially known as the State of Rhode Island and Providence Plantations, settled by a rebellious group from Massachusetts who did not see eye to eye with the Puritan preachers and their magistrates.

Roger Williams, a clergyman and the founder of the Baptist denomination, was unwelcome in the Massachusetts Bay Colony, where he strongly voiced his resentment against the granting of land that belonged rightfully to the Indians. In Salem his views on the separation of church and state were political heresy and he had to flee into the wilderness with a group of his adherents. These bellwethers of religious tolerance and the new democratic approach made their first settlement at Providence in 1636 on land purchased from the friendly Narragansett Indians.

In 1638 William Coddington, John Clarke, Anne Hutchinson and numerous other Puritan exiles purchased, with the aid of Roger Williams, the island of Aquidneck from the Narragansett Indians and there established Portsmouth.

Coddington and Clarke withdrew from Portsmouth because of factional differences and founded Newport in 1639 on the southwestern side of the island. Massachusetts and Plymouth started to agitate and press their claim to the area. Roger Williams counteracted through influential friends and secured a parliamentary patent in 1644 under which a code of civil law and organized government was established for the existing four towns — the fourth being Warwick, established by Samuel Gorton in 1642.

The persistent Coddington received a commission in 1651 annulling the patent but the commission was revoked the following year through the efforts of Roger Williams and Clarke, and the four towns were reunited in 1654.

The charter granted to Roger Williams in 1663 by Charles II assured the future stability and survival of the colony against boundary differences and pressure brought to bear by Connecticut and Massachusetts, but their agitations continued well into the eighteenth century.

When Roger Williams made it known that Quakers and Jews, unwelcome elsewhere in the colonies, would be accorded full religious freedom in Rhode Island, this grant from Charles II, with its guaranteed freedoms, was hailed as the most liberal document in all New England. All comers were welcome to share a democracy in which the State and the Church were at long last separated. The early settlers were for the most part English, all of them drawn to Rhode Island by the guarantees of religious freedom.

Quakers, who had a hard time elsewhere, arrived in droves, and not a few oppressed Jews settled in Newport during the first year of Roger Williams's presidency in 1654. The early settlers owned the land which they purchased from the Indians — a practice Roger Williams encouraged.

The cordial existence between the settlers and the Indians persisted, and trading and fishing went on amiably as a supplementary living to those who tilled the soil. It was an agrarian democracy which Rhode Island's neighbors accepted with mixed loathing and mistrust; Rhode Island was never admitted to the New England Confederation. But she shared equally the devastations of King Philip's War.

Newport until the American Revolution did a thriving business with the other New England ports on the "triangular trade" in rum, slaves and molasses. Due to Rhode Island's irascible attitude towards British mercantilist policies, she constantly violated the Molasses Act of 1733 and the Navigation Acts. Narragansett Bay became a notorious haven for smugglers and privateers.

Rhode Island renounced its allegiance to George III one year after the Militia under Nathaniel Greene joined the Continental Army at Boston in 1775. From 1776 to 1779 the British forces were in occupation, but they abandoned it when news arrived of the approaching French fleet.

With the Revolution won, Rhode Island, jealous of her independence and nurturing a kind of congenital stubbornness, was one of the states responsible for the failure of the Articles of Confederation.

Rhode Island held out against the ratification of the Constitution until 1790.

The early years that followed the Revolution brought currency problems and bankruptcy. In the wake of despair her industrial greatness was born. The abundance of water power led to the rapid development of manufacturing, which attracted capital from merchants and shipping magnates who dominated economic life as well as the political scene far into the twentieth century.

Samuel Slater, who founded the American textile industry, served his apprenticeship in the English cotton-spinning mills and made himself thoroughly acquainted with the intricate machinery devised by Richard Arkwright and Samuel Crompton. In 1789, at the age of twenty-one, Slater came to America in disguise — textile mechanics were forbidden to emigrate and it would be a still greater offense to be caught with designs of textile machinery. Young Slater did bring with him the plans for textile machinery — every intricate piece of it, in his head instead of on paper — and proceeded to construct the machinery after meeting Moses Brown, who provided financial backing. A year later their machines were producing cotton goods for the American market.

It would be impossible to surpass Prospect Terrace on Congdon Street for a memorial to Roger Williams. This impressive, yet simple figure of Roger Williams was executed by the sculptor Leo Friedlander; the stone arch which frames the statue and the state capitol was designed by Ralph T. Walker.

First Baptist Meeting House

PROVIDENCE

Whether you look at a church as just another beautiful building in the community or evaluate its spiritual contribution, the First Baptist Church has occupied a high place in the development of Rhode Island since its founding.

The present meetinghouse on North Main Street was erected in 1775; it is believed to be the third oldest church of that denomination in America. The slim white spire was adapted from an illustration in James Gibbs's *Book of Architecture* (1728) by Joseph Brown, a capable amateur architect to whom was given the responsibility of making the final selection of a design.

University Hall, at Brown University, was built from one of Joseph Brown's designs. He was a trustee of the University and a member of the faculty and acclaimed a brilliant scholar. In 1773 Brown and Stephen Hopkins were elected to take charge of erecting the Market Building, which is still standing in Market Square, much smaller than University Hall but executed in the same style. Among all of Joseph Brown's architectural accomplishments, the First Baptist Meeting House was his most important commission. The body of the church was also adapted from designs by Gibbs and the interior is typically Gibbs in influence and feeling. The great columns are cut midway by the balconies; the doors, windows and the cornices are all illustrated in Gibbs's book.

Somewhere in the course of time, the body of the church was lengthened and minor changes effected. When the church was built there was no organ in the west end gallery — instead there was a second balcony where Negroes were accustomed to sit during services. The Palladian window in the east end, set within an arched design, was originally flat and had small panes of glass.

The old square pews and the pulpit were removed in 1832 and presented to another Baptist Church in Centerdale. When the error was recognized, the old pews later on were duplicated and reinstated. In the pulpit end of the church the baptismal font and the stained glass window are slightly at variance with the original appearance.

From all angles the church is perfectly preserved — an outstanding and beautiful example of a typical eighteenth-century English baroque edifice.

Joseph Brown was versatile — his own house at 50 South Main Street, which he built a year before the Baptist Meeting House was erected, is an unusually inspired piece of architecture. The gable is shaped as an ogee pediment, and the

First Baptist Meeting House, Providence

house originally had its main entrance at the second floor, approached by a double flight of steps that led to a pedimented doorway, in which the architect repeated the ogee lines of the gable above the door. The house was later adopted by the first bank in Providence.

The Stephen Hopkins House
PROVIDENCE

Many old houses impress you with their pretentiousness, others have their own secret charms for wooing you, but the Hopkins House has its inalienable simplicity.

Stephen Hopkins was a self-educated man, a believer in the merits of education who contributed generously towards the purchase of books for a public library, and a close friend of many noted men of his time. He was Chief Justice of the Superior Court and the first Chancellor of Brown University, was nine times Governor of Rhode Island, a member of the Continental Congress. A signer of the Declaration of Independence, he was affected with palsy at the time, but remarked, "My hand trembles, but my heart does not."

Stephen Hopkins was born on March 7, 1707, in Cranston, Rhode Island, of a staunch Puritan family. After the death of his first wife, he married Mrs. Anne Smith and formally joined the Society of Friends, becoming a close associate of Moses Brown and other prominent leaders.

In the spring of 1776, while Hopkins and his wife were in Philadelphia, his stepdaughter received George Washington as a guest. Today the room he occupied is furnished to simulate the period — a canopy bed, a graceful highboy, a chest of drawers and a four-hundred-year-old Bible. Throughout the house the wide floorboards are worn smooth by many feet.

The original part of the house, built in 1707, consisted of two rooms and an unfinished attic. The house stood on the corner of Town Street and Bank Lane, now South Main Street and Hopkins Street. Stephen Hopkins purchased the small house in 1742, and the following year he added the other rooms. The house was moved halfway up the hill in 1804 and moved to its present location in 1927, nearer Benefit Street. The members of the Society of Colonial Dames in Rhode Island and Providence Plantations succeeded in preserving it as a historical landmark and restored the building as accurately as possible under the able supervision of the eminent architect Norman Isham.

The big door in the "Keeping Room" was formerly the main entrance. When the house was moved to its present location it was turned around; the present front door replaced a window and was designed by Norman Isham to conform to the mid-

Terraced beauty — the corner of Benefit and Hopkins Streets, Providence

eighteenth-century classic doorways. It has a triangular pediment, a turned-up backband that breaks the horizontal elements of the architrave, and Doric pilasters on high pedestals.

The stairway has the closed string course, ornamented with heavy moldings, and stubby turned balusters and plain handrail which butts directly into the newel post — a common mode of construction in the plain period houses. The simple acorn-shaped drops are also typical of the same period.

The parlor has a charming fireplace with Bolection moulding and recessed shell shelves. The corner posts and high narrow windows in the room to the ceiling are indicative of mid-eighteenth-century construction, as are the hand-hewn woodwork and the doors.

After the house was restored it was furnished with authentic period pieces, donated by members of the Society of Colonial Dames and their friends. The house is maintained by the Society, but is owned by the State of Rhode Island.

The Hopkins House shows how unpretentiously some of the "great" men lived before the sea brought tremendous wealth to Rhode Island.

Just off Benefit Street is the John Brown house, which is now occupied by the Rhode Island Historical Society. John Quincy Adams described it as "the most beautiful house on the Continent."

The Old Colony House, with its back door on Benefit Street, was built in 1762. From the steps of this building the independence of Rhode Island was proclaimed from England May 4, 1776, two months before the joint Colony declaration took place.

The Birthplace of Gilbert Stuart
SAUNDERSTOWN

This gambrel-roof house is located in the Pettaquamscutt Valley, where a small stream once ran four early American water-driven power plants and where each spring one of nature's unsolved secrets prompts the spawning alewives to leave the sea and enter the swollen fresh-water stream to reach the pond above the dam.

A portion of the dam still stands at the site of the Mumford Mill which was built in 1686 and which once furnished lumber, and functioned as a fulling mill. The gristmill ground corn for the famous Rhode Island Johnny Cakes.

The house is built on a sharp slope of land at the head of the Mattatucket River. The stream that flows past the house operates a huge wooden waterwheel which turns the wooden gears and teeth of the mill on the lower floor of the building where Gilbert Stuart's father erected the first snuff mill in New England. The

Gilbert Stuart's birthplace, Saunderstown

143

present mill is over 175 years old — it was shipped over from England in 1932 as a gesture of goodwill.

The birthroom of Gilbert Stuart is left of the entry. The furnishings are simple and approximate the period: a three-legged candlestand, a red pine cradle with hood, a betty lamp and a roped bed with a blue coverlet; a deer-hide trunk, a brass warming pan, a blanket chest and a mirror with a primitive painting.

Gilbert Stuart's father, who was unsuccessful as a snuff maker, offered little encouragement to his son, who desired to be an artist. Gilbert Stuart sailed to London to study art but his early days there were fraught with want. Unable to seek help from home, he was driven to appeal for work from Benjamin West, who immediately assisted him by inviting him into his home. Stuart became West's pupil-assistant in his studio.

Within six years Gilbert Stuart acquired enough training to enter his work at the Royal Academy. He won fame immediately and opened a studio in Dublin in 1787. There he became so successful that it went to his head. He spent money carelessly on parties and high living, and eventually, in order to escape the pursuing sheriff, he and his wife returned to America in 1792 and settled in Philadelphia. In 1805 he moved to Boston, where he spent the rest of his life.

Few artists of the mid-eighteenth century had their work so widely circulated. His likeness of George Washington, which is on our currency, is a masterpiece — and Gilbert Stuart knew it. He prized it so highly the portrait never left his possession. Those of the same subject we see in museums are copies of the original — he sold copies for sums ranging from five hundred to eight hundred dollars each, and there are seventy-five copies that are accounted for. The original rightfully belonged to Martha Washington, who ordered the painting and prevailed upon George Washington to pose for it, but Stuart maintained the excuse that it was not finished and avoided handing it over to her. The "unfinished" portrait is acknowledged as the best likeness of Washington. Stuart painted three portraits of George Washington. His first, the so-called Vaughan Type (1795), is a bust with the right side of the face shown; the original has disappeared, but at least fifteen copies are known to exist. The second, the Lawnsdowne, shows the President standing, full length, his left hand outstretched. The original is in the Pennsylvania Academy of the Fine Arts. The third, unfinished, the Athenaeum Head, remained in the artist's possession until after his death. It was acquired by the Boston Athenaeum and loaned later to the Museum of Fine Arts, Boston.

Some of Stuart's well-known sitters were Jefferson, Madison, Monroe, Judge Story, Jacob Astor, John Jay, Edward Everett and Jerome Bonaparte. He also painted portraits of his fellow artists John Singleton Copley, Benjamin West, Sir Joshua Reynolds and Washington Allston.

St. Paul's Episcopal Church

WICKFORD

Wickford was laid out as a real estate development in 1707, which accounts for the number of eighteenth-century houses — far more than are found in any New England village of equal size — but Wickford also has one of the largest marinas in the East.

St. Paul's Church was built in 1707 and moved from Tower Hill to Wickford in 1800. It is a fine example of the fresh approach to architecture brought to Rhode Island by the Church of England. In 1702 the Society for the Propagation of the Gospel in Foreign Parts prevailed upon the authorities that Narragansett needed a missionary, and the Reverend Christopher Bridges arrived in 1706.

The church at first had neither pews nor galleries and it was not until 1721 that the parish voted to procure timber for constructing them. When the settlement at Tower Hill dispersed, the church was moved to its present location.

The church has a pitched roof; the ceiling is arched, following the curved forms of the ceiling beams. The pulpit, designed by Norman H. Isham, is of the wineglass type which was not uncommon in New England in the eighteenth century. The exterior exemplifies the classic spirit, with roundheaded sash windows of Georgian design symmetrically placed on either side of the door, and a cornice of classic moldings.

The doorway has the characteristic feeling of the early construction, exemplified by the nearly semicircular high segment of the pediment, with its curving cornice overhanging the supporting entablature; the scrolls of the pediment are carved with interesting rosettes of Jacobean type. The clapboards were laid in the manner of the very early construction — close together at the base of the building and farther apart as they approach the top, with the ends feathered and lapping over each other, and nailed with wrought-iron clapboard nails.

In 1721, the portly and bewigged Reverend James MacSparran was called as a missionary to take up his duties as rector of St. Paul's parish. In the ensuing thirty-seven years of Dr. MacSparran's devoted service the community of Tower Hill became an intellectual and spiritual center; somehow, after Dr. MacSparran's death in 1757, the settlement gradually dissolved.

Chiseled in a stone set into the walk that goes to the church door, and where everyone may notice it, are the following words:

TO THE GLORY OF GOD AND IN MEMORY OF
GABRIEL BERNON, BORN IN ROCHELLE, FRANCE 1644,
DIED PROVIDENCE 1736, A SEIGNEUR, A CITIZEN OF
RHODE ISLAND, A FOUNDER OF THIS CHURCH.

White Sand

WICKFORD

Narragansett Bay cuts its way deep into Rhode Island, extending as far inland as Providence. Numerous islands spot the Bay standing guard over the sub-bays favored by yachtsmen, but the entire perimeter of Narragansett Bay is one of New England's finest summer resort areas.

Wickford and Narragansett are situated on the western shore of the Bay where the beaches reach, almost without interruption, as far as Watch Hill in the southwestern part of the state after rounding Point Judith, just south of Narragansett.

Point Judith is well known to mariners and feared by them — over a hundred ships have been wrecked in the vicinity which sailors call "Old Point Jude." The lighthouse was built in 1810; the Coast Guard Station on the point has from time to time rendered heroic assistance to shipping in distress. Among the well known ships lost off Point Judith were the *American Eagle,* the *Swallow* and the *Acushnet.*

Nine miles offshore lies Block Island with its high bluffs, the feet of which are brushed by Atlantic currents. Sportsmen know the tuna and swordfish well but frequently have to settle for a bluefish or a cod.

Quonset Point, and the United States Naval Air Station appear on this drawing, but blend into the horizon. However, aircraft constantly leaving or returning to base remind one of a hornet's nest with its inhabitants buzzing about.

On the eastern shore of Narragansett Bay, going southward from Providence, the road passes through Barrington and Warren — both shellfishing centers — thence to Bristol, one of the best-known seaports of early Rhode Island, where some of the finest sloops have been built, many of which have successfully defended the America's Cup.

Bristol was settled in 1680 by several well-to-do members of the Massachusetts Bay Colony, and remained a Massachusetts town until 1747. The character of Bristol right from the start differed from other towns in Rhode Island.

St. Paul's Episcopal Church, Wickford

In 1698, Joseph Reynolds built his house soon after his arrival in Bristol from Boston. Nearly one hundred years later his house became the Bristol headquarters of General Lafayette. There is an interesting story told about preparations being made for Lafayette's arrival on a certain day. A young French officer appeared at the house and asked for something to eat. He was warmly ushered to the table prepared for the general. When the unknown officer tarried too long over his meal he was requested to leave by the lady of the house to permit them to prepare the table for Lafayette. To her great shock and chagrin the officer replied, "Madam, I am Lafayette."

Spotlight on Newport

There is much more to Newport than a casual visit reveals. Newport has over 400 houses and buildings built between 1675 and 1820, widely different in character and interest, which make the town one of the nation's preeminent monuments to Colonial and Revolutionary times.

In the minds of many visitors Newport is synonymous with great wealth. This is a deduction induced by the famous palaces on Bellevue Avenue which made their appearance in the 1890's, and were dubbed "cottages." Left stranded by time, they are now out of place and incongruous with the architecture of eighteenth-century Newport.

The Newport Preservation Society keeps a watchful eye on Newport, always ready to buy notable landmarks whenever and wherever threatened by developers, in order to assemble enough of historic Newport to complete the story of architecture and history from colonial days to the present.

The Elms, The Breakers and Belcourt are now open to visitors, who troop through the elaborate gardens and the buildings — containing as many as fifty furnished rooms — to see how society lived in its era of splendor. The excesses represent a way of life the pioneers wished to leave forever on the other side of the Atlantic.

The notorious Jazz Festivals further depress the tone of Newport when hundreds of jazz enthusiasts converge upon the town, snarling traffic and pitifully jamming the approaches, the ferries, and creating unendorsed chaos by capers that try the patience of the residents and the police.

When scheduled, the America's Cup Races are held in mid-September, and Newport braces herself for another invasion. This time society, the sight-seer, and the town watch the harbor fill up with costly yachts from round the world, and social activities return to frenzied heights with formal dinner parties and festivities.

Quonset Point and Naval Air Station in the distance

Thoughts return, in spite of distractions, to old Newport where the visitor or the antiquarian reaps his greatest rewards. In the center of the old part of town is Washington Square, where the weary pedestrian may rest in the shade or examine the large seated statue of Commodore Perry with his back to the Colony House nearby. This building is one of Richard Munday's architectural masterpieces, built of brick in 1739 and influenced by the work of Sir Christopher Wren.

From 1739 to 1776 this charming building served as the Colony House, and from 1776 to 1900 as the State House where the assembly met and governors were inaugurated.

Some stirring scenes were witnessed by Newport's public buildings, the Colony House in particular. From its balcony in 1761 the death of King George II of England was officially proclaimed, and the ascendancy of King George III was celebrated here by a large banquet. In 1776, the people gathered at the Colony House to rejoice over the repeal of the Stamp Act, and during the Revolution the building was used by the British and the French as a hospital. When George Washington came to visit General Rochambeau he was entertained at dinner in the Great Hall.

The Vernon House
NEWPORT

William Vernon purchased the house located on Clarke Street at the corner of Mary in 1774 from Metcalf Bowler, another Newport merchant and shipowner, and it remained in the Vernon family until 1872. It was later purchased by Harwood Read, who sold it to the Charity Organization Society, now known as the Family Service Society, the present owners.

When the British occupied Newport in December 1776, William Vernon, then owner of the property, left to become identified with the newly formed Navy Board of the Colonies in Boston. It is quite possible that the British may have occupied Vernon House during their stay in Newport.

With the arrival of the French in Newport the best houses in town were requisitioned for living quarters, and the commander-in-chief was assigned the Vernon House. Vicomte de Rochambeau used the front north room on the ground floor for his headquarters and entertained many prominent guests in this spacious house. The pressing need of a meeting place for his officers made it mandatory to build an assembly hall which was erected just north of the house in the garden in 1780; later it was incorporated into the stable which once stood on the site.

The Colony House

Vernon was irritated by the building of French Hall, and questioned the right of Rochambeau to erect it in his garden. Later, the General, when in Boston, called to pay his respects to Vernon, at which time he probably explained his actions. When the French departed from Newport in 1782, Vernon asked to be reimbursed for damages of $450. Apparently the elegant balls held in Vernon House had wrought considerable wear and tear which Vernon was less prone to overlook than the French.

All social affairs were climaxed by Washington's visit to Newport on March 6, 1781, at which time, after the conclusion of a ceremonial review of the troops on the Parade, Washington went to Vernon House to spend the night with Rochambeau, and remained in Newport for ten days.

In September 1908, a bronze tablet was affixed to the house by the Alliance Française in memory of Rochambeau. Count de Chambrun, a lineal descendant of Lafayette, delivered an address, and Julia Ward Howe pulled the ribbons which released the Tricolor covering the tablet.

In 1937, a noteworthy discovery was made in the house when some wooden panels were removed for repairs. Beneath them were hidden some unusual murals, painted on the plaster of the exterior walls of the north front room on the ground floor, which were restored by the Newport Historical Society. The panels were replaced with hinges so that they may be opened to expose the murals, which have caused considerable speculation and interest as to their origin. The character of the work unquestionably points to their having been executed by a Chinese artist, or someone exceptionally acquainted with Chinese art.

Trinity Church

NEWPORT

No major wooden structure of Colonial America has been as carefully preserved as Trinity Church, erected in 1726 under the leadership of the Reverend James Honyman, who was minister from 1704 until his death in 1750. The present building replaced an earlier one which the congregation outgrew.

Trinity Church was built by Richard Munday, who also constructed the Colony House, as well as many of the finer homes in Newport. Munday incorporated in the church special features found in several of Sir Christopher Wren's London churches, but it is impossible to substantiate the claim that Wren actually drew the plans for Trinity Church.

In 1762 the church was enlarged by cutting it apart in the middle and lengthened two bays. The delicate proportions of the superimposed piers supporting the galleries and ceiling, the airiness of the groined ceiling, the balance of the triple-decked wineglass pulpit in the center aisle — the only pulpit of its kind left

Revolutionary Headquarters of Rochambeau — the Vernon House, Newport

153

in America — and the carvings throughout the interior, the sturdy paneling of the box pews and the windows testify to the genius and great skill of Richard Munday and his fine workmen. Pew Number One at the left rear is the one Munday and his wife occupied — a modest choice.

Although the Church of England had come to Virginia in 1607, there were no permanent established Anglican Churches north of the Mason and Dixon Line until almost the end of the seventeenth century. The first Church of England parish in the north was King's Chapel, founded in Boston in 1683. This was followed by Christ Church in Philadelphia in 1695, Trinity Church in New York, 1696, and Trinity Church in Newport in 1698.

The revocation of the Edict of Nantes in 1685 drove many prominent Huguenots to America, where the freedom of Rhode Island appealed to these persecuted Frenchmen. Their ritualistic leanings and abhorrence for excessive Puritanism moved the Huguenots to join the colonists loyal to the Mother Church.

The first missionary served for only two years before he died suddenly. His place was filled in 1704 by the Reverend James Honyman, who became the real father of the parish.

The simple table which served as the altar, first used in 1698, is among the treasures that may be seen. Other priceless treasures include the first chalice and paten given to the church in 1702 by the London Society for the Propagation of the Gospel in Foreign Parts. The famous silversmith Daniel Russell, of Newport, made two pieces of silverware — the Kay Memorial baptismal bowl, considered by many to be one of America's finest pieces of silverware, and a smaller bowl which is still used weekly as an alms bowl. The baptismal bowl has been in use since 1734. Benjamin Brenton, equally famous for his craftsmanship, made two large silver flagons for the communion service between 1733 and 1734.

The bell in the Tower Room bears the date 1702 and is believed to be the first church bell rung in New England. A larger bell was given to the church by Queen Anne in 1709 but has since been recast.

The original casework of the Bishop Berkeley organ is complete with its royal crown and bishop's mitres. Bishop Berkeley, Newport's most distinguished colonial visitor, resided here from 1729 to 1731; he preached on numerous occasions and after returning to England gave the organ, which was installed in 1733 — the second such instrument in America.

George Washington made his first visit to Newport in 1756 as the guest of Godfrey Malbone, a Trinity Vestryman. Pew 81, where Washington worshipped on his visits to Newport, is just to the right of the great pulpit in the center aisle.

Since 1733 the black and gold altarpiece has been in the same place, though minus the British Royal Arms which surmounted it — destroyed by patriots after the British evacuated Newport. Fortunately, no further damage was done by the mobs, and Trinity remained intact as "the supreme and matchless reminder of Colonial America."

PHILIP KAPPEL

George Washington worshipped here — Trinity Church, Newport

Touro Synagogue

NEWPORT

The Redwood Library was Peter Harrison's first important architectural commission in Newport, in 1748; his second was the Brick Market, built in 1762, to provide Newport with an adequate granary and market, with the upper part divided into stores for dry goods. The third commission, and perhaps Peter Harrison's most distinguished building, is the Jewish synagogue, built in 1763.

Jews emigrated to Newport from Spain as early as 1655, and from Holland in 1658. The Lisbon earthquake in 1755 forced sixty families to settle in prospering Newport, where in 1758 Rabbi Isaac Touro, a renowned scholar and theologian, established the first Jewish congregation. Five years later he established the first synagogue in America; and since 1946, a national historic site. This two-story square brick building with its flat hipped roof and severe exterior ornamented by a modillioned cornice, roundheaded windows and a one-story Ionic porch, was considered exceptional in its day. However, prior to the Revolution, porches were rarely without chambers above them — besides, the classic entrance porch seldom was seen in New England. This arched porch with columns was indeed unique in Rhode Island.

The interior of the Touro synagogue is its chief charm. No one knows what prevented vandalism during the Revolution from destroying the synagogue, but it has survived as one of the few unaltered colonial shrines in all New England. Harrison's ability as a great designer is nowhere brought to the fore with greater ingenuity, since he had to meet the uncommon demands of the Jewish ritual. The synagogue scheme had to be superimposed upon the ritual of the Temple of Solomon in Jerusalem, which included twelve columns representing the twelve tribes of Israel, as well as a gallery especially designed for the use of women — for Jewish practice dictated that women shall enter the synagogue from a stairway built in a small addition at the side. The wall of the Ark of the Covenant was always oriented to the east, which necessitated placing the synagogue where it is in relation to the street.

PHILIP KAPPEL

Touro Synagogue, Newport

157

New Hampshire

Portsmouth

Portsmouth has watched one irreplaceable landmark after another disappear, replaced with stores and businesses. Those who were apprehensive about this historic area succeeded in establishing Strawbery Banke, Inc., "to acquire, hold, care for, invest in, operate, administer and otherwise deal in such real and personal property as may illustrate and be a part of the early history of Portsmouth, the Piscataqua River, and the state of New Hampshire." This ambitious nonprofit organization intends to restore a ten-acre area which was the original site of Strawbery Banke. It became the business district of colonial Portsmouth, and was also known as Puddle Dock. Sea captains and successful tradesmen built their homes near the water; but in time the area lost its charm and became slums. When I last saw Portsmouth, these were cleared to receive the thirty old houses and other buildings which will restore a way of life between the years of 1775 and 1820. Famous old Pitt Tavern stood there when George Washington and John Paul Jones, Lafayette and Louis Philippe, who later became King of France, shared the hospitality of the inn.

Twenty years after the founding of Strawbery Banke, the colony grew to a fair-sized seaport which was rechristened Portsmouth, after the home city of its founder, Captain John Mason. In colonial times, Portsmouth was the capital of New Hampshire, and here the American Navy was born with the launching of John Paul Jones's flagship, the *Ranger*.

Few cities in the United States offer the visitor more examples of lovely dwellings that belonged to the early settlers or exemplify the splendor of the Royal Governors. Portsmouth was the home port of some of the wealthiest colonial traders whose magnificent estates and belongings remain unsurpassed.

The Governor John Langdon Memorial, on Pleasant Street, is considered to be one of the great Georgian houses in America. It was built in 1784 for Governor Langdon, who became the first president of the United States Senate.

On Mechanic Street stands another magnificent example of Georgian architecture built in 1760 by Madam Mark Hunking Wentworth as a gift to her son Thomas, the younger brother of John Wentworth, the last of the Royal Governors. It is said that at one time the Metropolitan Museum of Art planned to move the building to New York.

The Macpheadris-Warner House

The Moffatt-Ladd House, situated on Market Street, was erected in 1763 by John Moffatt for his son Samuel, who had serious business reverses and fled Portsmouth; but somehow the elder Moffatt managed to rescue the house from the creditors. The French scenic paper in this mansion, depicting the Bay of Naples, is among the best on the Eastern seaboard.

Another house which still gives the illusion of being occupied by people of rank, is the Macpheadris-Warner House, situated on the corner of Chapel and Daniel streets. This house, perhaps the finest example in New England of an important brick urban dwelling of the first quarter of the eighteenth century, has been designated as a Registered National Historic Landmark by the Secretary of the Interior. Captain Archibald Macpheadris built the house about 1716. His daughter married the Honorable Jonathan Warner in 1760 and they lived in the house until the death of Warner in 1814. Collateral descendants occupied the house until 1931, when it became the property of the Warner House Association. Of special interest is the lightning rod on the west wall which was installed under the supervision of Benjamin Franklin in 1762.

Just beyond the Macpheadris-Warner House, on the crest of a hill, is St. John's church which was built in 1807 of brick on the site of the old Queen's Chapel on Strawberry Bank. The bell was taken from the French in 1745 at Louisbourg and recast by Paul Revere in 1807. The communion silver was given by Queen Caroline in 1742 and the church has an English organ that is reputed to date back to 1710. Daniel Webster and Benjamin Franklin were pewholders. In the graveyard near the church are the tombs of Royal Governors and patriots of the Revolution.

At the foot of Little Harbor Road and situated at the water's edge, two miles from Portsmouth, is one of those rambling houses of great age, the oldest part of which was built in 1695 — becoming by stages a mansion of consequence. It was occupied by Benning Wentworth, governor of the province when Portsmouth was the seat of government.

The Victorian Rockingham Hotel is, in its own way, a historic landmark. It occupies the site of the colonial mansion which was once owned by the Honorable Woodbury Langdon, a member of the Continental Congress. The original hotel was built in 1833, but sixty years later it was leveled by fire. Fortunately the famous Langdon Room was saved and incorporated in the new building.

Next to the hotel stands the John Paul Jones House, a dignified gambrel roofed building that has been since 1920 the headquarters of the Portsmouth Historical Society. The house was built in 1758 by Gregory Purcell, a sea captain and merchant who maintained a shop on Long Wharf. He married Sarah Wentworth, a niece of Benning Wentworth. After her husband's death in 1776 she conducted a "genteel boarding house" in her home to support herself and her seven children. Among her boarders was the youthful Captain John Paul Jones, in Portsmouth to supervise the outfitting of the *America*.

PHILIP KAPPEL

The John Paul Jones House, Portsmouth

Peripheral Journeys in New Hampshire

WAKEFIELD

The superhighways between the large cities along the Merrimack River — Concord, Manchester and Nashua — offer fast and easy access to strategic sectors of New Hampshire, but New Hampshire imparts a feeling of majestic isolation when one travels the secondary roads. Especially delightful are the trees on "dress parade" in the fall when New Hampshire is a fairyland — narrow roads arched by trees of scarlet and gold, the roadsides bordered by ferns and colorful underbrush, with vistas through the clearings of panoramic breadth or cloud forms reflected in the numerous ponds.

The small villages spaced miles apart entice the motorist farther away from home; on one such trip that started in a casual way I found myself at Wakefield in eastern New Hampshire. The deep ravines locked in the grip of evening, conjure the hazards the pioneers endured by coming to this virgin country, which in the end turned out to be too rock-riddled to substantially support them. Many of them, spirited away by the opportunities offered by the American West more than a century ago, left the farmhouses, pastures and orchards to the mercies of the second growth timber that superseded everything won by hard labor. Today, the testimony of the past lies deep in the woods; in the stone walls that at one time defined the boundaries of old farms.

In the Monadnock region there are numerous charming late eighteenth-century villages, and Hancock is one of the most charming. It was granted a charter in 1779, named after John Hancock, who owned much of the village. The lumber mills and the tanneries are gone now — all that remains is the essence of charm.

One should not drive through Hancock's main street; a stroll under the trees that line both sides of the street is more rewarding in welcoming doorways and delightful fences. At one end of the street is the brick building, at one time a tavern, which presently houses the Hancock Historical Society. At the other end stands the white Congregational Meeting House which serves as town hall and church. The bell hanging in the church belfry was cast by Paul Revere.

Though the village of Wakefield, near the Maine border, is widely separated from Hancock, they do not differ drastically. The central feature of my drawing is the Roberts place in Wakefield, built about 1800. It was at one time the home of Dr. Roberts, a prominent physician. The house to the right of the Roberts place is known as "Erna Tulip's House." Most of these houses were originally one-and-a-half-story and were raised to two-and-a-half from about 1825 to 1840 — a commonplace procedure during the nineteenth century when additional living space was required.

Wakefield Village

The original Wakefield Congregational Church with its fine steeple, built about 1790–1810, stood opposite the Roberts house. It was destroyed by fire in 1957 and rebuilt, but architecturally it is not in the same class as the old church.

Mountains and Lakes

New Hampshire has the shortest seacoast in New England — only eighteen miles — but the state is tall on mountains.

If he is not lured by the mountains, the vacationer has a choice of superb bathing anyway, in New Hampshire's 1300 lakes and ponds.

The highest bodies of water in the state are two barren, rock-rimmed basins named Lake of the Clouds, a mile above sea level on Mount Washington. The lake was discovered by Darby Field in 1642 when he made the first recorded ascent of Mount Washington. In the northernmost part of the state at Pittsburg a series of three lakes are the headwaters of the Connecticut River.

The largest lake in New Hampshire is Winnipesaukee — 71 square miles of water surface punctuated by over three hundred islands. Second in size is Lake Wentworth, not far from Lake Winnipesaukee. Wolfeboro on Lake Winnipesaukee has the reputation of being the oldest summer resort in New England. Nearby are the Belknap and Sandwich Ranges, and the Ossipee Mountains, also Copple Mountain, making the region notably scenic.

Colonial Governor Wentworth had his summer home in Wolfeboro and carried on the functions of government from there for many years. The old foundation of the Wentworth mansion is not far from the shores of Lake Wentworth; the relics excavated by the state of New Hampshire from the site are exhibited in the Libby Museum along with other interesting items of local interest, including a model of the wooden sidewheeler S.S. *Mount Washington,* launched in 1872 and burned at the Weirs Docks in 1939.

The replacement of the S.S. *Mount Washington* on Lake Winnipesaukee during a single season carries 50,000 passengers on cruises, besides making scheduled stops. A century ago, horseboats plied the lake at four miles an hour as ferries, driven by horses that walked on a treadmill attached to a paddlewheel on each side of the boat.

Each new season in this distinctive vacationland offers fresh appeal. The quiet Indian summer days of September and early October lure thousands into the state to witness the phenomenon of nature's curtain call, an extravaganza of gold, scarlet and yellow that is spellbinding.

Long before the snow starts falling, the ski tows are conditioned and the facilities for the skiers and the non-skiers are made ready to accommodate them from

Hopeful angler on lake Winnipesaukee

mid-December to April. The skiers reluctantly leave the slopes when the thaws arrive, and New Hampshire hangs the pails on the maples in the sugar-bush. It is maple sugaring time, which is a brief season, requiring many hands and experience. The salmon and trout fishermen arrive after ice-out, thousands of them.

When the spring season is well along and the soft air becomes irresistible, Mr. American Motorist infiltrates New Hampshire's deep ravines and makes a try at reaching the summit of Mount Washington as soon as the road is free from late snows. Others are content to motor through Franconia Notch and take pictures of the Old Man of the Mountain or travel in a gondola to the summit of Wildcat Mountain, 4100 feet above sea level, for a breathtaking panorama that extends to Canada and the Atlantic Ocean.

The state's abundance of historic lore is equally inviting. New Hampshire was settled under the authority of an English land-grant in 1623, and was the first of the states to declare her independence, in January 1776, and the first to adopt her own constitution. New Hampshire was the ninth and deciding state to accept the Federal Constitution, binding together the original thirteen states as a Republic.

The first recognized aggressive act of the Revolutionary War was the removal, by a small band of patriots in 1774, of the powder and guns from Fort William and Mary in New Castle, east of Portsmouth, at the mouth of the Piscataqua River. New Hampshire troops were in the fighting of Bunker Hill; and the state is proud of General Stark, whose victory at the Battle of Bennington was of tremendous importance.

Durham is one of New Hampshire's earliest settlements — founded in 1635 — and it was in the church where the patriots hid the powder and arms they captured from the British at New Castle in 1774, before they were secretly moved to Cambridge by oxcart. General John Sullivan's house is near the site of the church.

Cultural shrines in New Hampshire are so numerous that only a few can be mentioned here. One of these is the Saint-Gaudens Memorial at Cornish where one of America's most famous sculptors maintained his home and studio. At Peterborough, where composer Edward MacDowell once lived, many creative artists, musicians and writers live in a wooded retreat at the MacDowell Colony, created by his widow as a memorial. The Currier Gallery of Art, at Manchester, has a permanent collection of art that is worthy of the most fastidious attention, and also offers special exhibitions and lectures on art.

The homestead where Franklin Pierce was born is located just west of Hillsboro. It was built in 1804. Pierce was New Hampshire's only President of the United States. Between Salisbury and Franklin is the house where Daniel Webster was born. It is partially restored at present.

Open Season — *the sight of a retriever sloshing ashore,*
  holding a duck in his mouth, is cause for jubilation

Happy Corner Bridge

PITTSBURG

A fly-fisherman will often try his luck in the pools beneath Happy Corner covered bridge spanning swift flowing Perry Stream that cascades over rocky outcroppings near the Canadian Border. This covered bridge is one of the oldest in the northern part of New Hampshire, but its exact age is unknown. It is one of the unusual Burr-type bridges, few of which are still in use.

There are about sixty covered bridges in New Hampshire — fifty of which are used by vehicles and six for the exclusive use of railroads, and one is intended for the sole use of the pedestrian.

On either side of the Connecticut River, where bridges crossed it, towns flourished, and traffic between Vermont and New Hampshire was willing to pay toll charges. The ferries were slow and carried the bulk of the traffic prior to the coming of the covered bridges.

The Windsor (Vermont)-Cornish (New Hampshire) covered bridge is almost one hundred years old. Until 1943 toll was collected — the cost was two cents on foot, four cents for a horse, two cents for a cow, and fifteen cents for a cord of wood. During the winter it was customary for an appointed individual, who was paid a fee, to haul snow inside the covered bridges to facilitate the passage of traffic which was on runners.

Covered bridge over Perry Stream, Pittsburg

Railway to the Clouds

MOUNT WASHINGTON

The Mount Washington Cog Railway was the first mountain-climbing railway in the world. It has been in continuous accident-free operation since 1869, except at intervals during the two World Wars and after the great hurricane of 1938, which destroyed much of the trestle.

The cog railway starts from Marshfield Station at the foot of the mountain. The railway is 3½ miles long, most of it on trestle which ascends the west slope of the mountain. The average gradient is one in four, or 25 per cent; the steepest grade is slightly more than 37 per cent on Jacob's Ladder. The operation of the odd-looking locomotive depends on a cog rail bolted to the crossties of the road, into which the toothed wheels under the engine mesh.

Above the timberline the mountain is brutally barren, but beautiful Alpine flowers blossom among the crags, unmoved by the ferocious winds. Here and there within sight of the trestle commemorative signs tell tragic tales of those who didn't quite make the summit while hiking. The hikers use a trail that runs along the crest of the Presidential Range to Mount Washington's 6298-foot summit. The area above timberline is about eight miles long and two miles wide — the largest Alpine zone in the Eastern United States. The trail is marked by rock cairns at close intervals to prevent hikers from getting lost when clouds envelop the peaks or when sudden snowstorms descend during the fall months.

172

Mount Washington cog railway

Maine

The Western Coast

From Kittery to the Bay of Fundy, the Maine coast is slightly under two hundred and fifty miles long. This coast is not straight, but crumpled and indented, with numerous inlets, bays, rivers, coves and about two thousand islands, large and small. If they could be unraveled to make a straight line, the distance would come to thousands of miles.

The western sector of the Maine coast extends from Kittery to Portland, with few exceptions level or modestly rolling country. Miles of beaches alternate with exquisite inlets, and stretches of marshland and waving metallic-toned salt hay. The water is warmish, and swimming is inviting and delightful as far as the east coast of Casco Bay, where the water suddenly turns icy cold. Therefore it is not surprising that the beaches between Kittery and Cape Elizabeth are popular and congested. Thousands of people from out of state, returning year after year, generate the developments with small summer cottages, accompanied by garish roadside eating places, amusement areas, honky-tonks, and the billboards, which are wholly inconsistent with the natural beauties of Maine, as is the litter this careless public leaves behind.

Mount Agamenticus, in York, is the tallest hill in the area, 673 feet, from which mariners for years have taken their bearings while cruising along the coast.

At Ogunquit there are many old houses on tree-lined streets, and hotels where "senior citizens" sit all day on porches or front lawns to watch the crowds. But the real activity is found along the beach, or at attractive Perkins Cove, where the Art Colony flourishes. Within this area artists, artistic aspirants and poseurs live as a closed society in fishermen's shacks, brilliantly painted in raw colors and draped with fishnets and lobster floats. For added attraction, beards and abbreviated shorts set the mode of fashion for the artistic set.

Not until you get to Portland Head will you be able to look out upon the blue water of Casco Bay and the Calendar Isles (the first of the important Maine islands) without being distracted by countless numbers of vacationers, swimming pavilions and snarled traffic. The best of coastal Maine still lies ahead — just beyond Portland, the largest city in Maine.

Kittery is refreshing to look upon with its storehouse of historic lore and drowsy charm. Not far from downtown Kittery is the U.S. Naval Base, established in 1800, where such wooden fighting ships as the *Franklin, Saratoga* and *Congress*

Fort McClary, Kittery Point

were launched. Today, nuclear submarines for our modern navy are assembled here.

The frigate *Ranger* was built on Badger's Island. She was the first ship of the Continental Navy flying the American colors — under the command of John Paul Jones — to receive the salute of a foreign power.

Along Route 103 there are numerous historic houses. One of the most renowned is the Lady Pepperell Mansion (1760), which was built for Lord Pepperell's widow by British workmen brought over by her ladyship. It is a gleaming white shiplap-styled mansion, elegant in its proportions and patrician in character. On the opposite side of the road is the First Congregational Church and parsonage, constructed in 1730.

The Sir William Pepperell Mansion (1682) is another fascinating landmark. It is a two-and-a-half-story gambrel built of wood, with much of its interior paneling extending from floor to ceiling. The furnishings are Queen Anne and Chippendale; the silver, floor coverings and pewter are all handed down from the Pepperells. A complete eighteenth-century library contains many rare items, among which may be found the diary of Chief Justice Samuel Sewall, a judge at the Salem witchcraft trials and a grandfather of Lady Pepperell.

The John Bray House was built twenty years before Sir William's and retains many of its features; it is attractively furnished and looks out upon a bay filled with boats. It is said that the Bray house is the oldest in the state. Another important landmark of local and national interest is the birthplace of General William Whipple, a signer of the Declaration of Independence.

Fort McClary, situated on Kittery Point, has long been associated with the defense of Portsmouth Harbor. The fort overlooks the Piscataqua River, with a magnificent sweeping view of the harbor and the distant Isle of Shoals. The fort was originally called Fort William but after the Revolution was renamed in honor of Major Andrew McClary, the highest-ranking officer killed in the battle of Bunker Hill.

The site was fortified as early as 1715 by the Province of Massachusetts to protect the Massachusetts merchants (Maine was then a part of Massachusetts) from "unreasonable duties" imposed by the Colony of New Hampshire. The first fort was completed in 1809; the present restoration is a six-sided blockhouse with a first story in granite topped with an overhanging wooden second story.

William Pepperell, after whom the original fort was named, came from England as a young man and was placed in command of the fortifications. Pepperell subsequently became Maine's most distinguished citizen and one of the wealthiest men in New England. His son, Sir William, served on the Massachusetts Governor's Council for thirty-two years, and as President for sixteen. He further distinguished himself by successfully leading the Louisbourg Expedition against the French in 1745, towards which he contributed 45,000 pounds.

A short distance past Kittery, a church spire catches the eye — the First Parish Church in York, a dazzling white building standing on the green where sixty York minutemen assembled before marching off to fight in the battles of Lexington and Concord. The church was organized in 1673, and the cornerstone laid in 1747, which makes this church the oldest religious society in Maine. The church was completely remodeled in 1951.

Among York's many noteworthy houses with historic backgrounds, one has special interest as the oldest English public building in America still in use. Situated on high ground facing the green, the somber Old Gaol was built in 1653. You may now see the criminals', women's and debtors' cells, surrounded by stone walls three feet thick. A pillory that used to take care of minor offenders stands in front. The gambrel-roof building presently houses many items of local interest.

The Old Burying Ground, opposite the First Parish Church, is a captive of the languid shadows cast by neighboring trees. Their indigo patterns move stealthily over the tombstones from dawn to dusk while the summertime traffic rolls past.

One stone marker has a touching account of the Candlemas Day Massacre of 1692 when the Abenaki Indians attacked the settlement on the dawn of a cold January morning, killing or capturing three hundred of the inhabitants, of whom forty lie buried here in obscure graves. The others marched to Canada, many dying along the way.

The King's Highway at one time ran past the Old Gaol. It was later incorporated into the Old Post Road which ran from Portland to Boston, crossing Sewall's Bridge over the York River. This bridge was used by the York minutemen on their march to Lexington. The present pile bridge is a replica, but without the original drawbridge section.

The Hancock Warehouse, beside the river, belonged to John Hancock, who acquired the building through a foreclosure proceeding and held it until his death in 1794. I am told that the warehouse is the only Colonial commercial building still standing.

Farther along the coast, in Brunswick, is Bowdoin College, chartered in 1794. Nathaniel Hawthorne and Henry Wadsworth Longfellow both received their degrees with the Class of 1825. Sarah Orne Jewett was the first woman to be honored with the degree of Doctor of Letters by Bowdoin College, in 1901. Her book *The Country of the Pointed Firs* has become a classic.

Harriet Beecher Stowe wrote *Uncle Tom's Cabin* at Brunswick, where she lived with her husband, Calvin Ellis Stowe, when he became a professor at Bowdoin College.

At the mouth of the Kennebec River, the Pilgrims exchanged corn for beaver skins as early as 1625. Deep in debt, they sought a major water route into the interior to set up a trading post. Since the French controlled the region from the Penobscot River eastward, the Pilgrims procured a patent for the Kennebec region, where they firmly established a post at Augusta and did so well by trapping and trading they were able to liquidate all payments for the *Mayflower* within ten years!

Beyond Brunswick the Maine coast changes drastically. The granite promontories become numerous, extending southward like multiple fingers from the coast — identified as part of the "drowned-coast" of glacial times and continue all the way Down East as far as the Bay of Fundy.

Pemaquid Point Light

At the end of the Bristol Peninsula, where spruce and fir grow nearly down to the water, the Pemaquid Lighthouse completes one of the most photogenic spots on the Maine coast. The lighthouse, a white pyramidal tower built in 1827, has a capacity of 11,000 candlepower. The light stands 79 feet above the water and warns shipping far out to sea, for if by some misfortune a skipper hears heavy surf breaking against the rocks of Pemaquid Point in dense fog, it's too late.

The Pemaquid area was among the earliest parts of the coast to be settled; in 1605 Champlain visited the vicinity while charting the coast and discovered that a settlement had already been established there. Mystifying to historians are the cellar holes and bits of street pavement at Pemaquid Beach, which antedate the Popham settlement; many theories have been advanced concerning their origin but none agree. Captain John Smith made a note of the site in 1614 and mentioned that it was opposite Monhegan Island.

Pemaquid has had a tempestuous history. The first fort erected on the point made its appearance in 1630 and was promptly demolished by the Indians. It was replaced by a more substantial structure in 1677, under orders from Governor Andros, but this was also destroyed — by pirates. Sir William Phipps raised a still better fort on the same spot, considered at the time to be impregnable, but it proved otherwise when Baron de St. Castin swept down with his Indians and leveled the fort to the ground. For good measure he killed everyone in the garrison when he discovered that one of his Indians had been chained inside the fort and mercilessly tortured.

A fourth fort was built in 1729, in the same place. The jinx made itself felt when the fort was again destroyed — this time by the Americans during the Revolution, to prevent the British from using it against them.

The present fort is the fifth and is actually a replica of Phipps's Fort William Henry, a cylindrical stone structure with loopholes and embrasures. Inside there is a collection of Indian relics and ancient military equipment.

The first land purchased from the Maine Indians was bought from Samoset and Unonquil at Pemaquid, on July 15, 1625, by John Brown of New Harbor, Monhegan Island, for fifty beaver skins; the territory included what now encompasses Jefferson, Bristol, Nobleborough and Newcastle. The deed transferring this

Lighthouse tower, Pemaquid Point

property to John Elbridge and Robert Aldworth, in 1626, was the first deed made in all New England.

An epochal one-hour naval engagement took place on September 5, 1813, off Pemaquid Point, between the Yankee Brig *Enterprise* and His Majesty's Sloop-of-war *Boxer*. Both captains were killed in the engagement, and their double funeral was held in Portland. The bodies were placed on two separate barges draped in black and slowly rowed by muffled oars to the landing while all the ships in the harbor fell in behind. Bells tolled and the guns of the artillery fired at one-minute intervals as the English Captain Blythe, twenty-nine years old, and the American Captain Burrows, only twenty-eight, were laid to rest side by side in Portland's Old Eastern Cemetery as comrades in death.

Longfellow's poem "Lost Youth" immortalizes the battle. Longfellow, whose boyhood home is one of the most cherished landmarks in Portland, unquestionably witnessed the battle and saw the arrival of the *Enterprise* in Portland Harbor with the defeated *Boxer* in tow.

Between Portland Head Light and the head of Penobscot Bay, there is a string of white historic towns strung out one after the other — rich in fine old captains' houses, beautiful doorways and ancient trees. Many pages could be written about Damariscotta, at the head of the Damariscotta River, where in the spring the alewives come to spawn. Shipping was the common interest in all the eighteenth-century towns along the coast, but what a variety of ships — clippers, four- to eight-masted schooners and stone barges. Boothbay Harbor and Wiscasset still have some of the old schooners, rotting away, caught in the shallows of the harbors — going nowhere, just making pretty pictures for the artist.

At Waldeboro, ten miles from the sea, the *American Eagle* was the first three-masted schooner built; it was followed by the *Governor Ames* which was the first five-masted schooner ever launched. Rockland was too busy burning limestone to be interested in much else until the industry was crippled by the adoption of steel and Portland cement in construction, but Rockland still remains a sizable producer of lime. Today, Rockland's fine harbor is noted as the largest distribution center for lobsters.

Montpelier, built in 1795 at Thomaston, was the home of General Henry Knox, Chief of Staff and Secretary of War under George Washington. The house was rebuilt in 1929 and furnished with antiques and the General's personal possessions.

Among the beautiful towns down the coast, Camden is one of the most appealing. Camden is a perfect example of a dying seaport and shipbuilding center converted into a resort town with scrupulous taste and discretion by its wealthy benefactors, among whom Mary Louise Bok has been responsible for many of Camden's cultural advantages.

Approximately six miles north of Belfast, which was founded in 1770 by thirty people of Irish descent who arrived from Londonderry, New Hampshire, is the delightful town of Searsport, located near the head of Penobscot Bay. Searsport was at one time a very prosperous and cultured community left stranded by the decline in shipping. Over one hundred and fifty ship captains made their home there and it is said that over ten per cent of the captains who manned the American Merchant Marine between 1870 and 1880 lived in Searsport. When prosperity collapsed the entire town slowly ebbed away. The fine old houses still face the harbor, waiting, perhaps, for the return of the tall ships.

Down East — The Middle Coast

The Boothbays, situated on a peninsula between the estuaries of the Sheepscot and Damariscotta rivers, lie in the Middle Coast area of Maine, a region extending from the west bank of the Kennebec River to the east bank of the Penobscot — both vital and important rivers commercially and historically.

The Indian Wars of 1668 made the Boothbay settlement untenable and forced its abandonment thirty-eight years after its start. David Dunbar dreamed about that abandoned piece of real estate. He sought and received a grant from George II in 1748 and brought to the peninsula a group of Irish and Scotch colonists, carefully selected for their pioneering capabilities and reliability. They excelled in shipbuilding, did some farming, made much of fishing and were exceptional traders.

With the decline of shipping, the area sought supplementary means of livelihood and the resourceful Maine folk found a way; tourists were invited to live among them.

Beside Boothbay, Boothbay Harbor and the East and West Boothbay Harbors, there is a vast area widely acclaimed by the tourists and summer residents for its exceptional beauty — such places as MacMahan Island, Squirrel Island and isolated Monhegan Island, which lies ten miles offshore. Also worthy of mention are Newagen, Southport, Fire Islands and Christmas Cove — there are others, of course, but the focal point for all is Boothbay Harbor by boat or road.

There is inconclusive evidence that the Norsemen had been here a thousand years before. But there is definite proof of an English Colony as early as 1607 near the mouth of the Kennebec River, on a site overlooking the present delightful settlement of Popham Beach. Captain George Popham was sent over with a group of settlers; they underestimated the severity of the Maine winters, and in about a year the discouraged survivors were removed to England leaving behind over half of their original number beneath the sod, including Popham himself.

PHILIP KAPPEL

Accouterments of the lobsterman

Low tide, West Boothbay Harbor. Squirrel Island in the distance

Main Street
CASTINE

Castine changed hands many times in the battles waged by the sovereigns of Europe; Richelieu and Mazarin, churchmen, politicians and ambitious men, intrigued to possess her. Myles Standish, Clarendon and Thurlow were also among those who had a hand in Castine's destinies.

Castine was the key position in the struggle for European supremacy in New England.

Situated beside the Penobscot on a peninsula extending south of Bucksport, Castine today is a backwater, out of reach of twentieth-century traffic problems and most of the altercations that accompany tourism. What happened to Castine is chronicled by markers throughout the town, but the vibrant past is felt the moment you enter it.

Castine has a snug harbor; the Vikings nearly a thousand years ago may have been the first to moor their ships there while probing the coast. Gomez and Verrazano were probably acquainted with the peninsula when they discovered the Penobscot early in the sixteenth century; Gosnold and Weymouth could scarcely have passed it by; but the Pilgrims of Plymouth were the first Europeans to settle at Castine, in 1629, where they established a fur-trading post with full knowledge that they were trespassing on French territory. Two years later they were thrown out.

The French then built a stockade around the Pilgrim trading post and turned it into a fort of questionable strength. Soon thereafter the English returned; this time they swept the place clean of Frenchmen and regained control. The area was returned to France in 1670 by treaty and Chevalier de Grande Fontaine moved right in with his soldiers and Indian followers. Among the officers who came with him was a brilliant young ensign named Vincent Baron de St. Castin, to whom Fontaine assigned the responsibility of the fort.

St. Castin had forsworn a life of luxury and his estates to marry the daughter of the Indian chief of the Tarantines on the Penobscot. Fontaine was crafty and calculating — he recognized at once the built-in favors such a marriage carried. He reasoned that though he had few troops for a major job, the Indian warriors were numerous and would remain dependable and loyal under the command of their chief's son-in-law. St. Castin governed the French settlers well and in peace on the banks of the Penobscot. Their luck ran out four years hence when the ship *Flying Horse* sailed up the bay brazenly flying the Dutch colors. Jurriaen Aeronouts, who commanded the invasion force, expected an easy victory. Rather, it proved to be a costly one, but he succeeded in overpowering Castin, who had to flee into the surrounding woods, from which he made the Dutch victory hardly worthwhile. Any Dutchman who came within range of an arrow never made it back to the fort from the brook nearby which was the only source of fresh water. The area between the fort and the shore was likewise rendered untenable by the deadly arrows of Castin's Indian allies.

The Dutch recognized their hopeless position and evacuated Fort Pentagoet. Close on the heels of the fleeing Dutchmen, Castin reentered the fort and set to work erecting a stronger and larger fortification. Nothing remains of the fort today, but the site is well marked at the foot of Perkins Street.

The exhaustive work by Castin to make an impregnable fort was all for naught. Eight years later Sir Edmund Andros led a British contingent of troops into Penobscot Bay; he broke Castin's resistance and the fort remained the undisputed territory of the British for almost a hundred years. As a warning to all with designs on retaking Castine the British fortified themselves by building earthworks of formidable proportions.

The fortification, Fort St. George, faced its first testing in 1779, in a battle that fizzled out shamefully. Two thousand Continental troops under the command of General Lowell and Paul Revere in command of artillery sailed for Castine with forty-four vessels. The Americans, however, lost the initiative in spite of holding high ground above the fort and never fired a single shot. When five British frigates were sighted the Americans scrambled down to the shore, fired their vessels, and retreated in haste on foot back to Boston.

At the close of the Revolution, Pentagoet was renamed Castine in tribute to the man who was the implacable opponent of the British during the fierce struggle between France and England to gain control of Maine.

A stroll through Castine's shaded streets and quiet green will confirm that this is indeed legendary territory; the claws of progress have not yet deflowered its charm. The houses are impressively neat and trim, with gardens of riotous color. The relationship of the village with its surrounding open spaces is judiciously conceived, and the disposition of Castine is restful and retiring. The summer residents and the natives many years ago arrived at a nodding understanding and appreciation of each other. This is how I found Castine during many widely separated visits with friends who settled there.

"Maine Gothic"

CASTINE

Probably nothing along the Maine coast, with the exception of its breathtaking beauty, is more expressive of its flavor than the people themselves — like their surroundings, they have been shaped by the sea which formed their rugged independence, tastes and self-reliance!

Main Street, Castine

A short distance beyond this typical waterfront scene, the 7000-ton training ship *State of Maine* is warped to her pier — literally a floating classroom for over five hundred midshipmen who practice aboard ship what they learned in their textbooks at the Maine Maritime Academy. At the conclusion of their four-year course, the midshipmen are ready to serve as officers of the U.S. Merchant Marine.

The Academy buildings are located just off Main Street, where in the heyday of sail, merchants and shipowners built their delightful homes and planted the trees which tower above them today. The Maritime Academy occupies the site of the old British barracks near the ruins of the British Fort George, the outlines of which are plainly visible today.

The local Masonic Lodge at Castine has a charter dated 1794, signed by Paul Revere of Massachusetts, as Grand Secretary. The Unitarian Church (1790) is the oldest meetinghouse in Maine that still holds regular services. It has a Bulfinch steeple and a Paul Revere bell.

Between 1780 and 1790, Castine was a nest of Tories who harassed shipping between Boston and the towns on the west shore of Penobscot Bay and the river.

Massachusetts claimed Maine almost from the beginning. During the Cromwell period, Massachusetts extended its authority over Maine, and representatives from that state sat in the Massachusetts Legislature. When Charles II ascended the throne the claims of Massachusetts were disallowed.

Maine, the largest of the six New England states, was not one of the original thirteen; it was admitted into the Union in 1820.

Antiques for Sale
CASTINE

A casual look at this unabashed display of "antiques" is indicative of New England frugality, the urge to save everything, however inconsequential. Prominently displayed are two seats that formerly graced a privy; other obsolete and tattered items in various stages of wear are also waiting for buyers.

Antique collectors and bibliomaniacs occasionally discover a "sleeper" of value among such wreckage. Such good fortune is more likely to happen in seaport towns. Sea captains were avid collectors — not always knowing or astute, but having a sentimental desire to bring home to their families gifts from foreign lands that ultimately find their way into the antique shops. My first charming piece of Chinese porcelain, purchased many years ago at Bath, in an antique shop similarly cluttered, was the forerunner of a collecting spree that has gone forward unabated.

PHILIP KAPPEL

Display of antiques on a street in Castine

192

Waterfront scene, Castine

Young herring gull poses involuntarily with William MacKaye on Pond Island.
Nearby, among the flora detailed in the drawing, the mature gulls secrete their nests
with nearly perfect success.

193

Pond Island

During one of my visits to Castine, my hosts, William and Katy MacKaye, suggested that if I wanted to visit an uninhabited Maine island they would arrange a picnic party to join us aboard their ketch, *Tasman,* and explore Pond Island, one of the numerous islands in the mouth of Penobscot Bay, with which the Penobscot River merges as it flows southward past Castine.

Once we were under way the shore line expanded like an open fan as we entered the broad bay, sparkling under a brilliant blue sky. The helmsman called out, "We're almost there," and after a short interval he came about and ordered Admiral W. W. Warlick, who was at the time superintendent of the Maine Maritime Academy, to let the anchor go. Without protest the order was promptly executed and naval dignity was further compromised when Warlick manned the oars of the dinghy to get ashore.

We were at once greeted by hundreds of herring gulls that rose from the underbrush like sputtering helicopters; we had invaded their sanctuary and the young gulls were still in their downy nests. The protests of the gulls became deafening; the air was filled with their squawking. In a sense it was pitiful to watch them swoop down, vainly trying to frighten us off the island. Eventually they disappeared as fast as they appeared, in a fluttering mass of wings caught in a whirlpool of upward air currents. They had abandoned their young to our mercy. Nothing stirred in the underbrush — the camouflage was perfect — but knowing where to look, you could withdraw a baby gull from its nest. It's shockingly large, has web-feet, and is a dull gray-brown which becomes lighter with maturity.

Then the mosquitoes arrived — platoons of them determined to lay away enough blood to last until the next invaders arrived. The brilliant sky, the shimmering bay and the smells of pine and salt water became as dull as funeral crape. Nursing our wounds we returned to the dinghy.

The landing party — Pond Island

Stonington

DEER ISLE

Southeast of Castine, down in the eastern corner of the thirty-mile-wide Penobscot Bay, lie a group of small and large islands. Collectively they are known as Deer Isle — the more important islands are connected by causeways and bridges and are therefore linked to the mainland.

The largest of four hamlets is Stonington. You know that the inhabitants depend on fishing and lobstering for their livelihood by the overwhelming number of lobster pots lying about in various stages of repair or neatly arranged in piles against the fish-houses adorned by colorful marker buoys.

Stonington is quaint, delightfully reserved and charming — an artist's paradise. The houses are for the most part perched atop the pink ledges without a formal plan. Large trees are nonexistent, because of the shallow soil on the rocks; but wherever soil has collected between the crevices of the rocks, gardens bloom continuously, well into frost time, due to the tempered fogs and the rocks beneath the thin layers of soil that store and retain the warmth of the sunshine.

Deer Isle is also famous for its superior granite, which is sporadically quarried for building purposes and much of which was shipped by barge to New York for construction of the Triborough Bridge. Deer Isle granite was also used in the construction of New York's great Cathedral of St. John the Divine.

"Any more questions 'bout lobsters?"

Fisherman examining lobster pots

"Sea-dog" awaiting the return of the fishermen

The Inimitable Moods of Maine

Mt. Desert Island, lying between Blue Hill Bay and Frenchman Bay, is the most famous island of Maine, and the largest — sixteen miles long and twelve wide. Before going on to Mt. Desert it is well worth one's time to ramble along the back roads that circle and crisscross the area between Penobscot Bay and Blue Hill Bay.

Here and there among the wooded hills and ponds are clearings of pasturelands with cattle grazing, hemmed in by spruces and hemlocks, within the hamlets of Sedgwick, Brooksville, Penobscot and Brooklin. The white houses with their very steep-pitched roofs suggest the kind of winters the Maine folk anticipate — the roofs are built that way to permit the snow to slide off easily. Another feature, though not entirely belonging to Maine alone, is the habitual attachment of the barns to the houses, with well-stocked woodsheds serving as passageways between barn and house.

The doorway to Mt. Desert Island is Ellsworth, where in the days of the railroad the wealthy arrived in their private cars with servants and baggage. The remaining distance was negotiated by carriage or automobile over the bridge that connects Mt. Desert with the mainland.

From the eastern half of the island, Cadillac Mountain rises to a height of fifteen hundred feet above the sea — the highest mountain on the Atlantic coast. Bar Harbor is nestled at the foot of the mountain facing Frenchman Bay and its numerous small islands.

By 1890, Bar Harbor was the social capital of the United States — or perhaps shared this honor with Newport, R.I. Large estates belonging to the Morgans, Rockefellers and Satterlees, to name a few, left their imprint on Bar Harbor with less striving for the fantastic extravaganzas of other social centers. Bar Harbor is relatively free from that fenced-in feeling and the ever-present sense of hostility towards outsiders which is characteristic of Newport.

In addition to owning very large houses on Mt. Desert, the wealthy maintained modest cottages in the woods where they sought relief from social engagements.

One of the highlights of a visit to Bar Harbor in the 1920's was a beach picnic arranged by my host. The pièce de résistance was not such an elegant gastronomic delight as Oysters Rockefeller, instead we had eggs plebeian style cooked on bricks heated in an open fire of driftwood! I question whether I could ever attend another picnic like it with feigned expressions of delight without some help from John Barleycorn.

Sailing in Frenchman Bay

Across Frenchman Bay, Schoodic Point juts out into the gray-green water of the cold Atlantic. The rocks are a warm red and pink in color and pleasantly modify the bleakness of the point, which has scarcely a tree to clothe its nakedness. From here on, down the rest of the Maine coast, the land flattens out and is covered with scrub oaks and blueberry barrens.

The mountain region of Maine lies deep inside the state and is more extensive than most of us realize. The tallest mountain, Mt. Katahdin, situated in the densely forested and lake region of the north country, rises to a height of 5268 feet to catch the first rays of the morning sunshine in the U.S.A.

All Is Not Lobstering in Maine

As early as 1850 Bangor was the lumbering capital of the nation and all of central Maine was engaged in lumbering. Long before then, the early settlers had built their homes of wood and shipped much elsewhere. During our Colonial days the King of England claimed the best of Maine's straight, tall white pines for the Royal Navy, and none over twenty-four inches in diameter a foot above the ground could be cut by the colonists — surveyors from England cut a broad arrow in this choice timber. But the colonists did cut them whenever they felt obliged to do so.

The wild life of the dense Maine woods frequently determined the beginnings of Maine's early towns. Deer, moose, bear, beaver, otter, fox and mink were prevalent and still exist, under protective laws, but the hunter today, obsessed by sport rather than food, may not be mindful of the early settlers whose survival depended on the meat he shot. Also, the clothing they made from the pelts of animals was available from no other source within convenient distances.

Since 1890, potatoes have been grown in astonishing quantities on the rolling hills of Aroostook County. The rotated crops and the cool climate, plus the favorable soil, produce disease-free tubers in profitable quantities.

Maine still has another major crop, blueberries, which are shipped out of the state fresh or canned. This has been going on since 1870. The wild, lowbush variety of blueberries are usually smaller — and tastier — than the highbush cultivated farther south, but the latter do not survive the northern climate. Blueberries grow best along the coast east of the Penobscot River, and the poor soil in which blueberries will thrive is useless for other crops.

Lumbering site

The Ruggles House

Columbia Falls is located in that section of Maine designated as the Eastern Coast — a division of the Maine coast extending from Frenchman Bay to Passamaquoddy Bay, a vast area sparsely peopled. Out of a total of over a thousand communities, Eastport has the largest number — slightly more than twenty-six hundred.

The settlements are separated by wide stretches of barren country containing stands of stunted trees; the soil is too shallow to farm commercially, and the countryside as a whole does not attract vacationers — the ocean is frightfully cold for swimming and too dangerous for small craft.

But lobstering and fishing are predominantly good and Maine folk take their share out of the waters off the treacherous rocky headlands and in the quiet bays — a way of life that suits their temperament. Down-Easterners wouldn't swap their part of Maine for any place on earth.

Columbia Falls at one time was a prosperous shipbuilding center. There is very little left to show that it had ever been grazed by prosperity, but one architectural gem, the Ruggles House, built in 1818, stands as the lonely spokesman for those bygone years. It is an exquisite piece of country Adam with an unusual divided flying staircase which many experts say is the finest in New England. The Ruggles House also has a drawing room and a chimneypiece of such superb cabinetry few believe that the carving was done by an unknown whittler whose tool was only a penknife. The Ruggles House was selected by Arthur Train as the setting for his short story, "The House That Tutt Built."

Sardine-packing and freezing plants are today Columbia Falls's supporting industries, to which may be added the seasonal blueberry crops of the marginal farms which are being absorbed by the large packing companies better equipped to make the farms pay.

The famous Pinky, a small seaworthy boat once very popular along the Maine coast, originated in the nearby Millbridge shipyards.

The excellent deep-water fishing off Jonesport attracts many sportsmen. Across the strait a Coast Guard station is situated on Wass Island. It is said that dense fogs hide the station just about half the days of the year.

East of Columbia Falls is Machias, on the banks of the Machias River, pervaded by the roar of its falls. Machias is located in a sheltered place easily approached from the sea but hidden from sight, just the place for the Pilgrims of Plymouth to establish a fur-trading post after their first post was destroyed at Pentagoet by the French. The French destroyed the post and abandoned Machias, and it remained unoccupied for many years. Attracted by the seclusion of the place, pirates began to operate out of Machias to attack foreign shipping. They

The Ruggles House, Columbia Falls

were superseded by the notorious Samuel Bellamy, who forcibly took possession of the place, lock, stock and barrel as his own stronghold. Bellamy's arrogance was overplayed when he attacked a French corvette of thirty-six guns on her way to Quebec with troops, and his ship was badly damaged. However, he managed to escape under cover of darkness and sailed his crippled *Whidaw* southward right into the trade lanes along the Massachusetts coast. He encountered the *Mary Anne*, a whaler out of New Bedford, off Nantucket Shoals, and easily captured her. Bellamy then tried to win over the skipper of the whaler to join him in piracy. The Yankee cunningly feigned compliance, believing it to be the wisest move for the time being. The skipper of the *Mary Anne* agreed to lead the way through the treacherous shoals off Eastham, Cape Cod, at Bellamy's request, and a lantern was placed on the stern of the *Mary Anne* which the pirate ship faithfully followed. The skipper of the whaler then deliberately ran aground and both ships piled up on one of the bars beside each other. Cape Codders who went down to the shore to salvage the ships soon discovered the Yankee's ruse and took the pirates into custody, tried and hanged them.

The Machias breastworks and the moats are still faintly defined, but the rest of the pirate installations rotted away many years ago.

The first permanent English colony in Maine was established at Machias in 1762. The settlers established a successful shipbuilding and lumbering center which prospered for a number of years.

Vermont

Historic Old Bennington

In flavor and character, only Vermont could double as Vermont. This is notably apparent to motorists soon after they enter the state when a broad eye-filling valley suddenly appears extending northward into the blue haze of distant mountains. In the hollow of this peaceful valley lies the village of Pownal, dubbed the Gateway to Vermont. It is one of the oldest white settlements in Vermont; here the Dutch settled temporarily about 1724, crossing over from New York State.

Up this broad valley came the pioneers from Connecticut, among whom were men like Thomas Chittenden, the first governor of Vermont, and Ethan Allen, who shaped the destinies of the state.

Just west of Pownal is North Pownal, where two Presidents taught school at the beginning of their careers. Chester A. Arthur taught Pownal youngsters in 1851. Later James A. Garfield did likewise while an undergraduate at Williams College.

The best route to western Vermont from Massachusetts is U. S. 7, the Ethan Allen Highway. The highway skirts the valley east of Pownal, twisting and turning as it follows faithfully the side of a mountain to Bennington, where Ethan Allen and his Green Mountain Boys once quaffed their rum at Catamount Tavern. Bennington also figured prominently in the New Hampshire Grants, chartered by Governor Benning Wentworth, who parceled out lands later claimed by New York. With help from the Green Mountain Boys the settlers disputed the New York patents, issued to countermand the New Hampshire Grants, which led to bitter fighting and the creation of the independent republic of Vermont in January 1777. After fourteen years of independent statehood Vermont was admitted into the Union.

With the coming of the railroad, Old Bennington was left on high ground to mellow and accumulate historic charm while the villagers flirted with nineteenth-century progressiveness at Bennington.

The Bennington Historical Museum, located midway between Old Bennington and Bennington, contains treasures of regional significance. Among its chief attractions is the oldest Stars and Stripes in existence; it was raised over General John Stark's company in the Battle of Bennington. Also on exhibition is Ira Allen's writing-chair, upon which he wrote the constitution of Vermont.

Highway U.S. 5, situated east of the Green Mountains, parallels the Connecticut River for much of its length and is called the Calvin Coolidge Memorial Highway. Coolidge was born in the isolated hilltop village of Plymouth, located a considerable distance from the Connecticut River, in a simple house adjoining a

A church in old Bennington

country store which attracts thousands of visitors each year. So does the homestead across the road where Calvin Coolidge lived from four years of age and where, by the light of a kerosene lamp at 2:47 A.M. August 3, 1923, he was sworn in as President of the United States by his father, Col. John C. Coolidge, a notary public.

Northwest of Plymouth are located the second loftiest mountains in Vermont — Pica Peak, Blue Ridge and Killington. Collectively, the mountains of the state are known as the Green Mountains and consist of four distinct groups, all of which traverse the state in a general north-south direction. The largest and most important are the Green Mountains proper, which extend from the Canadian border to Massachusetts down the center of Vermont.

The Green Mountains, older than the Rockies, are actually mainly a deep lush green in summer, and a galaxy of riotous hues in the fall. The Taconic Mountains, which occupy the southwestern sector of Vermont and spill over into neighboring Massachusetts, contain the state's valuable marble deposits. East of the Green Mountains, and extending from the Canadian border to somewhat below the middle of the state, are the Granite Hills.

Bennington Battle Monument

This granite battle monument was dedicated in 1891 and marks the site of the storehouse that General Burgoyne lightheartedly ordered captured; it dominates not only Monument Avenue but the whole countryside. It is the tallest battle monument in the world, rising three hundred and six feet above the hill on which it stands, from the top of which there is a sweeping view of the rolling country and the snaking Walloomsac River. No statue of Ethan Allen is among the monuments at Bennington but there is a statue of him in the portico of the State House at Montpelier. The statue of Colonel Seth Warner is conspicuously situated as it faces Monument Avenue — a reminder of his success against General Burgoyne's rash order.

Warner was born in Roxbury, Connecticut, and moved to Bennington, where he became one of the leaders of the Green Mountain Boys. Warner was not a land speculator, as Allen and other leaders were. Soon after the American Revolution broke out, Warner accompanied Allen to Ticonderoga and was given charge of the detachment that took Crown Point May 11, 1775.

In July 1775, when the Green Mountain Boys were organized as part of the Continental Army, Warner and not Allen was elected to command. From that

Bennington Battle Monument and statue of Seth Warner

time forward the two men became estranged, Warner devoting his life to the cause of the colonies as a whole, not to Vermont alone.

In the Quebec campaign of 1775, Warner distinguished himself in an engagement at Longueuil before the Green Mountain Boys were dismissed in November after their term of enlistment was completed. He was called back to Canada in January 1776, at which time Burgoyne was scoring an effective advance. Warner was in charge of the rear guard protecting Arthur St. Clair's retreat from Ticonderoga. Though Warner fought well when set upon near Hubbardton on July 7, 1777, he was defeated, but he redeemed that failure and became the hero of the Saratoga campaign.

Warner continued to serve his country until late in the war when wounds he contracted on the campaign forced him to retire; he died at Roxbury, Connecticut, in 1784. Colonel Seth Warner's remains lie beneath a tall granite shaft in the center of Roxbury. Those of General Ethan Allen, who died in 1789, are in the cemetery at Burlington, Vermont. Even in death the two onetime friends remain parted.

Bennington

Bennington was the first town settled in the state west of the Connecticut River, receiving a grant from Governor Benning Wentworth of New Hampshire and named in his honor in 1749; it also has the distinction of having the oldest town charter in Vermont. Here the first meetinghouse was built in the state.

Bennington is a magic word in Vermont. This was where the Vermonters challenged the "York State" lawyers who laid claim to their lands. They had come up from Connecticut and Massachusetts with their household belongings to start a new life, but the British Colonial courts declared invalid their titles to the land they cleared in the wilderness.

Monument Avenue in Bennington recalls these days. Here on the wide slope the first settlers built their homes facing the green; here too was built the first meetinghouse, and nearby both British and American soldiers killed in the Battle of Bennington lie in the oldest cemetery in Vermont. Also buried here are five governors of Vermont, the author of Vermont's Declaration of Independence and scores of loyal New Englanders, among whom was recently laid to rest poet Robert Frost beside his wife. Beyond the graves rises the graceful steeple of the First Congregational Church, built by Lavius Fillmore in 1805–1806. Fillmore was guided in the design by Asher Benjamin's book, *The Country Builder's Assistant*. Indicative of the Benjamin treatment, the building has round-topped windows on the second story, Palladian windows above the door and in the square part of the tower,

Façade of the Old First Church, Bennington

oval windows in the octagonal lantern, all of which add variety to the church and make it one of the most interesting and beautiful in Vermont.

Many remarkable scenes took place in the first meetinghouse which the present church replaced; here the Vermonters met in prayer to ask for assistance against the oppressive measures of New York and the might of George III. Hither the settlers returned from the capture of Fort Ticonderoga, the Battle of Bennington, the surrender of Burgoyne, to offer up their thanksgivings, and here were also brought the 700 prisoners captured on August 16, 1777.

Here met the convention, consisting of one delegate from each town, which on January 10, 1791, ratified the Constitution of the United States by the signatures of 105 out of 109 delegates, thereby preparing the way for the admission of Vermont into the Union as the first state after the original thirteen.

A bronze catamount on Monument Avenue marks the site of the Catamount Tavern where the Green Mountain Boys used to meet. It was formerly designated the Green Mountain House, but its sign, a snarling catamount with open jaws, gave it its more familiar name. Before the Battle of Bennington, British soldiers sent a message to Stephen Fay, the landlord, ordering him to have dinner ready when they entered Bennington in triumph. As the British prisoners, guarded by the men from Vermont, came down the road that humid, hot evening, attired in their battle-stained scarlet uniforms, Fay welcomed them politely and announced: "The dinner you ordered is ready, gentlemen."

In 1793 the first Bennington pottery made its bow and became famous throughout the land. A comprehensive showing of Bennington pottery may be seen in the museum in Old Bennington.

Another first by a white man was the making of maple sugar in Bennington by Samuel Robinson in 1752.

Reflections in the Walloomsac

NORTH BENNINGTON

The best way to see Vermont is simply to wander on the back roads where many pleasant surprises await those who take any turning that comes along.

By sheer chance and without prior knowledge, I recently came upon three covered bridges a short distance apart, spanning the placid Walloomsac River in North Bennington, making rustic compositions of extraordinary charm. And if you have an ear for bells it is possible to hear the old bell tolling in the steeple of the First Church located in Old Bennington where the Green Mountain patriots listened to the preaching of the Reverend Jedediah Dewey, the first pastor of the church.

Covered bridge over the Walloomsac River

There are over one hundred covered bridges in the state still spanning languid rivers and turbulent mountain streams — more than in any other state in New England. The first framed timber bridge in America was actually built in Vermont by Enoch Hale, in 1785, across the Connecticut River at Bellows Falls.

Bennington College is located a stone's throw from the Walloomsac River, in North Bennington, on an exquisite site overlooking Mt. Anthony and the Bennington Battle Monument. The college, which was opened in 1932, is comparatively a newcomer among the important New England colleges. Bennington sponsors a new concept in educational experimentation in which over 350 students participate, living in cottage-type houses in a traditional New England atmosphere.

Shaftsbury

Anyone with a penchant for historic houses couldn't possibly pass through the village of Shaftsbury without stopping to admire the old Jonas Galusha homestead with its fine Palladian window and decorative cornice with its remarkable sophisticated detailing. The house is situated close to Route U.S. 7 about four miles north of South Shaftsbury. Built in 1783, this splendid white frame building emphasizes that our modern homes, to a large extent, are utterly uninspired.

The Galusha house, attributed to Lavius Fillmore, the noted architect of the Middlebury and Bennington churches, was always well cared for; consequently everything is still intact, even the window panes and hardware. Wall paintings done in 1810 by an itinerant French artist adorn the southeast bedroom.

Jonas Galusha, extraordinary Revolutionary hero who was nine times elected Governor of Vermont, was born in Norwich, Connecticut, on February 11, 1753. He moved to Shaftsbury with his father's large family in the spring of 1775, just as the Revolution was breaking at Concord and Lexington. His father had four wives, whom he catalogued in the following manner: "I have been twice in heaven, once on earth and once in hell." All but one wife bore him children — a total of sixteen.

The Galushas were a credit to Shaftsbury — they served both in the government and in the armed forces during the Revolution. Jonas Galusha was at the head of his company when Burgoyne surrendered at Saratoga. In 1778 Galusha married Governor Thomas Chittenden's daughter, Mary. She died leaving nine children to rear, but Galusha married three more times, adding one more child to his progeny.

In 1809, Jonas Galusha was nominated for governor and was reelected every year through 1812. He was back in office in 1815 and reelected every year through

The Governor Galusha House, Shaftsbury

1819. Thereafter he declined to hold public office. When Shays's men fled into Vermont from Massachusetts in 1787 after the failure of their rebellion, they met at Shaftsbury with the purpose of extending the movement in Vermont. Galusha attended the meeting with other prominent citizens and emphatically warned Shays's men to withdraw from Shaftsbury at once.

Galusha never joined a church but attended services regularly. When nearly eighty he made plans to attend a "protracted meeting" — now called a revival meeting — in Manchester, to make a public profession of his belief, but was felled by a stroke from which he failed to recover.

Another prominent man of the area was Jacob Merritt Howard. He was born in Shaftsbury on July 10, 1805, where he was raised and educated. Howard distinguished himself by being the man who drew up the resolutions adopted by the first Republican State Convention held in Jackson, Michigan, July 6, 1854, on which the Republican Party was founded. He was also the sole author of the 13th Amendment to the Constitution.

In 1840, Howard won his first seat in the House of Representatives. He was a strong opponent of slavery and prognosticated that slavery would plunge our nation into war. His native state of Vermont became the first in the country to prohibit slavery by writing it into its constitution. In 1862, Howard was appointed to fill out the unexpired term of a U.S. senator who had died. He was reelected in 1865 and served as senator until a month before he died in Detroit on April 2, 1871.

The simple brick house in which he was born in Shaftsbury still stands on a little-traveled back road. His parents are buried in the graveyard just north of the Baptist Church, built in 1846. (The first Baptist church in Vermont was organized at Shaftsbury, in 1768.)

One late fall day, I walked between the regimented gravestones silhouetted against the blue haze of the mountains. I recognized many that were incised by Zerrubabel Collins, who migrated from Connecticut in 1778 to settle in Shaftsbury. His distinguished stone carving on slate and native marble has a flair and style that sets his craftsmanship apart from that of his contemporaries.

Another of Shaftsbury's famous residents was Robert Frost, whose poetry is so expressive of northern New England life. Frost was of New England ancestry but was born in San Francisco, where his father moved after the Civil War. The family returned to New England in 1885, after the death of Robert Frost's father. Except for several years in England, Frost lived in Vermont and New Hampshire. The stone house in Shaftsbury into which he moved in 1920 is located near Route U.S. 7, one mile south of South Shaftsbury. He moved to another house later because the stone house was too accessible to his admiring and overzealous public.

Governor Benning Wentworth signed the fancy piece of paper which gave to one small part of the western wilderness the name of Shaftsbury on August 20, 1761. Those who settled there were hardy and self-reliant. Many arrived during the closing years of the French and Indian War from Connecticut and Rhode Island.

Ethan Allen had acquired 45,000 acres of land at the mouth of the Onion River along Lake Champlain which he wanted to sell at a profit but his claim was rendered worthless by New York State's legal action against the Hampshire Grants. Both large and small parcels of land were in jeopardy, and the manner in which the Green Mountain Boys conducted themselves to remedy the situation is history. New York spared no pain to keep matters off balance and made several attempts in the vicinity of Shaftsbury to enforce its claims by arresting settlers who refused to be ejected.

In 1772, John Munro of Shaftsbury, a New York justice of the peace, led a New York posse to the home of Remember Baker at Arlington. Baker was seized and bound, thrown into a sleigh, and driven towards Albany. When the news reached Bennington, ten indignant Green Mountain Boys rode after Munro, caught up with the sleigh, and routed the posse. Munro was taken back to Shaftsbury, where he was severely punished. Throughout the Revolutionary War, Munro remained a Royalist, but Vermont countered his obstinacy by confiscating all his property.

Peregrinations and Interludes
MANCHESTER CENTER

Eighteen miles north of Shaftsbury, the Ethan Allen Highway descends into the orderly and well-shaded village of Manchester — a long-time cultural center and one of the oldest summer communities in the East.

Manchester and Manchester Center lie within one of the major ski areas in Vermont. Nearby are Big Bromley, Stratton Mountain, Snow Valley and Magic Mountain. Mt. Equinox forms the backdrop for Manchester and may be ascended by a private toll road. The summit, overlooking Lake Catherine, encompasses a breathtaking panorama studded with the nearby Taconic peaks, Ascutney, Killington and Greylock (Massachusetts) and, on clear days, Monadnock in New Hampshire.

On a less dramatic level those who wish to enjoy, in a leisurely way, the beauty and quiet of the countryside prefer to use and explore the old "shunpikes" that form an elaborate network of back roads — laid out to shun the toll roads in the state.

The toll pikes were entirely maintained from tolls collected at turnstiles instead of from gasoline taxes. By the time this country entered World War I, Vermont had abolished all toll roads except the one up Mt. Mansfield. The Peru Mountain road entering Manchester was the last to go; at one time it was one of the main stagecoach routes to Saratoga Springs from Boston and netted a fortune for its operators in toll charges. The old charter attained the ripe old age of one hundred and three years, but the stagecoach days, the turnstiles that swung open after the required fees were paid, have faded into limbo.

Manchester's estates, with well-tended grounds and large mansions overshadowed by ancient trees, keep their enchanted distances, but the clusters of white houses, snugly nestled in the valleys, with church steeples rising above them and the groves of trees in which they lie half hidden, are characteristically Vermont.

The numerous dairy farms delight the eye with their variations in construction, indigenous to New England. Red barns, white houses, weathered lean-tos and silos blend into one homogeneous and continuous utilitarian group.

The Vermont farmer needs all his industry and indomitable spirit to hang on to the soil he loves in an era in which mechanization threatens his very existence. His land is sanctified; in it rest the bones of generations of his own blood kin. In spite of themselves many farmers, tricked by fate and forced to retreat from their farms, have sold out to eager summer people who restored them with affection.

Many prominent artists and writers settled also in the neighboring townships of Dorset and Arlington. Some came to spend their summers and stayed on as year-round residents, leaving their imprints on the villages; but nowhere were the changes drastic enough to impugn the physical charm of the villages — instead each community became famous for its cultural pursuits.

Mrs. Abraham Lincoln and her son Robert came to Manchester to spend their vacation during the Civil War, and later the son returned to live there.

The object of a trip to Vermont from my home in Connecticut, one week late in October, was to reinforce my notes and sketches, to catch Vermont off guard. The timing was just right because it was too late in the season for tourists and too early for the influx of skiers.

The mountains had already received a light dusting of snow. The tree-clad slopes were no longer green but etched by gray skeletonized deciduous trees tinted with powder snow. Somber-toned evergreens were likewise tinted but retreated almost entirely into the purple shadows of the slopes.

I pressed northward from Manchester Center on Route 30, the Seth Warner Memorial Highway, towards East Hubbardton. The highway takes you almost to East Hubbardton and the Hubbardton battlefield, before sweeping past Lake Bomoseen and penetrating the Champlain Valley as far as Middlebury.

The Hubbardton Battle Monument marks the place where the only battle of the Revolution was fought on Vermont soil, on July 7, 1777. Recalling the Battle

A Vermont idyl

of Bennington, August 16, 1777, the average man assumes that this engagement was also fought in Vermont. The impressive 306-foot granite monolith in Old Bennington commemorates an encounter which was actually fought just over the border in New York State. Valuable stores and supplies were stocked on what now is the site of the Bennington monument and the British were eager to capture them.

The engagement at Hubbardton did not end as a victory for the Americans who were retreating from Fort Ticonderoga. After two hours of furious combat the British held the field but were so badly mauled that they were unable to pursue the Americans at once.

The main portion of Colonel Seth Warner's Green Mountain Boys and Massachusetts men, among whom were a handful of New Hampshire soldiers, met about eight hundred elite troops of General Burgoyne headon in three successive counterattacks. The delay enabled General St. Clair of the Americans to change his course and march to Fort Edward in New York, where he joined the forces of General Schuyler on July 12, 1777.

Castleton, which is situated south of East Hubbardton, was founded in 1761 — a colorful community where, in 1775, at the Remington Tavern, Ethan Allen rallied his Green Mountain Boys for the bloodless assault on Fort Ticonderoga.

Trout Pool

Trout fishing time starts the first of May in Vermont. Anglers foregather well in advance to appraise the best pools of past seasons and add to their collection of lures.

Fishermen who court the small streams and relatively short rivers are a breed apart, willing to stand up to their armpits in frigid water for hours, and endure without complaint the biting insects, for the sheer joy of catching fish.

Many fishermen travel hundreds of miles for the privilege which Vermonters seldom venture far from home to get — good fishing is always handy. Vermont and New Hampshire fishermen have a high regard for the Connecticut River. Its deep mysterious waters in the vicinity of Bradford, Newbury and Fairlee seldom disappoint the angler of experience.

Trout pool in Connecticut River

The Village with Four Revere Bells

WOODSTOCK

Woodstock is the shire town, or county seat, of Windsor County, located on the Ottauquechee River, west of White River Junction, in a preserve of nature. It seemed natural for the village to grow into a summer and winter resort center. Woodstock's image was not accidental — it was achieved by resisting material progress and negatively responding to factories and commercial encroachment. When the railroad was discontinued in 1933, no tears were shed, but when the old covered bridge, imperiled by recurring spring and fall floods, had to be replaced by a modern one Woodstock regretfully parted with a segment of its nostalgic past.

Woodstock possesses four churches, and an equal number of bells cast by Paul Revere and his sons. Only eighty-seven Revere bells exist today out of hundreds cast. Bells were necessary adjuncts to village life. Each ring had its individualistic message; a certain ring awoke the parishioners, another urged haste in getting to church. The ringing of the "pudding" bell served notice to anyone in charge of the kitchen to get dinner ready. The "passing" bell tolled when villagers died — one ring for a man, two for a woman and three for a child, followed by one peal for each year of age.

Timothy Knox, a Harvard man, was the first settler in Woodstock. He traveled alone up the Connecticut River in 1765 and entered the wilderness until he reached the Quechee Valley. He made his way to a point one and a half miles from the present village green (laid out in 1830), where he built a hut. For a period of three years he was the only settler in the township, but by 1771 ten families, with a total of forty-two people, formed the nucleus of the village. The first frame building built near the green was erected in 1772 and soon thereafter a church was built, a preacher found, and schools established. The first town meeting took place in 1773, at Joab Hoisington's inn.

Woodstock has given to the world an astonishing number of prominent men. Among the most eminent citizens was George Perkins Marsh, born in 1801, author, and Congressman of note. While serving in Washington (1843–1849) he helped to found and guide the Smithsonian Institution. President Lincoln appointed him the first U.S. Minister to the new Kingdom of Italy, and he held this office until his death at Vallombrosa, in 1882. During his sojourn in Italy, Marsh wrote *Man and Nature,* in 1864, considered his greatest work. He has been called "the mighty prophet of the whole American conservation movement."

Hiram Powers, the most celebrated American sculptor of his day, was born on a farm near Woodstock in 1805, the son of a poor farmer and ox-yoke maker. By 1835 his fame had risen to spectacular heights; in Washington, he modeled portrait busts including one of President Jackson. In 1837 he left for Florence, Italy, where he was influenced by classic art and lived luxuriously to the end of his days, but his renown failed to survive him. Powers's *Greek Slave,* showing a young

The village green, Woodstock

Greek woman offered for sale in the Turkish slave market, was first shown in 1843. Immediately it became a conversation piece, in fact the most sensational piece of sculpture of the day in America and Europe.

The brick building shown in the drawing was built by Charles Dana in 1820. From that time until 1906 it housed a dry goods store and carried a wide variety of household goods. The sons and grandsons of Charles Dana conducted the business on Elm Street until the Elm Tree Press was started, in 1910, under the guiding hand of Edward Dana, who got a reputation for well designed and creative printing. All subsequent owners followed in the footsteps of Dana's tradition.

The charming house below the Press building was built in 1807 by Charles Dana as his home. Three generations of his descendants occupied the house until the death of Edward Dana, in 1943. The Woodstock Historical Society purchased the house and established a valuable historical library and museum.

Woodstock was an early publishing center. The first Greek Lexicon printed in North America was printed on the famous Stephen Daye press, brought to Woodstock early in the nineteenth century and later removed to Montpelier. The printing press arrived in this country in 1638, accompanied by Stephen Daye, who operated the press in Cambridge until 1649.

Agriculture was, and still is, the most important industry around Woodstock. Captain Jarvis, the first to introduce Merino sheep in Vermont, brought them over from Spain in 1809 to his farm at Weathersfield, southeast of Woodstock. Every farmer had a flock of sheep and sheep-raising brought fame and profits until the bottom fell out of the market. President Cleveland's administration brought ruin to the farmers by repealing the duty on wool, and the price dropped from forty-five cents per pound to twelve cents. The resourceful Vermonters sold their sheep and went into dairying.

In 1791, Justin Morgan, a schoolmaster, brought to Vermont a colt of such fine quality that it sired a whole new breed known as the Morgan horse. His stallion Justin Morgan is the only horse to have a legislative resolution passed in his honor, and Woodstock points with pride to the years 1800 and 1801, when the famous stallion was stabled in the village, a claim that carries with it the same feeling of status enjoyed by New Englanders elsewhere who can prove that "George Washington slept here."

T-Bar Ski Tow

When snow falls on New England, and Vermont in particular, newspapers and radios start reporting the skiing conditions. The slopes are accessible all winter, thanks to an efficient system of road plowing — Vermont could hardly afford to do less for the skiers, who contribute generously towards the state's annual revenue of

Ascending a Vermont ski slope

about $120,000,000 from tourism, matching as accurately as can be ascertained, the sum received from agriculture and industry!

Interest in skiing has made phenomenal growth since the first ski hill was built at Brattleboro, Vermont, in 1922. The first ski tow in America was built during the winter of 1934 at Woodstock — a primitive rope tow powered by a Model T Ford engine. Today, ski trails, ultra-ski tows, modern lodges and chalets costing millions are being built at breakneck speed to keep up with the popularity of the sport.

In the 1920's, a 250-mile hiking trail was built, stretching from Massachusetts to Canada down the backbone of the Green Mountains through the most unspoiled mountain peaks in the East. The Long Trail or "Footpath in the Wilderness" personifies the remoteness and inaccessibility of the mountains; however, in recent times hikers, much to their dismay, have been unable to avoid coming upon the terminal towers of one ski lift after another every twenty miles — harsh reminders of the paradoxical wonders of progress!

Back in 1936, Vermonters turned down, by referendum, the government's offer to build a Green Mountain Parkway, fearful that such a parkway might destroy the character of Vermont and its natural beauty. Sometime during the intervening years a change of heart permitted the building of an atrocious television transmitting station on the summit of Mount Mansfield, Vermont's highest and loveliest mountain. The mad rush to have Vermont catch up with the times is dangerously toying with the destruction of legendary Vermont where Yankeeism survives against all odds.

To this lovely New England state, which has a long history of courage and individualism, many famous personalities have come to work or retire, confident that Vermont would remain an everlasting spring of peace.

Rudyard Kipling made his first trip to Vermont in the winter of 1892 and succumbed to Vermont's winter grandeur. He later built his home at Dummerston, near Brattleboro, and named his India-type bungalow "Naulahka." Among the rolling hills Kipling floundered amateurishly on skis and wrote books, among them the *Jungle Books, Captains Courageous* and *The Day's Work*. After several years of living next door to a troublesome brother-in-law, Kipling and his Brattleboro-born wife, Caroline, whom he met in London, left the country in 1896. In his book *Letters of Travel*, Kipling describes graphically the isolation of being snowbound and the fascination of a Vermont blizzard.

The World's Largest Granite Quarry

BARRE

Vermont leads the nation in the production of granite. The industry's center is located around Barre, where a top grade of granite is quarried and converted into monuments or building stone. Barre was first organized as Wildersburgh, in 1793,

The Rock of Ages Granite Quarry

and has since been dominated by its famous quarries, which were developed after the War of 1812. The granite for the State Capitol at Montpelier was supplied by the Barre quarries, in 1836. The Rock of Ages Granite Quarry is the largest of its kind in the world. Visitors are invited to gaze into its awesome man-made canyon, covering 20 acres and 350 feet deep.

Vermont also produces 95 per cent of the nation's asbestos, which is mined not far from Hyde Park. Still another gift from nature is marble, and Proctor boasts one of the nation's largest marble quarries. The village of Proctor has many buildings constructed of marble. Redfield Proctor, who developed the great Vermont Marble Company, was a Vermonter of many facets. He served in both houses of the State Legislature; one term as Lieutenant Governor (1876–1878), and as Governor from 1878 to 1880 before becoming United States Secretary of War in 1889, a post from which he resigned in 1891 to enter the United States Senate where he served until his death in 1908.

Sugaring in New England

Sugaring is indigenous to New England. The pioneers were taught the art of making maple syrup and sugar by helpful Indians. No other continent grows the sugar maple tree and in no area in North America does it grow more luxuriantly. The sugar bushes of Vermont produce a third of the annual supply of maple syrup; a Vermonter will never admit that good maple syrup is made elsewhere, just as Maine folk believe that good lobsters can only be caught in Maine. But New Hampshire is also a heavy producer of maple products.

It is not surprising to learn that recently the plastic tube has invaded the maple syrup industry. Plastic tubes are still not in general usage, but the theory is simple — the trees are tapped and a tube is inserted to carry the sap by gravity to the gathering tank; thus eliminating the men who customarily collect the buckets and empty them by hand. Otherwise sugaring has changed very little since the Currier and Ives lithographs of it.

The Indians coerced the flow of sap by cutting a "V" shaped slash in the bark and leading the sap by a piece of wood so it would drop into a wooden trough. Later, wooden spiles or spouts were inserted in the trees to catch the sap in wooden buckets. The pioneers used open kettles over fires to reduce the sap to syrup; as the level of the kettle dropped more sap was added. This method of long boiling produced maple syrup of a very dark hue.

The modern method is the same in principle, but better processing methods produce a purer product. The sap is today collected in metal buckets holding 12 to 16 quarts. The sap flows through a three-eighths-inch hole bored in each tree, to

Sugaring in New England

a depth of from slightly over one inch to as much as two inches, three feet above the ground. A spile is then driven into the hole, which slightly slants upwards towards the center, and the bucket is hung on the spile's hook — usually one bucket to a tree, though as many as four may be hung on very old trees. A maple has to attain an age of forty years before it is commercially profitable.

The filled buckets are emptied into a tank mounted on a sled and drawn by a team of horses or tractor through the forest. On arrival at the sugar-house the sled-load is drained into a storage tank — located on the north side of the sugar-house to avoid exposure to the sun. The large sugar and syrup producers in Vermont may have as many as five hundred trees tapped in a single sugar bush and may hang over one thousand buckets in a single season.

The sap is boiled down the same day it is received from the sugar bush. One gallon of syrup requires from thirty-five to forty gallons of sap.

The sweet aroma of steam rising out of the evaporator may last a few weeks in the spring, if the frost comes out of the ground too fast, or a month if spring takes its time arriving. Generally, sugaring begins in March when the first warm days arrive and the mounds of snow accumulations begin to melt. At best, the sugaring season is brief and packed with frenzied work.

Connecticut

The Burning of Danbury by the British

Danbury's Scott-Fanton Museum and Historical Society occupies this house at 43 Main Street; from basement to attic it is a treasure trove of early Americana. It was built about 1750. Prior to the Revolutionary War a Tory lived here, therefore, when General William Tryon raided Danbury, he obligingly spared the house from the torch. When the British troops withdrew in the direction of Ridgefield early Sunday morning April 27, 1777, Danbury was left a smoldering shambles.

The British had destroyed the stockpile of Revolutionary Army supplies, burned nineteen homes, sacked and destroyed twenty-two stores and barns. They spared the Episcopal church, but the stores inside the church were removed and destroyed.

Joseph Plumb Martin, a Revolutionary soldier who wrote an account in 1830 of his adventures under Washington, Lafayette and Steuben, described the destruction of Danbury as an eyewitness: "The town had been laid in ashes, a number of the inhabitants murdered and cast into their burning homes, because they presumed to defend their persons and property, or to be avenged on a cruel, vindictive invading enemy. I saw the inhabitants, after the fire was out, endeavoring to find the burnt bones of their relatives amongst the rubbish of their demolished houses. The streets in many places were literally flooded by the fat which ran from the piles of barrels of pork burnt by the enemy. They fully executed their design."

Due to Danbury's strategic position on a good road from the Hudson River to Long Island Sound, the American Army commissioners ordered, towards the end of 1776, the removal of medicines and military supplies from Stamford to Danbury. General Tryon's Tory spies went to work promptly. On the basis of their information, British troops gathered in the North River, New York, to move on Danbury. Governor Trumbull and his Council ordered General Stillman to watch developments in the enemy's maneuvers.

On April 25, 1777, twenty-six sailing ships appeared off the Norwalk Islands. They anchored at four P.M. off Compo. By ten P.M. more than two thousand men had landed on Compo Beach and began their march on Danbury, where they arrived the next day at two P.M. The British column was first fired upon from Major Daniel Starr's house at the corner of Main and Boughton Streets, on the site of the present Junior High School.

The cruelties inflicted on the residents of Danbury can be judged by the statements attributed to the Earl of Falkland's son, who entered Major Starr's house after the British were fired upon. He excused their conduct by saying that "their

The Scott-Fanton Museum and Historical Society, Danbury

constant practice, when they found people shut up in a house and firing upon them, was to kill them and burn the house. Tories were excepted."

The militia company of one hundred men, under the command of Colonel Joseph Cooke, and a handful of Continental troops, hopelessly outnumbered, were forced to abandon the town.

Soon after the arrival of the British the first wisps of smoke began to rise from the houses set afire; the conflagration spread rapidly. Everything of military value to the Americans was destroyed; the homes of the Yankees were set afire for spite. The night was spent by the British troops in debauchery. The casks of rum stored in Danbury found appreciative guzzlers; the troops were so anesthetized and disorganized the Americans could have destroyed them all had they arrived on time.

General Tryon, alarmed by the gathering militia under General David Wooster, withdrew from Danbury to nearby Ridgefield on April 27, where General Wooster was mortally wounded and died on May 2, 1777, in the house where a short time ago Tryon's men made merry. The general was laid to rest May 4, 1777, in the old town cemetery on the corner of Main and Wooster streets. His remains were removed April 25, 1852, to Wooster Cemetery, named after him, where a fitting memorial stands.

In another cemetery not far from Danbury rests the heroine of eastern Putnam County, whose nighttime ride through the countryside on April 26, 1777, when she was sixteen years of age, alerted her father's men to assemble for the march to Danbury. Sybil Ludington, the "female Paul Revere" of Putnam County, had by her courageous action made one of the principal contributions towards the British defeat in the area. A bronze statue of Sybil Ludington was cast by Mrs. Anna Hyatt Huntington, a longtime resident of Redding. She presented the statue to the Mary Wooster Chapter of the Daughters of the American Revolution, who in turn presented it to the Danbury Board of Education.

The French troops under Rochambeau, enroute from Yorktown, encamped in the vicinity of South and Triangle streets in October 1782.

General Israel Putnam's campsite in Redding, not far from Danbury, is one of our Revolutionary War shrines. There, from November 7, 1778, to May 25, 1779, Putnam's division of the Continental Army suffered untold miseries. On "Company Street" there is a double row of fieldstone campfire sites, 65 in number, around which the impoverished troops huddled during the harsh winter of 1778-1779. The officers' quarters were made of logs and stone in the side of a hill, a dugout with a chimney, which must have been luxurious living by comparison with what was endured by their men.

Among the fieldstones, here and there, are young oak trees. They are not ordinary oaks — they were planted from the acorns of the famous "Charter Oak" at Hartford in which the Charter of Connecticut was hidden when Sir Edmund Andros, the Royal Governor, threatened the liberties of the Connecticut people in

1686. Here in Redding, the oaks serve as a living reminder of how providently Putnam's army secured and helped to preserve our young nation's liberties.

Danbury was purchased from the Pahquique Indians, and was settled in 1684. From a mere handful of settlers the place grew into a vigorous city. As early as 1780 Zadoc Benedict established what is reported to be the first hat factory, with a daily capacity of three hats. From that humble start, Danbury became for a while the leading hat-manufacturing city in the United States. In back of the Scott-Fanton Museum stands the Barnum House, moved to its present site from 35 Main Street where it once stood from 1770 until 1957, but more significantly, this restored house was where the first hats were displayed in Danbury.

The Battle of Ridgefield

RIDGEFIELD

At the turn of the eighteenth century, twenty-eight families left Norwalk, Connecticut, and settled in Caudatowa, meaning "high land," which later became Ridgefield. The General Assembly permitted the Norwalk group to resettle and purchase the land from the Ramapoo Indians. Their chief sachem, Catoonah, closed the deal for £100 and turned the deed to 20,000 acres over to John Belden, Samuel Keeler, and nineteen other settlers from Norwalk and four from Milford, on September 30, 1708. The tract was bounded on the south by Norwalk, on the northeast by Danbury and on the west by New York State. Ridgefield was incorporated in 1709, the name suggested by the ridges in the terrain.

Large estates avoided in the nineteenth century any danger of Ridgefield becoming an industrial town, and its purely residential characteristics outlasted the small minor industries that flourished for a time. However, changes are impossible to thwart forever, and during the past thirty years they have crept into Ridgefield steadily. Many of the large estates were divided and the business characteristics of progress, rampant in many New England towns, have also reared their heads ominously in Ridgefield, checked to a degree by zoning laws that should permit the twentieth century to implant its mark with restraint and orderliness.

Ridgefield's broad Main Street, over a mile in length and 120 feet in width, is lined with many beautiful eighteenth-century homes, situated back from the road, amid well-cared-for groves of trees and lawns.

At the southern end of Main Street, opposite the fountain at the junction with West Lane, stands one of Ridgefield's major historic buildings of Revolutionary interest. At the time of the Revolution and well into the nineteenth century, the place was known as Keeler Tavern and owned by Timothy Keeler and his heirs. It was on the direct line of coach travel between Boston and New York.

The British started to burn the tavern but they were asked to desist by a loyalist living next door, since the flames would also destroy his place. The celebrated architect Cass Gilbert owned the old tavern until his death in 1934.

The Battle of Ridgefield followed the evacuation of Danbury by General Tryon, who entered the town by way of Ridgebury in order to outsmart General Wooster. Part of his troops went through Ridgebury Street and others turned east of the church through what today is an old wood road. Turning south on Ridgebury Street, the British continued toward Ridgefield. At Scotland District they stopped for breakfast on the plain near the schoolhouse. The main army was protected by detachments on the west.

General Wooster approached from Barlow Mountain with two hundred men and shot out of the woods east of where the British had stopped, seizing forty prisoners.

Wooster's second attack followed the first nearly two miles from Ridgefield Village. The British artillery in front and in the rear of their lines completely demoralized the militia. General Wooster rallied his men by calling out, "Come on, my boys, never mind such random shots," but he himself was mortally wounded.

Benedict Arnold took charge of Wooster's militiamen, and the Battle of Ridgefield commenced on Main Street near the Stebbins house, which no longer stands. General Arnold's horse was killed beneath him, and at the moment of being dismounted, a Tory approached him with fixed bayonet and demanded his surrender, whereupon Arnold whipped out a pistol and shot him.

Arnold ordered his men to withdraw after the barricade was forced by an overwhelming number of British troops. All day the battle continued and the British kept up the fire of their cannon in front of the Episcopal church, then turned upon the church and set it afire — it was jammed with American military supplies.

The British version of the Battle of Ridgefield is given in a letter to Lord George Germain from Sir William Howe, dated New York, May 23, 1777 — "On the 27th in the morning the Troops gutted Danbury and met with little opposition until they came near Ridgefield which was occupied by General Arnold, who had thrown up entrenchments to dispute the Passage, while General Wooster hung upon the Rear with a separate Corps. The Village was forced and the Enemy drove back on all Sides."

It is surprising the whole town wasn't burned, knowing General Tryon's proclivity for "playing with matches" in Fairfield, Norwalk and Danbury. The last building of six was burned near the old fair grounds and undoubtedly served as some kind of signal to those aboard the ships off Compo.

On the morning of the twenty-eighth, Tryon set out. The British marched through Wilton, demanding food as they went. Fearful of meeting trouble, Tryon

The text visible on the monument in the image reads:

IN DEFENSE OF AMERICAN INDEPENDENCE
AT THE BATTLE OF RIDGEFIELD
APRIL 27, 1777
DIED
EIGHT PATRIOTS
WHO WERE LAID IN THESE GROUNDS
COMPANIONED BY
SIXTEEN BRITISH SOLDIERS
LIVING THEIR ENEMIES DYING THEIR GUESTS

PHILIP KAPPEL

Monument to those who died in the Battle of Ridgefield

changed his plan to return to his ships through Norwalk, and instead took the Westport road.

Arnold pushed on from Ridgefield in pursuit of Tryon. Colonel Lamb, with three cannon, and Colonel Oswald's troops were posted on the line of Tryon's march through Westport at Old Hill where they waited for Tryon's appearance.

Tryon, having heard of Arnold's plan to trap him, again changed his plan of march and crossed the river three miles above the bridge. Under the protection of the guns from the ships, the British reembarked. Three hundred had not returned. At Westport General Tryon received slight wounds, and Colonel Lamb was wounded by grapeshot and suffered a severe concussion. A bullet passed through Arnold's coat and his horse was wounded. Had he not escaped the bullets meant for him at Ridgefield and Westport, he might have died a national hero. For Arnold's gallantry at Ridgefield, he was made a major general by Congress.

The accompanying illustration of the tablet placed by Miss Mary Olcott in the stone wall on the site of the Battle of Ridgefield is a touching tribute to our fallen patriots. The inscription reads as follows:

IN DEFENSE OF AMERICAN INDEPENDENCE

AT THE BATTLE OF RIDGEFIELD

APRIL 27, 1777

DIED

EIGHT PATRIOTS

WHO WERE LAID IN THESE GROUNDS

COMPANIONED BY

SIXTEEN BRITISH SOLDIERS

LIVING THEIR ENEMIES, DYING THEIR GUESTS

"IN HONOR OF SERVICE AND SACRIFICE

THIS MEMORIAL IS PLACED

FOR THE STRENGTHENING OF HEARTS"

Roger Sherman, New Milford's Illustrious Statesman

NEW MILFORD

New Milford green is one of the most attractive in western Connecticut, but within two decades, the steady growth of the town has modified its traditional character.

In order to forestall the complete takeover of the green, approval of zoning was sought through the polls. With customary Yankee contumacy many citizens emphasized that the fuss over zoning was, in fact, meddling in their personal liberties. Life for the liberty-loving New Englander today does not quite equate with what was at stake in 1775, but Yankee resistance and stubbornness certainly does.

Winter tracery, New Milford green

PHILIP
KAPPEL

As early as 1670, attempts were made by would-be settlers to purchase Weantenock (New Milford) from the Indians for a plantation. Since the lands were never taken up, permission in 1702 was given to the people of Milford, on the coast, to deal with the Indians, and in 1703 New Milford was founded. The Indians were given a tract of land for their own use.

John Noble, of Westfield, Massachusetts, came down through the wilderness in 1707 to become New Milford's first white settler, bringing with him his little eight-year-old daughter to "cook his victuals." He built a hut at the foot of Fort Hill but abandoned it later to build a finer house in the town plot at the south end of Aspetuck Hill, laid out with a town street and sixteen lots. In 1712, New Milford was incorporated. It is the largest township in the state of Connecticut with a rural area of sixty-four square miles.

The first homes were palisaded, to protect the settlers against the Indians, and to further that protection a garrison was stationed in the village in 1711.

Many years before the English settled in New Milford, the area was connected with other settlements by paths, including the ones from Farmington and Hartford, and between Woodbury and Waterbury. Later these paths became part of the general routes or roads from Boston to Philadelphia. An old milestone on Canterbury Hill, opposite the chapel of Canterbury School, is a reminder of the turnpike that passed to the right of the Knapp House and continued on over the hill. John Adams in his diary mentioned passing through New Milford on his way to Congress in Philadelphia.

Long before the Lexington alarm, New Milford was well aware of the deteriorating situation between the Colonies and England. At a town meeting held on September 20, 1774, the villagers resolved to implicate themselves in the crisis, whatever the cost. The following April, New Milford answered the alarm with men and supplies — 285 men enlisted in the Continental Army.

Most of us are familiar with the spirited painting in the Metropolitan Museum of Art in New York City, showing General Washington standing in the bow of one of the many boats filled with troops, negotiating the ice-blocked Delaware River. With Washington on that memorable day were Captain Isaac Bostwick of New Milford and his men.

New Milford was riddled with Tories, many of whom were brought before the Committee of Inspection when the Revolutionary War broke out, but they were pardoned. Others less fortunate were sent to the "gaol" in Hartford.

Nearly five thousand troops under General McDougall encamped on Second Hill for about a month in the fall of 1778. These three brigades brought to the town the real atmosphere of war. Patriotism always ran high among the villagers. When news of Benedict Arnold's treachery reached New Milford, a life-size effigy of him was carried through the town and, before many spectators, was formally hanged, cut down and buried!

New Milford's most noted resident was Roger Sherman, who came from New

Powder snow, Second Hill, New Milford, from Route 25

ton, Massachusetts, in 1743 to join his brother William, with whom he lived in Sherman for a brief period before making his residence in New Milford. When the present Town Hall was built in 1875, the huge flight of stairs in front of the building was built over Sherman's well. For many years the location of the old well was a puzzle, but recently, when major alterations to the Town Hall were instituted the well was rediscovered, complete with its original capstone. Roger Sherman's well has been incorporated into the new look of the Town Hall, and the state has put up a suitable sign marking the site.

Roger Sherman was born in 1721, and at the age of ten he was apprenticed to a shoemaker. At the death of his father, the youth fell heir to the responsibility of supporting the entire family. After three years of struggling to make the farm he inherited from his father pay for itself, he was forced to seek more remunerative employment. As Sherman sat at his cobbler's bench he snatched his education from the books he always kept nearby. He became a first-rate surveyor and won an appointment as surveyor of lands for the County of New Haven.

By 1750, Sherman had saved enough money to join his elder brother in the ownership of a country store in New Milford and another in New Haven with a branch in Wallingford. In 1761, Roger Sherman moved to New Haven, where he became its first mayor when that city was incorporated in 1784.

Roger Sherman, self-taught, became a colleague of Silas Deane in the Continental Congress. Sherman was the only man to sign three great State papers: he was a member of the committee which drew the Declaration of Independence, of that which reported the Articles of Confederation, of the convention that framed the national Constitution. Ellsworth and Sherman were associates on the bench of the Supreme Court.

Roger Sherman became Treasurer of Yale College and held that office until 1776, when the cause of American Independence absorbed his interest. In 1791 he was elected senator, his last public office before death came in 1793.

Pug Lane Farm; eighteenth-century residence of the author

Sunday Morning—New Milford Green

The First Congregational Church in New Milford was formally founded in 1716, although the congregation gathered for worship in a log cabin just north of the Lincoln Monument in 1712. Near the same place the first meetinghouse was completed in 1731, and Daniel Boardman was ordained the first minister of the church.

The second meetinghouse was located on the green opposite the present St. John's Episcopal Church, and finally a new church, built in 1833, which is illustrated here.

The Reverend Nathaniel Taylor was pastor during the American Revolution, serving the church from 1748 to 1800. The Reverend Nathaniel William Taylor, a grandson of Nathaniel Taylor, was born in the house just south of the church in 1786. He became a distinguished professor of theology at Yale Theological School. The Reverend Noah Porter, pastor of this church from 1836 to 1843, later became President of Yale. Roger Sherman, during his residence in New Milford, was appointed a deacon in this church in 1755.

Until 1745 the Congregational Church was the only house of worship in New Milford. People were called to worship by the beat of a drum, for which task the town paid a man.

St. John's Episcopal Church was completed on the green in 1883, but the first Episcopal service was held as early as 1742. The church of St. Francis Xavier, Roman Catholic, was built in 1860. Other early churches in New Milford were the Methodist Church at Gaylordsville, established in 1825, and the Methodist Church in New Milford, erected in 1849. The Baptist Church in Northville was founded in 1814.

Just north of the Congregational Church, where the school now stands, once stood the home of Nathaniel Taylor, Jr., who lodged General Lafayette for a night during the Revolutionary War; and south of the church, Reverend Nathaniel Taylor granted the hospitality of his home to Count Rochambeau for a night.

Churchgoers living on the west side of the Housatonic River crossed the river by boat which was maintained as a ferry from 1720 to 1737. The first bridge built across the Housatonic was at the foot of Bennitt Street, a short walk from the village green.

PHILIP KAPPEL

The First Congregational Church, New Milford

Canterbury School

NEW MILFORD

The first impression of Canterbury School suggests that nothing here is commonplace — even the location of the school is spectacular, occupying a hilltop overlooking the Housatonic River Valley.

The early settlers of New Milford were well acquainted with this view and at first aimed to drive stakes into the hilltop for their homes, but they changed their minds and laid out the plots for their abodes a half-mile further down the hill, near the present village green.

Back in 1915 three gentlemen, each a giant in his own field of endeavor, sat down together to discuss a new Roman Catholic boarding school, and plans once theoretical soon became a reality. Clarence H. Mackay, Henry O. Havemeyer and Dr. Nelson Hume guaranteed that henceforth Roman Catholic boys were able to attend a college preparatory school that equaled the nonsectarian schools without neglecting the doctrines of Catholicism. Canterbury School is operated by a board of trustees under the patronage of the Archbishop of Hartford, though not under diocesan control.

Dr. Hume was headmaster of Canterbury from 1915 until his sudden death in 1948. Canterbury was prepared for the inevitable, for Dr. Hume had notified the trustees that in any eventuality it was his wish to have Dr. Walter Sheehan succeed him.

So well has Dr. Sheehan filled the shoes of his predecessor that the school has sprung its seams, and the cry is for funds to provide a building program that keeps pace with growth. The kind of support which Sheehan receives from the alumni is evidence of their faith in his leadership.

Indicative of the school's religious pursuit and background, the chapel is the core of Canterbury and without a doubt the most beautiful structure on the campus. Inside the chapel the stained glass windows, which experts acclaim as among the finest hereabouts, filter the light which falls on the pews in gossamery patterns of subdued shades of color, connoting the spiritual theme which is the basis of Canterbury's existence, but not as a church school. The records show few students have received Holy Orders after graduation. One student who attended Canterbury for a short time became the President of the United States — the late John F. Kennedy.

The Chapel of Our Lady, Canterbury School

Water Power

It is impossible to tell how many towns in New England developed around water-driven mills, but it is reasonably certain that wherever mills were maintained, settlers built homes and their neighbors convened to have their corn ground, and timber cut into board feet.

When James Watt patented the steam engine in 1769, for the first time it was no longer necessary to put mills on riverbanks where waterwheels gathered their energy — men were able to move their operations anywhere they desired. Today, electric power runs every conceivable gadget in our homes, the machinery in our factories; it has become man's most powerful ally.

High in the Berkshires of western Massachusetts, the Housatonic River modestly starts on its meandering course towards the Sound, 130 miles to the south, through some of the most idyllic country in New England. The predecessor companies to the Connecticut Light and Power Company developed the first hydroelectric plant at Bulls Bridge in the 1900's, about six miles upstream from the Rocky River plant near New Milford.

The operation of the Rocky River plant is interesting, for only a few of its type exist in the country. A dam 950 feet wide and 100 feet high was built near the Housatonic River, creating one of the largest lakes in Connecticut, surrounded by high hills. Candlewood Lake is entirely man-made. The Rocky River basin was cleared by an army of five hundred men who removed all trees, homes and graves in preparing a reservoir of 4500 acres.

In February 1928 the powerhouse beside the Housatonic began pumping water from the river through a steel penstock directly into Candlewood Lake. By September 1929 the reservoir had filled to an elevation of 430 feet.

The real function of the Rocky River plant, with a capacity of 33,000 kilowatt units, is to regulate the flow of the Housatonic River, which operates two other hydroelectric plants below New Milford. Otherwise during dry seasons they would cease operating.

Since Candlewood Lake is a storage lake, water is released into the Housatonic when the river flow is low, making more water available at the Shepaug and Stevenson dams operating downstream. This also regulates the water at Bulls Bridge. To compensate the lake for its loss of water, the Rocky River plant pumps back into the lake an equal amount of water.

The 47,000 kilowatt Shepaug unit shown in the sketch is the newest dam — it was completed in 1954. The immensity of the project is indicated by the scale of the antlike workers and the equipment. This ultramodern Shepaug Hydroelectric Development, on the Housatonic River between Newtown and Southbury, created a lake with a depth of 200 feet at the dam extending as far as New Milford, where Lake Lilinonah obliterated the beautiful falls in the vicinity of Still River.

The Connecticut Light and Power Company's
Shepaug Hydroelectric Development on the Housatonic River

251

New England Farmlands

NEW MILFORD

The average New England farm today shows a tendency to favor herds of prize cattle. More and more, dairying is becoming the interest of the gentleman farmer, who will wryly admit that his milk costs him more than the champagne served at his parties. Yet the small Yankee farmer is still around, working just as hard as his forefathers, selling his milk and offering his friends hard cider; though the leisure time made available to him by modern machinery permits some pleasures denied his forebears. Two hundred years ago the majority of New Englanders got their living from the soil. Settlements were made near open fields, and the forests were the demarcation of the unexplored hinterland.

The roomy and charming New England homesteads attest to the success of farming as a family affair in the late eighteenth and the early nineteenth centuries. When the West was developed, many of the small New England farms were no longer able to compete, and so the farmers came down off the hills and emigrated to the west or moved to the industrialized cities. This change began just before the Civil War with the advancement of agricultural machinery, making possible the cultivation of food supplies that could be transported by the improved railroad facilities to the East.

Cattle as a source of beef were just as important to the early settlers as they are today. In order to expedite this vital food on the hoof many of our early roads were developed to provide safe passage for cattle from the farms around Plymouth to Boston and its surrounding areas.

It's seldom necessary to stray far from home to discover the latest innovations in husbandry if you live in traditional farming country. I called on Jake Sullivan, who has a farm nearby, to sketch and ask him why he leaves his young stock out all winter instead of keeping them in the traditional barn. He said, "They do better that way." And they do.

In this sketch, Jake is holding his working tool, just as his family has done before him for generations. On the ground a light dusting of snow fell during a January night. The thermometer stood at five degrees above zero at high noon and our breath froze as we chatted. Needless to say, I completed this sketch in my heated automobile. Jake was making his personal deductions on modern man — people were getting soft, or cows were getting tougher.

A neighbor's child who came along with me to see the cows suddenly crawled into my lap, looked up and queried, "Do cows get cold feet?" "Never!" I snapped, and stuck my own feet further under the heater.

Jake Sullivan on his farm, New Milford

Apple Time in New England

Apple trees in the month of May are gloriously exciting. The bare lifeless limbs of a few weeks before achieve a tracery of life with the arrival of the first warming trend, then break out with deep pink buds. When the petals are completely open the entire tree becomes narcissus-white, faintly tinted with pink and slightly perfumed. The tiny leaves are crowded from view by clusters of blossoms until the petals start falling like snow to the earth.

John Chapman, familiarly known as Johnny Appleseed, was born in Massachusetts in 1774. He was so obsessed by the beauty of apple trees that he propagated them wherever he went. From Pennsylvania, where he sold or gave away saplings and apple seeds to families migrating westward, he descended the Ohio River in 1806 with two canoes filled with bags of apple seeds; he stopped at inviting places to plant orchards in the wilderness.

Johnny Appleseed continued to wander up and down in Ohio, Indiana and Illinois for forty years, visiting his forest nurseries to prune and care for them, and assisted hundreds of settlers from the East in establishing their own orchards.

Scores of legends were told of him after his death in 1847, but few scoffed at him for his restless activities and obsessions. During the War of 1812 he sped thirty miles to summon American troops to Mansfield, Ohio, thus forestalling a raid by Indian tribes who were allied with the British.

Fifty years ago more than a thousand varieties of apples existed. Today only a handful appear on the market; those that fell from favor have become childhood memories. It is quite possible that modern storage methods are not suitable to the older varieties, I don't know, but they withstood the old-fashioned methods of being stored in barrels in the cold cellars of the old homesteads.

New England is the home of the McIntosh apple, among the first to appear on the roadside stands and in the markets to portend the coming of fall. The apple grower delivers the windfalls to the cider mill; the hand-picked fruit is attractively displayed in baskets and boxes to tempt the passersby. This drawing was made around the corner from my home. The roadside stand, a combination cider mill and farmer's outlet for apples, is typical of those found elsewhere in New England, but the effigy stuffed with straw and rags owes no allegiance to any state except Connecticut. This sometimes dignified gentleman serves as scarecrow in adjacent fields during the summertime and as mascot in the fall to bring good luck in sales.

The roadside stand

Rural Delivery

Neither snow nor rain nor heat nor gloom of night stays these couriers from the swift completion of their appointed rounds.

This sentence, on the façade of the General Post Office in New York City, was placed there by the famous firm of McKim, Mead and White, who planned the building, and is a worthy tribute to the men who handle the mails.

The quotation appears in Book 8, paragraph 98 of the works of Herodotus, where he describes the expedition of the Greeks against the Persians during the reign of Cyrus, about 500 B.C. The Persians had a system of mounted postal couriers in operation, and this sentence shows the fidelity with which their work was done. Our modern postmen making their rounds, irrespective of the weather, need no further comment or confirmation from those whom they serve, even though they are frequently taken for granted.

The morning mail

Horses vs. Tractors

As late as a decade ago the author's driveway was plowed out by horses as a friendly accommodation by Farmer Peet. He quietly arrived as soon as the snow ceased falling, standing astride his improvised homemade planked snowplow behind two snorting swaybacked mares to do a man-sized job with astonishing thoroughness.

The tractors of today may be able to plow your snow-filled roads faster, but horses were more picturesque. The cacophony of sputtering noisy tractors pressed into service after a heavy snowfall is indicative of the frantic effort to get the stalled wheels of a mechanized world moving again.

Plowing with horses — a man-sized job

Cracked Corn for Hungry Pheasants

Nature lovers appreciate the strutting cock pheasants and the hens that string out in a long line after them, gliding silently through the underbrush and crossing the open stretches to reach the berries sighted in the yard that are the fruit of bushes planted years ago for their decorative and food value. Neighbor Logan arrives with a supply of cracked corn to supplement my own just about the time the berries have disappeared — you can count on his punctuality.

When spring arrives and courting time for pheasants entices them back to the woods, the yard seems empty without them. The following winter the pheasants that have survived hunters and marauding animals return for the easy life in my yard.

Cracked corn for hungry pheasants

Washington

Washington lies sheltered amid the hills of Litchfield County. The township has four post offices: Washington Green, Washington Depot, New Preston and Marbledale. These areas, developed along plans suitable to each one, are collectively known as Washington. To appreciate how different this community is from the average town, one has to live here or nearby, to see the results of the effort that was made to retain its rural qualities. The residents of Washington, by and large, have developed a first-rate antipathy for anything that would disturb the prevailing peace.

The first settler in Washington was Joseph Hurlbut, who came in 1734 to what was known as Waramaug or Judea Society in Woodbury. He loved the rolling hills, the densely wooded areas and the deep ravines through which brooks and major streams tore their way through outcroppings of rocks. The potentials for water power were high and others soon followed Joseph Hurlbut and liked what they found. In April 1778 the inhabitants — 270 families — petitioned to be incorporated, and in 1779 the General Assembly acceded to their request and incorporated the first town in the United States to be named after George Washington.

George Washington passed through Washington Sunday, September 24, 1780, and breakfasted on bread and milk at the Cogswell Tavern in New Preston. It was May 18, 1781, when he set out for Wethersfield from Fishkill Landing to meet with Rochambeau and Admiral Barras, he arrived at Gideon Morgan's Tavern in Washington after a forty-three-hour ride from the Hudson River.

Frederick W. Gunn was born in Washington in 1816 and graduated from Yale in 1837. His need for money to study medicine made teaching at the Academy in Washington a necessity, but he was encumbered by his adamant stand on Abolition, which irritated many in the town. Other idiosyncrasies such as complete abstinence further isolated him, and his impertinences matched those heaped upon his head. During all the controversy, Frederick Gunn found an ally, Abigail Brinsmade, the daughter of General D. B. Brinsmade, with whom he fell deeply in love. General Brinsmade received Gunn's request for his daughter's hand in marriage with coolness, and suggested that the pair wait awhile.

The caldron of insults was overflowing, and few residents in Washington avoided being embroiled in the controversy over Abolition. And if anyone made a good scapegoat, it was Frederick Gunn. But just when the insults became merciless, General Brinsmade reversed his former position and gave the young couple his blessing. They were married in 1848. The following year Gunn resumed his

The Congregational Church on the green, Washington

teaching at the Academy and in the fall of 1850 he and Abigail embarked on their greatest undertaking — the founding of the Gunnery. The school was first called a family school and became endowed with the personalities of its founders.

Today, the Gunnery has an enrollment of more than two hundred boys; if its founders could return and witness to what extent their school has grown they might feel vindicated for all the heartaches they experienced at the start. However, the Gunnery barely missed tragedy in 1947 when the school stood on the brink of failure. The Gunnery is one of the few preparatory schools for boys that maintains a studio to encourage the fine arts. The students receive no credits for the work, but they flock there nevertheless. The cultural advantage of such a program is tremendous.

The Gunn Memorial Library, on Washington green, was erected to memorialize Frederick W. Gunn and his wife.

The First Congregational Church on the green is as much a part of the Gunnery as it is of Washington at large. The entire community and the school have been bound by close ties for over a century. Gunnery students of Congregational background have attended services here through the years, other denominations by choice. Customarily they sit on the right side of the church. Graduation ceremonies of the Gunnery are held in the church each year. From this church Abigail Gunn and her husband Frederick Gunn were borne to their graves. Henry Ward Beecher delivered the principal address before a crowded church October 12, 1882, on the occasion of the unveiling of the Gunn Monument which Senator Platt presented to the family at the cemetery after the church service.

The complete story of this church is that of a meetinghouse that rose from a log shed in 1742, to a frame building erected in 1754 which burned to the ground in 1800. Undaunted, the parishioners built the present church and held their first service on Thanksgiving Day, 1801. The original spire and belfry were restored in 1910. The church clock and the Westminster chimes were installed at the same time.

Adding to Washington's fame as a town of preparatory schools, the Wykeham Rise School for girls, founded originally in 1902 by Miss Fanny Davis and subsequently closed for a number of years, has recently been reopened with the support of the alumnae and the townspeople.

The Old Burr Calhoun Place

WASHINGTON DEPOT

The severity of New England winters, I am told, is a state of mind, but whose mind? As a longtime resident of Connecticut I could argue that point to a draw. It all depends on who has to wade through the snowdrifts and for what purpose. Those who are keen on winter sports and wait gleefully for the snow to fall may love it, but for the rest of us, winter is a headache. In the days when this old Burr homestead was built, winter could not have been accepted with less disfavor. Just keeping logs moving to the multiple fireplaces will take the starch out of anyone who at first looks on country life as a mere conditioning. But there were no utility poles to fall in the dead of winter, sending someone to a telephone screaming for plumbers, electricians and specialists because the electric well pump had stopped and the furnace was out cold. A useless pushbutton has its day of reckoning, as New England discovered November 9, 1965, the night of the Great Blackout, when the anachronistic few who had candles and firewood on hand basked in comfort while the modern world ground to a bewildered halt.

This red one-story saltbox house was built around 1750 by Burr Calhoun. The gnarled maple is estimated to be of matching age and has lasted because it received extensive care and tree surgery. It would seem improbable that the house or the tree could sustain the idyllic setting without each other. The Stephen Landons acknowledge this and treat both with tremendous sympathy and lavish their affection on the interior of the house as well.

Four generations of Calhouns occupied the house and in their neglect hastened the property towards total disintegration, which was fortunately arrested about the turn of the twentieth century when new owners made extensive restorations. It was at that time the original hearthstone turned up in the orchard and was brought back to the house by oxen.

When Mr. and Mrs. Stephen Landon purchased the property a short time ago, it needed minor alterations, but great care was exercised to avoid drastic contrasts. The house has its original hand-hewn oak floorboards fastened with hand-wrought iron nails. There are three fireplaces, old woodwork and iron hardware — all of special interest to the antiquarian. The gardens are a harmonious assemblage of flower beds in constant rotating bloom and nearby is a reflecting pond and numerous outbuildings as old as the house. This rambling farm was not an accident — it was arrived at through planning and affectionate forethought. Inside the house there is an important collection of furnishings, including a painting by the celebrated Trumbull of Mrs. Peter Augustus Jay, the daughter-in-law of John Jay, the patriot.

The Old Burr Calhoun Place, Washington Depot

PHILIP KAPPEL

267

The Rebirth of Washington Depot

The relationship between Washington Green and Washington Depot is consanguineous, but in the former, commercialism is conspicuously absent, except for a drugstore and a post office on the green. At the foot of a steep hill west of the green lies Washington Depot, hard by the banks of the Shepaug River, where shops, two banks, the fire house, the Town Hall and the post office furnish everything any small community needs.

The defunct Shepaug Railroad once twisted through the Shepaug Valley and made scheduled stops at Washington Depot. The station stood about where the new bank is today, opposite the Washington Art Association in Bryan Plaza. The railroad made its first run through this beautiful valley in 1872 but shortly after the Second World War it was scrapped.

Until 1955 the Depot developed as it had a mind to within the framework of zoning, but the sector along the Shepaug River was intended to be commercial. But people resented the decay that had set in and secretly hoped one day to restore the Depot to refulgence. The contrast between the Green and the Depot was sharp indeed, but artists saw it with kindly eyes. They respected its quaintness, its hodgepodge, and shrugged off the shouting about too little parking space and the amenities of a large town. They were for little alteration and the status quo. People by and large liked to shop where parking was better and the shops more attractive. The flow of business was diverted elsewhere, and no one did anything about it.

An Art Association seemed a necessity in the community; the resident artists were too impatient to go through the throes of raising money for their own quarters and settled for the next best thing. The Washington Art Association was incorporated in 1952 and moved into an abandoned post office. The quarters were cramped and the executive committee was hopeful that someday, somehow, we would have our own quarters. One day in August 1955, with customary enthusiasm, the finishing touches were completed for the preview opening the following day. The punchbowl was placed in the center of the table, and the rubber doormat outside, with the letters W-E-L-C-O-M-E across its face, was swept clean for the occasion.

Heavy rain had been falling for days. The brooks looked ominously swollen and the lowlands were gradually filling. The Shepaug appeared unusually high, but it had been that way before, and few people gave it thought. But four miles above Washington Depot tragedy was gathering its forces. At Woodville where the Litchfield–New Milford state road crosses an earth embankment, the conduits through which the Shepaug flowed were blocked by debris and the earth embankment became a dam. The water which had been building up behind it burst the embankment and swept through the Shepaug Valley mixed with rocks, trees and parts of houses that served as a battering ram destroying everything in its path.

The Washington Art Association, Bryan Plaza, Washington Depot

All the major bridges except one went out. Washington Depot was shorn of whatever dignity it once had, its streets eroded to ribbons. This dismal picture greeted everyone, and apprehensively we returned to survey the damage to the art gallery. The pictures on the walls were sucked off their hooks as if a huge vacuum cleaner had removed them through the broken windows and the damaged walls. The pictures were scattered along the banks of the Shepaug. Many were found miles from the Depot, others were never located. But amazingly the punchbowl was still in its place of honor on the table, but filled with mud, and the doormat reposed exactly where it was left at the front door, welcoming, staring at the cleanup crew entering the mutilated building with shovels and brooms. If tragedy was to have its moment of comic relief, this was it.

Then came the reconstruction, and Washington Depot received painstaking rejuvenation. There are always some who would object to wholesale reconstruction, but it came anyway, due to the foresight of the few who had a constructive plan. Shops beyond repair were replaced by conforming colonial designs. Today the scars of yesteryear are gone and even the former skeptics admit it was a job well done.

The Washington Art Association sought a place of its own in the reconstruction plan of the town. One of the last of the derelicts still standing on the banks of the Shepaug was chosen as the Art Association's permanent home, and in January 1958 the trustees authorized the purchase of the old brick Hearn building. It was moved to its present site beside Canoe Brook and restored handsomely. Our first exhibition was held on May 27, 1959. The support we received was spontaneous and has kept on going since the day the old quarters were so thoroughly laundered.

Woodbury

Woodbury was a frontier town; during the spring of 1673 it was settled by fifteen families who left Stratford. The original grant was given by the General Court in 1672 to William Curtice, Samuel Sherman and a few others. The land in the plantation of Pomperaug (Woodbury) was purchased from the Potatuck Indians in 1673; they kept a tract for themselves and called it the Potatuck Reservation. By 1758 so few Indians were alive, the land was sold off piecemeal.

In 1779, about a hundred years after its founding, a part of Woodbury was set off to Washington, and another portion became Southbury in 1787. In 1796 still another part was sliced away to become Roxbury, and the final cut of Woodbury's territorial pie was lifted in 1807 to become Middlebury.

Predatory Indians were a major threat and worry, but when King Philip's War broke out in 1675, the Woodbury settlers lost heart and scurried back to Stratford.

The North Congregational Church, Woodbury

The present Main Street of Woodbury follows the original Indian trail. As early as 1675 highways were planned leading to important towns and the numerous milestones in the Woodbury area attest to their use and necessity.

The Washington turnpike was authorized to be built in 1803 from the center of Washington to the center of Woodbury. Another important turnpike in 1803, was built from Danbury through Woodbury to Farmington, and the road from Cornwall to Washington was continued to North Woodbury and in use by 1812.

The citizens of Woodbury were, from the start of hostilities with England, loyal to the cause of liberty. When Colonel Ethan Allen led his successful attack on Fort Ticonderoga, half of his men were from Woodbury. Woodbury during the Revolution had over 1400 men in arms; and it was a Woodbury doctor, Isaac Foster, who was entrusted with directing the program of inoculation, in 1778, of the men in the Continental Army.

At the time of the Revolution the population of Woodbury was slightly more than five thousand souls. It was a prosperous community and the numerous churches and charming houses still bear an air of sophistication; their sparkling white exteriors bear out the pride and interest their twentieth-century occupants are dedicated to preserve. The same spirit prevails in Southbury and Middlebury.

General Washington made his fourth journey through Connecticut in September 1780 and passed through Woodbury coming from the direction of Danbury, Newtown and Southbury, then proceeded through Waterbury, Southington, Farmington to Hartford. This was the protected route. The British troops offered no threat so far inland and safe passage was thus assured.

Rochambeau's troops on their way to Yorktown passed through Woodbury in June 1781 and returned as a victorious army on their eastward march to Boston at the conclusion of the victory at Yorktown.

The Glebe House is an architectural gem of special interest because there, on March 25, 1783, ten of the fourteen clergy of the Church of England in America in Connecticut, gathered to elect as bishop the Reverend Samuel Seabury, who was twice refused consecration by both bishops of England. Finally on November 14, 1784, at the home of Bishop Skinner in Aberdeen, the three bishops of the Church of Scotland consecrated him. For two years he was the only bishop in America. Since then, the Glebe House has been known as the birthplace of the organized Episcopal Church in the United States. The Seabury Society for the Preservation of the Glebe House was founded in 1925 and the house is open to the public.

To select one church of outstanding architectural purity from among those in Woodbury for its simple charm, I can in all honesty name the North Congregational Church (1816), situated on high ground at the northwest corner of the intersection of the Washington and Woodbury highways. The church is widely acclaimed as the only church in Connecticut to have an Asher Benjamin steeple.

Milestone on the old Albany turnpike, New Milford

Franklinstones and Markers

Motorists speeding along our highways seldom take notice of the few remaining historic milestones which stand inconspicuously by the side of the road. They served a useful purpose in Colonial New England, since the cost of stagecoach travel and the mails were based on mileage.

Benjamin Franklin, in 1753, as comptroller of the Colonial Post Office, spent ten weeks visiting the post offices throughout New England using an ingenious device for measuring distances, which he invented. The turns of a wheel attached to the wheel of his chaise measured each mile fairly accurately, and a stake driven into the ground indicated where a milestone was to be placed by the workmen who followed. These stones became known as Franklinstones, and a number of them still exist along the old Post Roads and Turnpikes.

One Franklinstone is located in Old Lyme, Connecticut, at the foot of Johnny-Cake Hill. A simple slab bears this inscription: "NL XIVM" — *New London 14 Miles.*

In Clinton, Connecticut, there is another Franklinstone near the Reverend Jared Eliot homestead on the Post Road. Legend tells how Franklin's horse wandered off the highway into the lane where Eliot lived; this incident led to a long friendship between Franklin and Eliot.

One Franklinstone in Woodbury bears only the letter L above the Roman numeral XVII with the letter M below; the L was an abbreviation for Litchfield, and the M for miles. At a glance the traveler knew he was seventeen miles from Litchfield.

The milestone illustrated here is not a Franklinstone. It stands beside the road that passes in front of the Canterbury School chapel. The road is restricted to local traffic today but is actually the long-lost Albany Turnpike of Colonial days, when it once was a main artery for travel between the Hudson River and Litchfield County by way of New Milford. The inscription on the milestone reads as follows: "84 MILES FROM N.YORK — 1 MILE FROM N.MILFORD — ERECTED BY ZACHARIAH SANFORD 1788."

The Church on New Preston Hill

Throughout New England the churches have a similarity — most are painted white if built of wood; a mellow pink if of brick; but the churches built of native stone are deserving of special attention. Our early New England builders relied on their eyes more than on the spirit-level. This is apparent in old houses and churches and drives the modern decorator frantic trying to measure windows for curtains. In my own home there isn't a single window frame that matches another, but what charm the builders have created without the aid of precision instruments.

Few churches have captured my appreciation more than the Congregational Church on New Preston Hill, built of stone with a wooden steeple. Its neglected condition recently prompted a handful of neighbors to restore the church to its former beauty. Their contributions of money and time effected the rededication of this noble edifice on Sunday, July 1, 1962. Nearby is the old manse in matching stone.

The first Ecclesiastical Society and the First Congregational Church of New Preston was established in 1757. The first building was constructed of logs; the second church was a frame building built in 1766. The third and present stone church was built in 1824.

The congregation built a fourth church in 1853 in New Preston village where services are now held. There is no church organization on the Hill for the membership in the New Preston Congregational Church in the village, but the First Ecclesiastical Society continues as a corporation.

This structure has been featured in books on early New England meeting-houses, but few have known of its whereabouts on its isolated hilltop site. Architects agree that seldom has the pulpit in this church been repeated elsewhere; it is situated at the entrance end of the room between the two doors opening from the vestibule, consequently the seats face the front of the building. Whatever the reason may have been, this unusual treatment makes the churchgoer's entry subject to scrutiny by the entire congregation.

At one time the church was almost completely overgrown with poison ivy. The markings left across the stonework by the ivy vines resemble the lines in an abstract painting. Today it stands as one of New England's most beautiful meeting-houses of the post-Revolutionary period.

New Preston, originally called the north purchase, includes the land in the town taken from Kent and New Milford. Edward Cogswell, an early settler, named New Preston after his earlier home in Preston in eastern Connecticut.

The historic Cogswell Tavern is still privately owned. Squire William Cogswell 1734–1787) was the moderator of the first town meeting in Washington. He was a major in the Revolutionary War and during his long absence his wife Anna brought up their family and managed the farm of two thousand acres. She also ran her home as a tavern, and it is located today, as a private home owned by the same family, at the foot of Baldwin Hill a short distance from the main highway to New Milford, and four and a half miles north of Washington Green.

A.D.1824.

PHILIP KAPPEL

Study in light and shade — the church on New Preston Hill

Fantasy in stone — the church on New Preston Hill

Litchfield

Litchfield's reputation stems from the illustrious list of important personalities who lived here, and from the number of old houses in existence which were once occupied by them, plus the fact that in this present unpredictable era of ours, Litchfield, miraculously unmoved by fads, remains unmolested as a living museum of bygone days. Tinges of commercialism have made their appearance but, by and large, they are too distant from the historic area to be of concern to the antiquarian.

North and South streets are essentially as they were at the close of the eighteenth century and the Revolutionary War; the Georgian houses are still well cared for — all are real homes to their present occupants.

Litchfield is one of my neighboring towns; for several decades I have had the good fortune to enjoy and share with my many friends there the subtle atmosphere and elegance that permeate the town.

In this rapidly changing world, that which is beautiful is seldom able to persevere or establish a protective shell around itself without concentrated assistance from public-spirited people. With some planning it is quite possible to keep the old, and still permit the new to flower, without forfeiting the grandeur and mellowness of great craftsmanship. If we relax and fail to hold what we have inherited, what would there remain to sustain us during the midseasons of man's fluctuating tastes?

Litchfield is situated in hilly terrain, specifically in those delightful rolling hills which are part of the Taconic Mountains. In May 1719 those who became enamored of the area sought to buy into it and settle here, which the General Assembly permitted them to do. The first settlers were John Marsh and Deacon John Buel of Lebanon, and fifty-five others from Farmington, Lebanon, Wethersfield and Windsor. Litchfield was incorporated as a town in 1719.

The present South and North streets run from the green in the directions their names imply. They were laid out as eight rods and twelve rods wide, respectively. The streets in Litchfield vary in width, but all are unusually broad.

In 1766 a post-rider had a route between Litchfield and Hartford. During the Revolutionary War, news was sent by expresses through Litchfield from Boston to New York, and from Hartford to West Point and other Hudson towns.

By 1798 the New Milford and Litchfield turnpike was operated as a toll-road — another turnpike was completed soon thereafter between Litchfield and Harwinton. The expanding road system included, by 1802, the Waterbury turnpike that also passed, and the Litchfield and Cornwall turnpike opened to traffic in 1814.

Five hundred and four men from the town saw service in the Revolutionary War. Provisions and military supplies were kept in storage houses near the Green.

Captain Bezaleel Beebe in January 1776, raised a company of men within seven days for the defense of New York. The following November he left with his select group of carefully picked men to defend Fort Washington near New York. Many of them were taken prisoner, and thirty died in prison ships or during confinement in New York.

The safe inland routes between Pennsylvania, west of the Hudson and New England, after New York fell to the British in 1777, passed through Litchfield.

The gilded leaden equestrian statue of George III, erected on Bowling Green, New York City, was destroyed by the Sons of Liberty the night of July 9, 1776, and secretly removed to General Oliver Wolcott's woodshed in Litchfield where his friends and family feverishly converted the molten metal into 42,088 bullets, allowing a few more or less for miscalculation. The bullets were referred to as "Melted Majesty."

About August 1776, prisoners taken by the patriots were sent from New York to the Litchfield "gaol." The present county jail, a dignified red brick building, was built in 1812 and is situated at the northwest corner of West and North streets; next to the jail is the First National Bank of Litchfield, established in 1815 — just north of the bank, removed by a few houses, is the famed Tallmadge House on North Street.

Some well-known prisoners arrived in Litchfield for safekeeping. One of them was the British Mayor of New York, David Matthews, who after his release gave his "pleasure carriage" to the wife of his guard, Major Seymour.

On April 30, 1777, the Governor was informed that the New Jersey Congress was sending Governor Franklin, the last royal Governor of New Jersey, a Tory sympathizer, and the only son of Benjamin Franklin, to the gaol in Litchfield.

Washington was in Litchfield five times during the Revolutionary War. Following the conference with Rochambeau and the French officers in Hartford in September 1780, he arrived in Litchfield with Lafayette on Saturday, September 23, and spent the night with Oliver Wolcott. Lafayette was entertained by Tapping Reeve at the same time. Washington passed through Litchfield twice in March 1781, and on the morning of May 19 he breakfasted in Litchfield. On Thursday, May 24, 1781, he left Hartford for New Windsor, New York, and lodged in Litchfield. In all probability he was entertained at Sheldon's Tavern.

Ethan Allen was born in Litchfield in 1737, but his residence here was brief; his parents moved around 1739 to Cornwall, where he spent his boyhood.

We have stressed the use of arms in these pages, but Litchfield harbored men and women who fought for causes with other types of weapons. If our new nation desired to be released from national slavery under a foreign power, thought Miss Sarah Pierce, then ignorance, on an individual basis, must be accepted as personal enslavement! She became a pioneer educator of young women.

To Miss Pierce's famous school, founded in 1792, in Litchfield, later came the youthful and serious-minded Harriet Beecher. When Harriet Beecher Stowe's distinguished career drew to a close in Hartford in 1896, she left a legacy of thirty-three volumes of her writings and a forceful message for posterity to remember. The house built in 1775 by Elijah Wadsworth on the corner of Prospect and North streets was moved by Dr. H. W. Buel about 1872 to Spring Hill, where it stands now as part of the Forman School. It is the birthplace of the Reverend Henry Ward Beecher and his sister Harriet, whose father, Reverend Lyman Beecher, owned the house. He was minister of the Litchfield Congregational Church from 1810 to 1826. The original site is indicated by a brass plate on the "Beecher Elm."

Oliver Wolcott, eminent American Revolutionary patriot, and a signer of the Declaration of Independence, came to Litchfield from Windsor after his graduation from Yale in 1747. He held several judicial posts and in 1775 was named an Indian Commissioner to keep the Iroquois neutral. Wolcott was a general in the Saratoga campaign, a delegate to the Continental Congress and Governor of Connecticut from 1796 to 1797. His house was built around 1753 on a tract of land inherited from his father, Governor Roger Wolcott, one of the original proprietors of Litchfield. This simple central-chimney house is the oldest in Litchfield. In this house on South Street Wolcott entertained many distinguished guests — George Washington, Lafayette, Alexander Hamilton and other Revolutionary heroes. It is still occupied by the family. Many consider this house the most interesting in the town. The porch is supported by Ionic columns upholding a fanlighted pediment.

Oliver Wolcott, Jr., like his father, also served in the American Revolution. He entered the practice of law after the Revolution, and in 1784, he and Oliver Ellsworth served as commissioners in adjusting Connecticut's claims against the United States. Wolcott served in the Federal Government under Alexander Hamilton, whom he succeeded in 1795 as Secretary of the Treasury. He supported Hamilton against John Adams and gained considerable unpopularity and in 1800 he was forced to resign. He served as a judge, was the presiding officer at the Connecticut Constitutional Convention in 1817, and from 1817 to 1827 was governor of Connecticut. His home on South Street was built in 1799 by Elijah Wadsworth.

Horace Bushnell was born in a house in Bantam, two miles west of Litchfield Hill, and spent his boyhood in New Preston, where he attended the academy which was opened there in 1818. He studied law and theology at Yale and moved to Hartford, where from 1833 to 1853 he was pastor of the North Congregational Church. The well-known park bearing his name was the result of his personal efforts to acquire it for the city, with an appropriation from the state — the first such acquisition by the state for such a purpose.

In the twentieth century, Litchfield continued to attract public-spirited people as residents, notably Alain C. White and his sister, Miss Mary W. White. As Horace Bushnell foresaw the value of open spaces in a growing Hartford, the Whites foresaw the advantages of great recreational centers around Bantam Lake and throughout the state; they preserved vast areas that might have been lost forever. Between 1908 and 1912 they purchased several large tracts of land extending north and east from Bantam Lake. In 1913 they conveyed them to the White Memorial Foundation with an endowment to help maintain and develop the sites to serve the public — 5500 acres of wildlife preserve.

The Whites were interested in the development of a state park system in Connecticut. The well-known parkland areas deeded to the state over a period of years, included Macedonia Brook and Kent Falls in Kent, Mohawk Forest and Mountain in Cornwall and Goshen, Campbell Falls in Norfolk and North Canaan, and the People's Forest in Barkhamsted. The Shade Swamp Sanctuary in Farmington, presently controlled by the Connecticut State Board of Fisheries and Game, owes its existence to the White Memorial Foundation.

The Congregational church on the green, Litchfield

Litchfield's Legacy

The Litchfield Law School was the first of its kind in America. The small frame building, twenty by twenty-one feet, is situated just south of the house. Judge Tapping Reeve in 1784 founded his law school, which he conducted until 1820, and his successor, Judge James Gould, continued the school until 1833. Over one thousand students passed through the Law School.

Tapping Reeve, a Princeton graduate, was born on Long Island and married Sally Burr, a granddaughter of Jonathan Edwards and a sister of Aaron Burr. Burr lived with the Reeves during his law studies. Judge Reeve entertained Lafayette and other persons of note at his home on South Street, built in 1773 nearly opposite the Wolcott residence.

Among the graduates of the Litchfield Law School was John C. Calhoun of Abbeville, South Carolina. He entered the school in 1805 and became Secretary of War from 1817 to 1821, and a vice-president of the United States from 1824 to 1832. Horace Mann, a native of Franklin, Massachusetts, was in the class of 1823. He became an educator of note and revolutionized the school systems of the country. He also laid out the plans for the normal schools in Massachusetts, the first normal schools in the country. Another celebrated student was Noah Webster of West Hartford, the lexicographer.

In 1784 when the American Bar was reconstituting the law of the United States there were no textbooks. Tapping Reeve's Law School produced many of them by assembling the lectures delivered before it.

In 1929 the Litchfield Historical Society purchased the building of the former Law School and moved it back to its original site.

The Tapping Reeve House, Litchfield, just north of the first law school in America

The Benjamin Tallmadge House

LITCHFIELD

It was natural for Colonel Benjamin Tallmadge to come to Litchfield and make his home here, for during the Revolutionary War Litchfield was a center for army supplies and personnel. Since the British held New York, Litchfield was on the inland route from Boston and Hartford to Washington's headquarters on the Hudson.

Colonel Tallmadge bought this house in 1782 from Thomas Sheldon, who had built it in 1775 as a tavern. Tallmadge remodeled the house after his visit to George Washington — in emulation of Mount Vernon, he added the abbreviated wings at the ends with two-story porticos, each supported by slender columns.

With the mounting discontent with British rule in the Colonies, Tallmadge enlisted in Colonel John Chester's Connecticut regiment with the commission of lieutenant. He became Chief of the Intelligence Service and a colonel in the Light Dragoons, and at the close of the war he was one of the founders of the Society of the Cincinnati.

In both official and social capacities, Colonel Tallmadge was the close associate of all the leading military figures of the day — Rochambeau, Lafayette, and Count d'Esaing, the Commander of the French fleet.

It was Tallmadge's activities as chief of intelligence that made possible the uncovering of the treasonable conniving of Major John André and Benedict Arnold, who had a master plan that might have easily lost the war for the Colonies. Arnold's escape left André to answer for their crime by hanging, alone — Arnold's life was spent in England in relative comfort.

Tallmadge and Nathan Hale were graduated from Yale in the class of 1773. The British hanged Nathan Hale without a trial on September 22, 1776, and thereby established the precedent that motivated the hanging of the British spy, André. Colonel Tallmadge was detailed to accompany to the scaffold the British spy, whom Tallmadge held in high regard as a personable and brilliant soldier.

To this house on North Street, Colonel Tallmadge brought his bride, Mary Floyd, a native of Long Island and daughter of General William Floyd, a signer of the Declaration of Independence. Tallmadge and his charming wife entertained lavishly. On one of the windowpanes of the ballroom, George Washington scratched his signature during one of his frequent visits to the Tallmadge house; on another windowpane in the same room, William Franklin, Benjamin Franklin's son, the last Loyalist Royal Governor of New Jersey, left his signature, together with several members of the Tallmadge family.

After the Revolutionary War, Tallmadge and his brother became pioneers in industrial projects and trade. Their firm, B. Tallmadge and Co., was tremendously

The Benjamin Tallmadge House, Litchfield

PHILIP KAPPEL

successful. Tallmadge became a member of Congress from 1801 to 1817. He appreciated the boldness of Alexander Hamilton's financial wizardry.

To Connecticut Tallmadge brought the fruits of his acumen and foresight far beyond his times; with his associates he made Litchfield, immediately following the war and during the early years of the nineteenth century, a cultural center and a business site in foreign trade only eclipsed in New England by Boston.

Sheldon Tavern
LITCHFIELD

The late Colonel Samuel H. Fisher, who lived here, had confidence in the perpetuation of Litchfield's colonial charm. The buildings on North and South streets are protected because they were made an historic area by law, but the old trees are more perishable! Ice storms, hurricanes and disease have gnawed away at their sturdy shapes. As early as 1790, an effort was made to plant the trees which today throw their shadows across the streets. Oliver Wolcott, Jr., and his brother Frederick planted many of the elms on South Street. One elm was planted by John C. Calhoun before 1805 on Prospect Street, and another on West Street. In 1825, elms were planted on the east side of North Street by James K. Gould, the son of Judge Gould, and Origen Seymour. The "whipping-post elm," planted by an unknown donor stands near the county jail and is estimated to be over two hundred years old. On good authority I was told that historian Hollister was responsible for the double row of elms on North and South streets.

Elisha Sheldon built the house on North Street in 1760 — later known as Sheldon's Tavern — on simple lines, and it remained so until his son acquired the place twenty years later and turned it into an inn. George Washington spent one night in the place and occupied the northeast room, which he mentioned in his diary.

Senator Uriah Tracy remodeled the house drastically after he purchased it about 1800 at which time the Palladian window was added. A sensitive architect, William Spratt, a Scotsman who had been an officer of Burgoyne's Army, was responsible for this architectural metamorphosis. After the surrender at Saratoga, Spratt came to Connecticut on parole, and the stamp of his craftsmanship is apparent on many of Litchfield's best houses.

The house later fell into the hands of Judge James Gould, the partner and successor of Tapping Reeve. The small building he built in the yard of the Sheldon house, and used for a time as a Law School, was moved elsewhere.

In drawing the house it was impossible to do justice to the impressive columned entrance, the Palladian window and the pediment above. The cornices under the eaves and over the first-floor windows, add that "quality touch" of the creative artisan that is seldom surpassed.

Sheldon Tavern, Litchfield

PHILIP KAPPEL

The William Spratt touch is apparent also in the Julius Deming House (1790–1793) on North Street — an elegant house that resembles the captains' houses along the New England seacoast, white and square, with tall chimneys, quoined corners, hip-roofed and balustraded all around.

The house, first called The Lindens, was built by a merchant who helped finance the Revolution. He lost his money through sentimental loans and rewon his fortune by participating in the lucrative China Trading Company with Oliver Wolcott and Colonel Tallmadge.

Covered Bridge

WEST CORNWALL

Unfortunately, there is little authenticated material on the local covered bridges. The one at West Cornwall is no exception — gossip and legend provide a multitude of stories, few of which carry factual weight. Sometimes the bridge is called Hart's Bridge, but for the most part it is known as the covered bridge at West Cornwall. It is about 212 feet long. Some say that the bridge was built in 1837, others insist that the date is 1841 and a few say that the bridge was erected in 1854 — any one of which might be correct. However, no one could deny that the bridge has stood over a century and has withstood numerous serious floods and ice jams. The Housatonic River in spate is vicious — here and there may be seen the abutments of bridges that have been swept away; at Gaylordsville a solitary ghost structure still marks the site of a former bridge bypassed by an iron one. A few miles north of it is Bull's Bridge, a covered bridge that crosses a deep ravine. Many years ago it served as a new route to the Hudson River markets for the products of an iron furnace run by Jacob Bull. By 1945 Bull's Bridge was in such disrepair it was threatened with destruction but the state of Connecticut made the necessary repairs, making two fine covered bridges that cross the Housatonic River.

Covered bridge over the Housatonic River, West Cornwall

The Antique Hunter's Paradise

Antique shops of every description may be found anywhere beside the highways throughout New England, in disheveled-looking shacks and barns or in converted buildings. They are as enticing to the collector as the more sophisticated shops in fine inns or located along the streets of the summer resorts. The motorist with a flair for antiques prefers to browse around in the roadside shops, where he is unmolested by the salesfolk. Besides, he enjoys the small talk between himself and the shop owner, which frequently leads to a pleasant exchange of views, and the fascination of probing the "junk heaps" and therein discovering something worthwhile, which Guy de Maupassant expressed so adequately and convincingly — "Oh! I am sorry for those who do not know the honeymoon of the collector with the antique he has just purchased."

During the past quarter-century the interest in antiques has risen enormously. At Sturbridge Village, Massachusetts, it is possible to visit a completely reconstructed New England Village of 1790 to 1840 where the past comes to life under the old conditions.

By and large, the roadside antique shops near or on New England highways resemble a forced dispossession of household goods, with antiques scattered over every foot of lawn in disorder, exposed to the weather, gathering patina and aging before the eyes of the public, and making a conglomerate mess.

This drawing shows one particular antique shop in western Connecticut, hard by the Housatonic River, which at one time served as a toll house to a covered bridge nearby. The dealer brings out his bait and withdraws to the interior of his shop to wait for his quarry.

Former toll house near the covered bridge, West Cornwall

Salisbury

There is more to this charming village, in the northwest corner of the state, than meets the eye. It has a traditional Congregational church — a very handsome one built between 1799 and 1800 and a town hall constructed in 1749. Salisbury has innumerable historic sites already preserved and many in the process of restoration.

Salisbury was incorporated in 1741. The first white settler was Thomas Lamb, who came from Springfield, Massachusetts, to work a forge at nearby Lime Rock in 1734. Salisbury, also known as Weatogue, was situated on an Indian trail that ran from Stockbridge, Massachusetts, to a point just below Kent, Connecticut. It was one of the earliest routes that went from Ore Hill in Salisbury to the ironworks at Great Barrington, Massachusetts, over which iron ore was transported by horses.

The first bridge that crossed the Housatonic River, east of Salisbury, was known as Burrall's Bridge. During the Revolutionary War travel was restricted to this route between the Hudson River and Massachusetts.

In January 1776, a meeting of the governor and the Council of Safety appointed Colonel Jedediah Elderkin to investigate the iron furnace at Salisbury. Subsequently the condition of the furnace was improved, and under Colonel Joshua Porter's supervision, pressing orders for the essentials of war were expedited. They included iron pots for the manufacture of sulphur, as well as cannon and balls for the Connecticut towns. In 1777, an order arrived for six hundred iron kettles for camp use. The workers at the site of the furnace were exempted from military duty by the General Assembly.

Sometime around 1731 iron ore was discovered at Ore Hill, near the New York state line. That same year a grant was given to Daniel Bissell of Windsor to use the ore, and later on to others. Ethan Allen bought his forge in 1762, belonging at the time to Benajah Williams. With other associates Allen developed the first blast furnace in Connecticut capable of producing over two tons of iron in twenty-four hours.

In 1768, Richard Smith, an Englishman residing in Boston, bought the property. During the Revolutionary War thirty-two-pounders were cast here and tested by Hamilton and Trumbull.

In 1810 the firm of Holley and Coffing developed the furnace on the summit of Mt. Riga, two thousand feet high, left idle since 1781. It was here that the anchor of the U.S. frigate *Constitution* was made and taken to the Hudson by six yoke of oxen. Here also were forged the *Constitution*'s eighteen- and twenty-four-pounder guns, as well as the guns for her sister ship, the *Constellation*.

During the Civil War large cannon were cast here also, and during the peaceful years at the turn of the twentieth century, most of the pig iron from Salisbury ore was made into railroad car wheels.

St. John's Episcopal Church, Salisbury

Following Burgoyne's surrender at Saratoga large numbers of prisoners, mostly Hessians, marched through Salisbury. Many of them camped at a site called Moore's Meadow, along the Salmon River. One of the Hessians hid in a haystack and made his appearance after the main body of troops passed. His presence was unchallenged by the Salisbury folk, for whom he ground corn for many years.

Henry Ward Beecher resided here for a time, and here he wrote his famous *Star Papers* in praise of the Salisbury countryside. Others who lived in Salisbury included Samuel Moore, mathematician and surveyor, who published the first book in America on surveying.

Hotchkiss School for boys brought to Lakeville the distinction of having one of the best of the preparatory schools in New England. The school was founded with a gift of $350,000, in 1892, from Mrs. Maria H. Hotchkiss of Salisbury. The school is located on Town Hill, a dramatic site overlooking lakes and mountains of three states.

Nearby Bear Mountain, 2355 feet above sea level, is the highest in the state of Connecticut.

The church shown in the sketch is St. John's Episcopal Church, which was built in 1824. On the left of the church is Ragamont Inn, built around 1800.

Farmington's Many Facets of Distinction

One year after the Fundamental Orders of Connecticut were adopted, a group of pioneers left Hartford to settle in the fertile and picturesque valley of Tunxis, through which the Farmington River contorts northward before entering the Connecticut River at Windsor. The name was changed to Farmington in 1645.

Farmington was the first inland town settled west of Hartford. John Haynes, on behalf of the colonists, and two representatives of the Tunxis Indian tribe signed a confirmatory deed April 1650. The Indians reserved certain rights, including protection by the English from other Indians. Until 1658 the tribe lived on the east bank of the Farmington River.

Sometime before 1658, the Stockbridge Indians battled the Tunxis tribe on Little Meadow and the local Indians came out the worse for their effort to fight off the Massachusetts intruders.

Indians continued to plague the area; Simsbury was destroyed on March 26, 1678, by fire during King Philip's War; Farmington was constantly asked to send aid to stricken settlements exposed to the harassments of Indians. The colonists of Farmington who answered those calls of mercy were rewarded with plots of land in recognition of their services.

After the atrocities the Indians committed at Deerfield in 1704, Farmington ordered seven of its houses on Main Street to be fortified. Regulations insisted that the doors of the houses be made of double plank, held together by nails driven so closely together they would make the doors impenetrable to Indian hatchets.

In 1708, Farmington was ordered by the General Assembly to maintain a garrison. The cupola of the second church provided a perfect lookout for the armed men stationed there to watch the approaches.

Greater protection was effected by paths cut in the mountains that separated Hartford from Farmington. In times of need, assistance could be expedited quickly. Soon, paths developed into roads. By 1783 Farmington's Main Street was part of the "Western Postroad from Boston to Hartford, Fishkill and Philadelphia."

The Talcott Mountain Turnpike and the Hartford and New Haven Turnpike Company were incorporated in 1798 — their roads ran through Farmington. By 1801 roads were constructed between Burlington and Hartford and that portion of the road between Hartford and Farmington became part of the Hartford and Danbury Turnpike.

A stagecoach line was formed as early as 1822 to carry passengers between New Haven and Hartford, a journey that took six hours to complete. Other stages passing through Farmington went between New Haven and Northampton, Massachusetts, and still another line served Litchfield and Farmington by 1823. Isolation was at an end.

Transportation became a major concern in the early nineteenth century, and James Hillhouse of New Haven conceived the advantages of water communications with the interior towns of the state. The Farmington Canal Company was chartered, and the estimated cost of $420,698 moved nearer to two million dollars necessary to complete the project, part of a grandiose scheme to create a water route from the St. Lawrence River to Long Island Sound, passing through parts of four New England states. A still greater ambition was to join New Haven with the Erie Canal and the Great Lakes.

The Farmington waterway was to tie in with the Hampshire and Hampton Canal to be constructed in Massachusetts. This was to follow the west bank of the Connecticut River to Brattleboro, Vermont, along the New Hampshire–Vermont border to Lake Memphremagog and hence to the St. Lawrence River.

On November 4, 1827, the first boat plied the waters of the canal between Cheshire and New Haven. The traveler could ride the eighty-odd miles of the canal for less than four dollars, including his food, in about twenty-four hours.

Taverns were built at points of vantage, property values rose on both sides of the canal, and in Farmington the Union Hotel was taking shape. The success of the project blinded everyone to the unforeseen trends that would within a few years kill the canals.

The Hartford–New Haven Railroad opened a line between Meriden and New Haven in 1838. The canal was unable to compete with the speed of the railroads that sprang up everywhere, and the last boat floated along the canal waters in 1848.

The defunct Farmington Canal exists as a U-shaped depression through the terrain; near Unionville, utility poles traverse the canal's empty length.

Farmington's early visible participation in the cause of the American Revolution was the erection of a forty-five-foot liberty pole on May 19, 1774, after the Boston Port Bill was signed March 31, 1774. A committee was appointed to receive and deliver relief to Boston, and seventy of Farmington's leading citizens agreed, on September 3, 1774, to ready themselves to go to Boston. On May 18, 1775, the first company of Farmington men left for Roxbury, Massachusetts. The Farmington men fought in most of the campaigns throughout the Revolution, but towards the end of the war they saw special service in the highlands above New York.

The General Assembly, in May 1776, authorized the mining of the lead deposits in Matthew Hart's Farmington lead mines for the manufacture of bullets.

Farmington was relatively free of Tories and her inland situation made the place safe for the storing of munitions. The fine road systems provided safe passage for all types of traffic. They included prisoners of war that poured into Farmington after Burgoyne's defeat, and his captured cannon, brought from Albany, were stored in a local apple orchard.

The freshman class of Yale was sent to Farmington in May 1777 and the sophomore class that October.

Washington passed through Farmington six times, and though his diaries mention having dined there, he omitted the names of his hosts.

Rochambeau's troops to and from Yorktown encamped on the flat lands south of Farmington on June 26, 1781 and October 29, 1782.

Noah Porter, D.D. (1781–1866), graduated from Yale in 1803. He was minister of the Congregational Church from 1806 to 1866 and was a vigorous preacher against slavery. In 1808 he built the brick house which he occupied until his death.

Noah Porter, D.D., the younger, was born in the Porter homestead on Main Street in 1811; a graduate of Yale in 1831, he became its president from 1871 to 1886.

Sarah Porter (1813–1900) established, in 1843, her school in a room in the store of Joseph R. Hawley. In 1850 Miss Porter acquired the brick building, erected by Major Cowles for an inn, called the Union Hotel. This unusual personality developed a boarding school for girls that is known throughout the world. The school buildings, eighteen in all, are situated on or near the Main Street of Farmington village; and the school farm is near the Farmington River.

The Third Meeting House was dedicated in 1772; the foundation was laid the year before, southeast of the old church, on Meeting House Green. The church was designed by Captain Judah Woodruff of French and Indian War fame. The paneling of the pulpit Captain Woodruff designed and executed with nothing more than a jack-knife. The meetinghouse is supposed to be Woodruff's one and only church, but some of his ideas are said to have been taken by Asher Benjamin.

Farmington in the days of the fugitive slave laws was an Underground Rail-

The Congregational Church on Meetinghouse Green, Farmington

road center on the route through New Britain and Southington to Simsbury. There were about thirty local abolitionists and stations, including the homes of Horace Cowles, George Hurlburt and William McKee.

There are many charming places in the town built prior to 1800. My first impression includes the Whitman home, restored by J. Frederick Kelly for the tercentenary celebration of the settlement of Connecticut. This house was erected in 1660, a superb example of seventeenth-century architecture with an overhang, and hand-hewn drops on the posts which run from the second floor to its roof. It is considered by many to be the finest house of its type in the country.

And another house, Old Gate, was built by the Reverend Samuel Hooker. In 1768 it was acquired by Samuel Cowles, a member of the Elijah Cowles importing firm that owned country stores in neighboring villages, as well as in Farmington, where East India and West India goods were sold over the counter.

After the Revolution the front of the Samuel Cowles house underwent alterations by William Spratt, and it is reported that the alterations were actually made by English carpenters from Burgoyne's captured army.

The Hill-Stead Museum, built in 1900, is a delightful mansion and speaks eloquently for the present century. The mansion was built for Mr. and Mrs. Alfred Atmore Pope with the assistance of architect Stanford White, and Miss Theodate Pope's designs. She was the wife of John Riddle, who was the former American representative to Russia, Turkey and Argentina; she also designed the famous Avon Old Farms school for boys near Farmington.

The house contains a remarkable collection of paintings assembled by Mr. Pope, one of the few Americans who recognized the value of the French Impressionists. His collections include paintings by Manet, Mary Cassatt, Monet, Degas and Whistler, as well as a collection of porcelains and china that blend admirably with the superb furnishings the Popes gathered together under one roof.

Windsor

The enthusiasm of a few individuals can accomplish mighty results. Nowhere is there greater evidence of this than the restoration of the Lieutenant William Fyler House, one of the few remaining authentic houses of early Windsor, which was settled in 1633 by William Holmes of the Plymouth Colony, on a site near the confluence of the Farmington and Connecticut Rivers.

The Fyler House is the headquarters for the Windsor Historical Society. In 1962 the Wilson Museum was built, connected to the house by a breezeway, to contain an important historical and genealogical library and a varied collection of Early Americana.

The Fyler House contains a collection of furniture consistent with its great age, in addition to which were added documents, papers and miscellany from various

The Fyler House, Windsor, in springtime

sources, among them an interesting order of payment to "Gen. Israel Putnam the sum of six pounds seven shillings and six pence money for his wages and expense in the alarm April 1775 marched for the relief of Boston."

The plot of land upon which Lieutenant Walter Fyler built his house in 1640 was a gift to him in 1637 for services in the Pequot War, and is located in an area once protected by a palisade, and where the settlers banded together for their mutual protection. Around the green were located the homes of the citizens, the church and all the leading establishments. Along the banks of the Farmington River stood the wharves, where sailing ships unloaded their cargoes. The Connecticut River was their gateway to the entire world.

Elmwood, the white clapboard Ellsworth homestead, is the birthplace of Oliver Ellsworth — intimate friend of George Washington, signer of the Declaration of Independence, and one of the first chief justices of the United States Supreme Court. In 1903, the Ellsworth heirs presented the house to the Connecticut Daughters of the American Revolution.

The house, which was built in 1740 by Oliver Ellsworth's father, contains notable antiques that belonged to the family, among which visitors may see the famed Gobelin tapestry presented to Oliver Ellsworth by Napoleon Bonaparte when he was Envoy Extraordinary to Paris. In a shed at the rear of the house is the carriage, mounted on runners, which was once used by George Washington on trips about the New England countryside in winter.

The Loomis Homestead, situated on a slight rise above a bend of the Farmington River, is just north of Founders Hall, Loomis School — a private secondary school for boys, founded by the descendants of Joseph Loomis. The Loomis Homestead, built by Joseph Loomis in 1640, has never been outside the family — a treasured memorial to an outstanding Windsor family and a museum mirror of life for over three hundred years in Connecticut.

Wethersfield

Wethersfield is on the west bank of the Connecticut River just south of Hartford; the Silas Deane Highway, built in 1930, gets you there fast. The traffic is unrelenting, and the gasoline fumes on a summer day are horrid, but worse still is the array of ugliness that flanks the highway, which luckily by-passes Wethersfield.

Leaving the concrete highway is soon rewarding — you will be traveling on the old middle Post Road that parallels the Silas Deane Highway and runs from New Haven to Boston. Immediately the sweet satisfying smells of cut lawns fill the nostrils and the long cool shadows of the trees that line the road spell relief. You are entering the main street of Wethersfield.

There are over a hundred homes in Wethersfield that were built before 1800.

I dread to think of what might have happened to Wethersfield were no alternate routes available to carry the traffic that each year increases at such a rapid rate.

John Oldham, who flirted with an adventurous life from Plymouth to Virginia, in 1624 was asked to leave Plymouth, but by 1631 he returned a wiser man and joined the church, and thereby became a freeman. Ingratiating himself once more, he left with John Hall and two others to trade in Connecticut with the blessings of the Bay Colony, for whom he would do a little exploring on the side. The route taken was surely by way of Springfield, Windsor, Hartford down to Wethersfield, along the Connecticut River, all of which were Indian towns and friendly.

Wethersfield was called Pyquag, or "clear land," under the domination of Sowheag, a sachem of the Wongunk Indians from whom the land for the town was purchased by the English. John Oldham's report to the Bay Colony emphasized the good treatment he received from the sachem; in September 1634 the Massachusetts General Court met and approved Oldham's plan to set out for Wethersfield with a party of eight. They arrived on the banks of Wethersfield Cove during the winter of 1634–1635, where they built crude huts to enable them to endure the winter. The following spring they planted grain, and when it ripened, they harvested it in preparation for the colonists who followed them the next year.

Hartford was first occupied by the Dutch, and settled by the English. Windsor was the earliest English settlement in Connecticut; the settlers were sent there by the Plymouth Colony as agriculturists and permanent colonists. But to Wethersfield came the first settlers acting as individuals, without a church organization. All the adventurers had plots as early as 1636 on Broad Street near the green. Another green was laid out which included the site of the present Congregational church, the parish house and the cemetery. All the meadows on the west bank of the Connecticut River and some upland on both sides of the river were divided among thirty-four proprietors, the town and the church in 1640.

During the American Revolution, Wethersfield sent provisions and money to relieve the suffering in Boston. In response to the Lexington alarm, Wethersfield sent Captain Chester to Massachusetts with what is considered by historians to be the largest company from the Colony in uniform, completely equipped.

On August 2, 1775, the Council of Safety ordered the *Minerva,* a brig of 108 tons, owned by Captain William Griswold of Wethersfield, to be converted to an armed vessel. Wethersfield was a very busy port on the river during its early existence. In a little over a month the "armed brig" was almost ready.

The General Assembly on December 3, 1776, appointed Hezekiah Welles captain of a company of volunteers, and Wethersfield's men were in most of the important engagements from Charlestown to Yorktown during the Revolution.

John Adams dined in Wethersfield with the widow of Captain William Griswold in 1771. In his diary he noted that between Hartford and Wethersfield was the finest ride in America — which our era has so effectively reduced to a blight of unsightliness.

Washington visited Wethersfield for the first time in 1775 en route to Cambridge to take command of the army. On the night of June 29, 1775, Washington was a guest at the home of Silas Deane whose house at 203 Main Street stands next to the Webb House, where Washington, on his sixth journey to Connecticut, attended a conference held in the south parlor of the Webb House on Tuesday, May 22.

"Hospitality Hall" was the name given to the Webb House where so many distinguished officers of the Continental Army and their young aides were entertained. Upstairs there are five bedrooms. On the right at the front end of the hall is the room where Rochambeau slept. Across the hall, precisely as it was in 1781, is Washington's room. Mrs. Webb, like any other hostess who expected distinguished guests, felt the feminine desire to tidy the house up a little, and she renovated the General's room with a very expensive dark red flock wallpaper that had recently arrived from France. Almost two hundred years later that paper is still on the walls of the Washington Chamber, as fresh and bright as the first morning the General saw it when he awoke.

The Congregational Church
WETHERSFIELD

This historic church is located near the site of the second meetinghouse. It was begun in 1761 and finished in 1764 — a beautiful brick building with a spire of three stories in wood with spirelets, with delicate urns on the four corners of the first story — an unusual architectural treatment. The lantern on the top gives lightness to the design. The bells are located in the body of the tower, constructed of brick — mellowed to a faded pink by age — part of which was laid in herringbone patterns.

There is a possibility that the architect of the Wethersfield spire was the same person who designed the spire of Trinity Church (1726) at Newport, Rhode Island — I myself sense the resemblance, having drawn both spires for this book. Furthermore there is a similiarity between the Trinity Church spire and that of the Old North Church (1723) in Boston which I also rendered as an illustration. This evidence suggests that William Price, who is supposed to have designed the Old North Church, may have been responsible for all three.

John Adams, during his stay in Wethersfield, worshipped here. Also, his diary mentions having climbed to the spire on Monday, August 15, 1774, to enjoy the view of the countryside, "the most grand and beautiful prospect in the world, at least that I ever saw." George Washington attended services in this meetinghouse, May 20, 1781, during the conference with Count de Rochambeau at the Webb House.

This meetinghouse was established in 1634. From 1660 to 1663 John Cotton, son of John Cotton of Boston, was its pastor.

PHILIP KAPPEL

The Congregational church, Wethersfield

The Buttolph-Williams House, 1692

David Buttolph lived here until 1698. When he left Wethersfield to start a tanning enterprise in Simsbury, the house passed into the hands of one Robert Turner, who paid £60 for the property and sold it again for £70 to Benjamin Belden, who made felt and was also licensed to run a tavern. Daniel Williams bought the place from Belden in 1721 and lived in the house many years. He paid Belden £245 for a £70 investment!

The house was restored by the Antiquarian and Landmarks Society as nearly as possible to its original state as ascertained from available records. The diamond-shaped panes in the casement windows were made by hand in England and secured to the frames with lead by stained-glass makers who inherited the art from their ancestors.

The Buttolph-Williams House is a typical seventeenth-century building of only four rooms, a downstairs front hall and an upstairs hall. The stair displays the early arrangement of "winders," or diagonal treads. The stumpy balusters and newel post are definitely Jacobean in style. Both are placed on top of a molded box string.

The kitchen served as the living room and on the right of the front door over the kitchen is the "kitchen bedroom." On the left of the hall is the parlor, and above the parlor is the "parlor bedroom." A secret passageway goes from the kitchen bedroom around and behind the chimney into the parlor bedroom, which was often used by guests. The purpose of the secret passageway is subject to conjecture — possibly for romantic reasons?

The kitchen is the finest room in the house — the most lived-in and the warmest during cold weather. Throughout the house the furnishings are authentic and fitting, but none were found in the house. When the Vibert family acquired the place in 1862, they did very little to keep the place up, except for the gardens. The hurricane of 1938 inflicted the coup de grace by toppling a huge maple across the roof of the house, destroying the chimney. After Frank Vibert died the Structure Committee entered the house in 1947 and found the place devoid of anything except a few pots, a portrait, some worthless personal effects and a battered trunk. For the first time in two hundred and fifty years the house was naked.

Dark and severe, the house has few windows to dispel its fort-like appearance. The narrow overlapping clapboards are delightfully weathered. Inside and out the perfection of the work and the special care in the preservation is joyously successful.

Around the corner is the Webb Mansion, beautifully urbane in contrast with the Buttolph-Williams House. Within a span of seventy-nine years the rise from a primitive existence to the success of those who lived in homes like the Webb Mansion proves how fast this nation was emerging out of homespuns.

Primitive Beauty — The Buttolph-Williams House, Wethersfield

The Old State House

HARTFORD

Thomas Hooker emigrated to Cambridge, Massachusetts, in 1632 with his congregation from Braintree, Essex, England; but his church did not remain long in Cambridge. Probers returning from the wilderness west of Cambridge, praised the Connecticut River Valley and its fertile soil, and Hooker did not delay pulling up stakes. He had good reasons, one of them being that the cattle were cramped for space.

The other reason was Hooker's desire to put as many miles between himself and controversial John Cotton as possible. Hooker was not in accord with Cotton. Both men were influential and there was too little room in the Massachusetts arena of operations for both to move without a collision.

Hooker was in sympathy with the liberal side in the Antinomian Controversy, and he was opposed to the Massachusetts policy of restricting the right to vote to church members only. Rather than make a spectacle of his convictions, he discreetly sought a way out. He petitioned the General Court for permission to move to Hartford, bringing into his scheme his entire congregation. Cambridge saw the last of them in June 1636.

A Dutch trading fort was already established at Hartford but Hooker and his congregation overruled by sheer numbers any Dutch protests.

Each succeeding month assured Hooker that he was making good on his notion to keep the Dutch out of Connecticut, the excuse he had used to offset the risk of opposition to his plan to leave Cambridge.

The freemen of nearby Windsor and Wethersfield assembled at Hartford on January 14, 1639, where all three towns drew up a constitution consisting of eleven articles — the "Fundamental Orders of Connecticut." For almost two hundred years they served as the law under which the Connecticut people ruled themselves. Charles II in 1662 granted a charter in recognition of the government then in operation.

The Dutch continued to deal with the Indians in furs, which had been a thriving business ten years prior to the coming of Hooker. To a point, the English and the Dutch tolerated each other, but eventually tempers got out of hand and the Commissioners of the United Colonies, Massachusetts, Plymouth, Connecticut and New Haven met at Hartford September 11, 1650, with Peter Stuyvesant, Director of New Netherland, to discuss the proper boundaries of Dutch jurisdiction.

By virtue of the discoveries of John and Sebastian Cabot in 1497 and 1498, the English argued their right to claim the territory of Connecticut. This territory was included in the grant to the Plymouth Company in 1606, but no colonization plans were undertaken by that organization. In 1635, the settlers came and took

The old State House, Hartford, designed by Charles Bulfinch

possession of the Connecticut Valley under the English flag, claiming the territory by virtue of the patents from the Crown.

The chief Sequossen, who ruled the river Indians, was paid for his lands. But when the Pequots challenged the right of Sequossen to sell their lands, the Colonists fell upon the Pequots and nearly annihilated the tribe.

The arbitrators recommended the transfer to the English of all the land lying west of the Connecticut River, except that occupied by the Dutch in Hartford, and giving the land east of the river to New Netherland — a decision that fostered ill will beyond repair. England declared war on Holland in 1653 and expected the colonies to consider the Dutch their enemies and seize all Dutch property.

James II ascended the throne in 1685 and made his authority felt by summoning the Governor and Company of Connecticut to appear and explain why they had misused their authority. In self-defense the Colony pleaded the Charter granted by Charles II and entreated the King to reconsider.

Twice more, writs of quo warranto were issued against Connecticut, but she refused to alter her stand or surrender the Charter, flouting the writs further by re-electing Robert Treat as governor.

Late in 1686, Sir Edmund Andros arrived with his royal commission as governor of New England. He was met at Hartford with great courtesy and civility by Governor Treat and his assistants. They conducted Andros to the Governor's seat in the council chambers, whereupon he read the commission from James II to Andros. At the conclusion of the reading, Andros held out his hand for the Charter.

Governor Treat and his assistants went into a filibuster that continued well into the evening, and then, under candlelight, the Charter was laid upon the council table in pretended surrender. Whereupon all the lights were extinguished by Connecticut men.

When the lights were restored the Charter had vanished!

Nimble-footed Captain Wadsworth, of Hartford, purloined the Charter and hid it in a hollow oak tree, five blocks away.

Andros returned to Boston without the Charter, but he declared the government of the colony to be in his own hands and annexed Connecticut to Massachusetts and the other New England colonies.

After the downfall of Andros in 1689, Treat resumed his position as governor of Connecticut, and the Charter reappeared from seclusion and continued to be the organic law of Connecticut Parliament during the remainder of the Colonial period.

The oak tree in which the Charter was hidden was a historic shrine until it blew down during a storm August 21, 1856. It is remembered as the "Charter Oak," and many of its descendants are growing in various places in the state.

A Madrigal for Hartford

By the mere favor of fate, my parents elected to live in Hartford as newlyweds, and had their firstborn in New England. During one of those raging snowstorms in February, the family doctor left his home by sleigh, bucking drifts and bitter winds to keep a date with me. He arrived exhausted and tardy early in the morning of my natal day and immediately went to my mother's side, where he discovered that I had arrived on schedule, unassisted — and in a fighting mood!

I return to Hartford infrequently, but my interest in it will never diminish. I received my early schooling there and made many lifelong friends, and I profited by its cultural institutions. From the earliest beginning, the town fathers stressed the value of education. The Hartford Public High School, for example, is the second oldest secondary school in the United States, dating back to 1638.

Hartford has gone in for wholesale redevelopment projects, and webs of new highways, with the inevitable dislocations of old landmarks. I witnessed the destruction of my old high school buildings to make way for an interstate highway. Whenever I return to Hartford I stand bewildered by these alterations, but I delight in the familiar institutions that were left unharmed, especially the Wadsworth Atheneum, and the Morgan Memorial Collections of Art.

For me, much of the contemporary scene is too close; the focus is blurred. We can see and touch what's there but the shapes are unfamiliar and foreign; the pulse beats in unison with the masses that demand efficiency, but the masses never determine what shall live after them. Not so with the past — its individuality was achieved through trial and error; its mellowness has all the charm of a personal gift just for your understanding of its purpose and its acceptance. Besides, it comes to us bereft of growing pains, turmoil, and the strain of progress, with all its attending noises and harassments. It is free of iconoclasms, and the diatribes of selfish people, leaving us the screened and purified mementoes of reflection, and their dignity to haunt us!

Even those bland juvenile days are enormously satisfying in retrospect, including the simple sorties into the woods or the parks. Hartford is rich in open spaces, many left as gifts to the city by its generous citizens, where we searched for chestnuts in prickly burrs that stubbornly surrendered their imprisoned nuts under our crushing heels. Chidren today never experience the excitement of looking for chestnuts, because, unfortunately, chestnut trees were removed by blight and are no longer with us.

Values are relative in each generation. In my youth the discovery of a patch of trailing arbutus in the woods was passed along in hushed tones only to our most devoted friends, lest someone overhear and betray our secret. Each spring we made our pilgrimage to the spot, and repeatedly, as one might go to a shrine.

But, best of all, possibly because it was forbidden, a sneak trip to the crumbling banks of the Connecticut River was the zenith of all experiences — it had all the glory and risks of youth from which I have never been set free!

Few of us ever doubted that Mark Twain's brainchild, Huck Finn, was the greatest of heroes. He was our silent exploring partner by adoption, with whom all mischief was conspired. Our worldly problems were ignored, especially our allegiance to school and teachers, and downstream we would go on the Connecticut River — our Mississippi — by boat or raft.

Young boys would be the first to discover old forts, long forgotten. I recall the Dutch trading fort on Dutch Point — at least we discovered that such a fort existed at one time on the Point, established there by the Dutch to insure the peaceful traffic in furs between themselves and the Indians.

The intrepid Adrian Block sailed up the Connecticut River in his 16-ton sloop, the *Unrest*, in 1614. After a brief stopover between Old Saybrook and Old Lyme to post "No Trespassing" signs, Block proceeded upstream to Middletown to explore the valley and then continued his sail as far as the falls at Enfield, above Hartford, and laid claim to all New England, or New Netherland, as the Dutch called it. This feat was accomplished six years before Plymouth Rock was sanctified by Pilgrim feet.

In the 1630's the English colonists swept past Block's "No Trespassing" signs and the forts. Since there were no Dutch colonists on hand to push them out, or relatively few, the English dug in at Windsor, Hartford, and Wethersfield.

Connecticut's Insurance Aristocracy
HARTFORD

Contrary to all appearances, Hartford, the state capital, famous today for insurance, education and manufacturing, was once prominently engaged in a lively export-import trade with the West Indies. Between 1750 and 1830, the banks of the Connecticut River were lined with wharves where ships unloaded sugar, rum, salt, coffee and molasses and took aboard salt pork, beef and fish. Behind the wharves stood the warehouses filled with exotic smells and outside, piled high with goods, were the freight wagons that rolled away to distant towns in northwest Connecticut. The upriver towns were likewise supplied by road or barge and everyone profited.

Packet lines ran on schedule between Hartford and Boston, New York, Baltimore and Norfolk. In my youth it was a constant delight to go down to the foot of State Street to wave goodbye to those bound for Long Island Sound. The packets have disappeared within my time, but barges filled with coal or oil still ply the river, though the romance is gone and the river now is confined between dikes. In the past, lower State Street, during major spring freshets, was always inundated.

It may be presupposed that Hartford's shipping interests prompted the need for insurance on vessels and goods. The risks Hartford merchants faced in the late eighteenth century through natural shipping hazards on land, and the lawlessness on the high seas, evoked a system of spreading the risks which developed into a full-fledged insurance program. Wethersfield is on record as having had an office for the purpose as early as 1777.

On April 14, 1794, Jeremiah Wadsworth, one of the wealthiest men in America, inserted an advertisement in the *Courant* announcing the "opening of an office for the purpose of insuring Houses, Household Furniture, Goods, Wares, Merchandise etc. against Fire."

A year later the first incorporated insurance group appeared in Norwich, and Connecticut was in the insurance business; but the testing was yet to come — how well could the business sustain a catastrophe? The great fire in New York of 1835, with a property loss of $15,000,000, bankrupted twenty-three of the twenty-six New York insurance companies. The conspicuous failures of the out-of-town insurance companies impressed upon the minds of those who had gone through the fire, and had difficulty in collecting on their policies, the integrity of the Hartford companies — who had paid all their claims in full.

The Aetna Fire Insurance Company in 1845 was caught with policies that totaled $115,000 on another New York fire that destroyed $6,000,000 worth of property. The company paid promptly on all its pledges.

In the great Chicago fire of 1871, which destroyed $140,000,000 worth of property, Hartford Fire carried its share of losses. The bank agreed to lend Hartford Fire funds to the limit of its resources, and the Connecticut Mutual Life Insurance Company loaned $500,000, which enabled Hartford Fire to pay off all claims — amounting to $1,968,225. Out of a total of 202 out-of-town insurance companies, only 68 survived and 83 settled their pledges partially. The Phoenix policy-holders found a representative on the scene promising on-the-spot payment — the consistent pattern of Hartford companies, with rare exception.

After the tragedy of the San Francisco earthquake and fire in 1906, Hartford Fire paid $11,557,365 in claims. This established an all-time high in disaster payments and solidified the position of Hartford as the Insurance City.

The integrity of the Hartford insurance companies soon spread to other forms of insurance. As the name implies, Travelers Insurance Company, whose tower is the most conspicuous in the Hartford skyline, was formed to underwrite protection against every conceivable risk in travel. The company was chartered in 1863 and later was revamped to include risks of many kinds, including automobile insurance, which Travelers was first to bring out, and workmen's compensation, another first, and yet another — aircraft insurance.

Hartford was slow to adopt life insurance — the English had a system of insurance that worked, but the Connecticut companies argued that whereas one might carry insurance against fire and never have a fire, sooner or later everyone dies; an indisputable deduction.

In 1846 the Connecticut Mutual Life Insurance Company was organized as the first to guarantee payment on every life insurance policy. It was followed by the American Temperance Life Insurance Company, which ten years later became the Phoenix Mutual Life, and next came the Connecticut General Life Insurance Company.

From the center of downtown Hartford and radiating westward for several miles, the massive insurance buildings are unmistakably handsome, surrounded by lawns and trees, and bear well the dignity of the insurance industry which collectively brought to Hartford the sobriquet "The Insurance City of the World."

The first name of the Connecticut General was the Connecticut Invalid Life Insurance Company. The founders intended to provide life insurance for people whose substandard physical condition made them unacceptable to other companies. Later the name was changed to the Connecticut General Life Insurance Company; the word "general" indicated that the company would insure standard as well as substandard risks. The company's charter was approved by the General Assembly on June 22, 1865.

By the end of 1880, Connecticut General was one of only six insurance companies organized in the 1860's which were still in business — a tribute to the resilience of the management. Thomas W. Russell was elected president in 1876. He guided the company through a maze of precarious situations in the insurance field left by the wake of the panic of 1873. Russell also successfully surmounted reverses of the 1893 panic, to such an extent that additional office quarters were required. The company moved from the four rooms on the fourth floor of the old Connecticut Mutual Building on Marble Street, to an entire floor in the Phoenix Mutual Building at 49 Pearl Street.

In 1957, while Frazar B. Wilde was president of the company, the new $20,000,000 home office building was dedicated in Bloomfield, surrounded by three hundred acres of beautifully groomed property. The Connecticut General's functional office building is so revolutionary that it attracts hundreds of people each year to "take the tour." It is one of the most elegant and practical "shops" in the country — done with boldness, conceived with an eye to the future and with an awareness of the rural potential as an aid to business. More than two thousand employees work in a miniature city with off-hours recreation facilities, a store, lending library, Japanese gardens within the building. A cafeteria, cantilevered over a reflecting pool on the south side of the main building, faces a tremendous oak tree surrounded by lawn. Nearby is a four-acre pond in which a pair of pure white swans were placed. Shortly after the building was dedicated, *four* swans were seen leisurely swimming in the pond one morning, but there was a definite conflict of color in the foursome — two were white and two dusky black. This was a competitor's prank successfully carried out one dark night.

The Connecticut General Life Insurance building, Hartford

Noah Webster's Birthplace

HARTFORD

Trees almost smother this humble homestead as if they were determined to shield this architectural treasure from further twentieth-century encroachment. It is situated on one of the busiest streets skirting metropolitan Hartford and is surrounded by developments; it would attract little attention were it not the place where Noah Webster's father received the news — "It's a boy" — in 1758.

Noah Webster, the lexicographer, graduated from Yale in 1778 and served in the American Revolution. He was admitted to the bar in 1781 and practiced law in Hartford. His *Grammatical Institute of the English Language,* published in three parts (1783–1785), was the first of a list of publications which made Webster the chief American authority on English for many years. The first part, frequently revised, became his famous *Elementary Spelling Book,* with which he hoped to standardize American spelling and to inculcate both morals and patriotism.

The difficulty of copyrighting his works in thirteen states led Webster to agitate for the enactment of national copyright laws. He became a pamphleteer for centralized government and regarded his sketches on American policy (1785) as the first proposal for a constitution.

In 1793 Webster left Hartford to support Washington's administration by editing the *American Minerva* in New York, later the *Commercial Advertiser.* He also wrote studies of the weather, the plague and American history.

During his late years Webster retired to New Haven, and he also devoted considerable time in the interest of Amherst College, where he served as a member of the first board of trustees.

Noah Webster's greatest accomplishment was his *American Dictionary of the English Language,* which was published in 1828; it included 12,000 words not in any previously known dictionary.

Noah Webster and America's Oldest Newspaper

In 1783, Noah Webster, who had been writing successful essays for the *Courant* in Hartford, submitted his manuscript of his Speller to Hudson and Goodwin, publishers and owners of the newspaper. Would they publish the book? Every important publisher had curtly turned Webster down — this was his last chance. The *Courant's* owners liked what Webster wrote and decided to take a chance on this twenty-five-year-old schoolteacher.

In spite of competition from Dilworth's English book, which was the established text in all the schools, Webster's book became an immediate best-seller. The

Noah Webster's birthplace, West Hartford

presses were unable to keep up with the demand and the *Courant* was forced to grant rights elsewhere, reserving New England for itself exclusively. One hundred million copies of the book were sold. With the royalties from the book, Webster went to work on his famous dictionary.

The *Courant* was established October 29, 1764, and has had its foot in the door of every crucial event in America and abroad since its inception. Widow Hanna Bruce Watson, at the age of twenty-eight, with five children to support and her husband's debts to liquidate, took over the newspaper in 1777 after her husband's death from smallpox. The times were fraught with uncertainties and tragedy. The survival of our nation was in jeopardy as the news from the front announced General Washington's troops retreating from the hard-hitting forces of General Howe. Then came the brutal winter at Valley Forge. Bewildered readers of the *Courant* relied on it for any bits of news that might bolster their hopes — and then came the shattering report that the paper mill which supplied the newsprint had burned to the ground. It was rumored that Tories destroyed the mill. Immediately the *Courant* cut the size of the sheet to conserve paper and kept the public informed of events on a limited basis. Widow Watson and widow Ledyard, co-owners of the paper mill, petitioned the Connecticut Legislature for a loan to rebuild it. The legislators authorized a state-run lottery which netted the *Courant* five thousand dollars, and within four months the mill was in full operation; suspension of publication was avoided by a narrow margin.

In 1869, when Charles Dudley Warner was editor of the *Courant* and General Joseph R. Hawley its president, Mark Twain tried to buy stock in the newspaper, but Warner and Hawley decided against it. For a time Mark Twain was hardly on speaking terms with the two, but when the thaw came, Warner and Twain teamed up and wrote *The Gilded Age* in 1874 on a dare from their wives. Hartford-born actor William Gillett was made famous by his New York debut in the stage version of the book in 1877.

Thomas Green, who founded the *Courant,* was able to print twenty-five copies of the paper an hour on a hand press in 1764. Today's presses are capable of printing 81,000 copies in the same time. The enviable record of two hundred years of continuous publication by the *Courant* is now being furthered by my longtime friend John R. Reitemeyer, president and publisher of the newspaper.

Hartford's Elizabeth Park

The Hartford Park Department, early in the spring of 1897, occupied part of the land given to it by Charles M. Pond as a memorial to his wife, Elizabeth Pond, and named it Elizabeth Park.

The first municipal rose garden — Hartford's Elizabeth Park

A small collection of roses was planted in a long border near the park road. Gifts of plants, cuttings and buds which the Superintendent of City Parks, Theodore Wirth, propagated, eventually increased the size of the border and the number of varieties to about one hundred, mostly the June flowering or hybrid perpetual type. The display of roses attracted so much interest that Mr. Wirth responded with the construction of a larger display.

The resulting garden is a square about one and one-quarter acres in area. From each corner and the center of each side it is crossed by tall wide rose arches converging at a rustic arbor grown over by climbing roses. The arbor is somewhat elevated, giving a delightful view of the one hundred and thirty-two rose beds. The whole is enclosed by a fence or trellis devoted to climbing varieties of roses and further enclosed by deep borders of perennials to give a degree of variety of blooms through the long spring, summer and autumn seasons.

Due to the increased interest in hybrid tea roses, a semicircular addition was made to the garden in 1912, and an area was set aside for the testing and judging of new varieties in cooperation with the American Rose Society. This was the first such trial garden for roses, followed in time by others in Washington, D.C., and Portland, Oregon.

Presently, over eight hundred named varieties of roses comprise the Elizabeth Park collection. From mid-May to early November some type of rose is in flower. The chief display occurs during the last three weeks of June. The autumn display comes late in September or October when the finest blossoms appear.

During the June season alone an estimated 400,000 people come to Elizabeth Park; in a typical year the park has over 1,000,000 visitors. It is significant and encouraging to discover that a garden of roses will draw as great a crowd as any major athletic event.

Harriet Beecher Stowe

On June 14, 1811, Harriet Beecher Stowe was born in Litchfield, Connecticut. She and her brother, Henry Ward Beecher, became outspoken supporters of the antislavery movement, and Harriet found the soil of her era just right for the seeds of her genius to flower.

The Fugitive Slave Law, and the evils of slavery in general, reached a powerful crescendo and she aroused millions of people in the North to come to the aid of the Negro with her book, *Uncle Tom's Cabin*, written in 1851 while the authoress resided in Brunswick, Maine, where her husband, Calvin Ellis Stowe, was professor of religion at Bowdoin.

73 *Forest Street, Hartford, home of Harriet Beecher Stowe*

The Stowes moved to Hartford in 1873. Their home, illustrated here, is located at 73 Forest Street, near Farmington Avenue. Just behind the Stowe house is the baroque home of another immortal — Mark Twain. Both houses are no architectural gems, but their style was determined by the taste of their day; the Stowe house is the more charming of the two.

Mark Twain wrote some of his best work while he lived in Hartford and his home became a landmark. Not too long ago, threatened with destruction and replacement by apartment buildings, an indignant and sentimental public saved the house and converted it into a memorial library.

The Saga of Newgate Prison

EAST GRANBY

At Newgate the wrongdoer was treated with brutality and scorn — he was fettered and confined in cells sixty feet below the surface of the ground in what formerly was a copper mine.

Counterfeiters, horse thieves and highwaymen were imprisoned here, along with a wide variety of law-breakers who at the height of the prison population between 1773 and 1824 numbered 100 inmates.

George Washington during his campaign around Boston in 1775 sent twenty-four ornery Tories to Newgate Prison; "some of the most atrocious villians," Washington called them. One day the guards relaxed their vigilance when the wife of one of the Tories obtained permission to see her husband. When the hatch of the shaft was raised, the prisoners poured out into the yard, precipitated a bloody battle, overpowered the guards and forced them into the caverns, and fled with the prison firearms. Henceforth, before the hatch was fastened for the night, the ladder to the caverns below was withdrawn. Prisoners were worked to exhaustion from 4 A.M. to 4 P.M., leaving little energy with which to plot an escape, but there have been exceptions.

In 1781 Congress made Newgate a jail for prisoners of war. The wooden palisade mounted with iron spikes gradually was replaced with a stone wall 760 feet long and 12 feet high in places.

Several prisoners succeeded in persuading the guards to permit them to occupy one of the cells above ground. Having obtained permission they secretly removed a stone slab from the floor and during the darkness of many nights, dug an escape tunnel across the narrow stretch of the prison yard, underneath that impregnable stone wall and into the woods beyond. One prisoner thin enough to crawl through the tunnel enjoyed his liberty two hours before he was brought back to assist his companions in filling the tunnel with rock, forever sealing it.

A more successful escape was made by a Tory named Henry Wooster who

Copper Hill, site of Newgate Prison

succeeded in unlocking his fetters and made his getaway through a drain with several companions. Wooster reached the New London coast and enlisted on a British vessel.

What remains of Newgate, the first Colonial prison in Connecticut, is today a tourist attraction maintained by the Newgate Historical Corporation. Most of the prison buildings are gaping ruins. The only building in good repair is in the center of the prison yard, formerly the guards' quarters, with a lookout tower. Today this building is a museum. Beneath it is the entrance to the underground caverns, unchanged and sickening. Tourists curious to see for themselves how the prisoners lived, descend the deep shaft by a perpendicular ladder. At once the musty dankness is noticeable, rising from the caverns below whose stone walls exude drops of moisture which made the prisoners' life anything but pleasant.

Returning into the brilliant sunshine from the dark caverns, the first object one sees is the awesome hanging post, standing a short distance beyond the exit.

Elsewhere in the prison yard is the old well. Sixty feet below the wellhead there is a gushing spring of pure water which supplied the prisoners. Between 1707 and 1773 the well was used as a shaft through which the copper ore was lifted to the surface with the aid of a winch.

At nightfall, the rope and the bucket were withdrawn to thwart designing prisoners from escaping. However, on the night of December 20, 1773, prisoner John Hinson used a lady accomplice to draw him up the well shaft. In 1827 all the prisoners were marched in chains to the New State Prison in Wethersfield eighteen miles away. The evening before the transfer, September 28, 1827, Abel Starkey was determined to make his escape. As a counterfeiter with a twenty-year term to serve, the future looked grim; any risk to be free again was worth the try. He succeeded in bribing one of the guards with his savings of one hundred dollars, earned by hard labor, to leave the well hatch open and the rope down — nothing more. Starkey tried to climb out of the well, but part way up the rope broke, cascading him into the water below, followed by the bucket which fell on his head as the coup de grace! The noise summoned the guards who discovered Starkey dead.

This drawing shows what remains today of the "ladybird" cell block, which was reserved for female prisoners, completed in 1824 and built of brown stone. Installed in this building was a treadmill for grinding grain for prison use. The huge treadmill was between twenty and thirty feet long, with horizontal flanges as steps, upon which the prisoners trod.

The prison stands in danger of complete collapse today. The windows with their iron bars are rusting away. The roof of the building collapsed years ago, and fell into the hollow shell, scattering itself as misshapen rubble among which trees took root.

Here in East Granby was the first copper mine in the state, which operated under a charter which was the first granted in America. The extracted copper was converted into many thousands of pounds of money.

The "ladybird" cell block, Newgate Prison

A hunter accidentally stumbled upon the telltale greenish outcroppings of copper on this site in 1705. His report set off a burst of mining activity which lasted from 1707 to 1773. Since English law prohibited smelting and refining on this side of the Atlantic, all the ore was shipped to England — but the ships sank with such regularity the mining venture failed.

John Higley from Simsbury, Connecticut, set up shop in East Granby, where he minted the first copper coins in pre-Revolutionary America from copper ore he gathered at the abandoned mine. Unless the metal weight was honest it was illegal to mint money, therefore, by way of proclaiming the genuineness of his 1737 pennies, Higley stamped his coins: "I am good copper" and "Value me as you will." Higley was also the first in America to experiment with the process of steel-making, in 1744.

The copper mines resumed operation again about 1831 under an incorporation granted to the Phoenix Mining Company by the Connecticut Legislature. Capital was raised and modern equipment installed, but the venture soon fizzled out. The remains of two smelters may be seen in the prison yard. The great shaft is there too, with its huge wheel once used to lower the massive bucket into the mines below to bring the copper ore to the surface.

Tobacco Jungle

Shade-grown tobacco is hand-picked by boys in their teens, preferably around fourteen years of age, lean and agile enough to pass between the long rows of growing tobacco without injury to the plants. The leaves are plucked close to the plants and deposited at their base to await collection. The bottom leaves are picked first, working upwards one row at a time until all the leaves are removed. The eerie light and the impenetrable array of growing tobacco that reaches to the top of the tent creates a jungle-like atmosphere — including the stifling humidity.

When I was fifteen years old and lived with my parents in Hartford, most boys in my neighborhood sought summertime jobs in Windsor during the tobacco-picking season. We received seven dollars for a six-day week's labor, out of which came trolley fares and food. We were collected at the terminus of the trolley in Windsor and transported to the tobacco fields in trucks. There was a certain amount of gaiety attached to a group of boys who were of all denominations and color — none had yet heard about segregation. Pushing along from plant to plant, our aim was to pick as much tobacco as possible and never submit to capers; but when the lad in the next row screamed *"Rattlesnakes, fellers,"* our reflexes responded immediately. Everyone disappeared to regroup in the open, shaking and wearing the

Tobacco Jungle

cadaverous pallor of fright! The overseer accounted for all the boys except Charlie, who had spread the alarm — he never returned even for his pay at the end of that week. The manner of Charlie's exit has never been ascertained, but after the snakes were disposed of by shotgun and we returned to our jobs, a sizable tear in the cloth above our heads was accepted as Charlie's escape route.

Tobacco — The Pampered Weed

The fresh-picked tobacco leaves are placed in canvas baskets and brought out to the end of the rows where they are placed on horse-drawn wagons or specially designed tractor-drawn trailers and transferred to the sheds, moving cautiously so as not to jar the fragile leaves in transit.

Inside the curing sheds dozens of employees are feverishly at work doing some specialized task. The canvas baskets are hauled inside the sheds and delivered to the workers at the assembly line, where women and young girls thread a needle through the stem of each leaf, which is then passed along to another operator who sews the leaves in pairs — twenty pairs to a string, hung on a wooden lath. The laths are then handed to the men aloft in the framing who suspend them from overhead crossbars where the tobacco remains for a period of eight weeks to dry.

While the leaves hang in the barn they slowly change color from deep green to a lighter green and then to a pale brown as the moisture gradually evaporates. This change in color is assisted by charcoal fires that are lighted as soon as the sheds are filled. In recent years the charcoal fires have been replaced by bottled gas, which furnishes an even, steady heat. Curing the tobacco is a long, delicate process.

The tobacco barns have slotted sides that may be opened or closed to supply the degree of ventilation or moisture desired; too much humidity could produce mold or rot, the bane of the tobacco grower.

Tobacco is taken down during moisture-laden days or days of rain before being placed in cases for removal to the warehouses where it is prepared for market. The final stage begins with the "sweating" or fermentation of the leaves arranged in bulks. Each bulk consists of three thousand to five thousand pounds of tobacco which is turned and rotated every eight or ten days. After being turned five or six times all the tobacco will have received sufficient fermentation to produce the proper color and taste. The tobacco is then ready for grading and sorting. Inspection will pass only the perfect leaves, which are then pressed into bales of 155 pounds each.

When the last bale has been completed, the grower once more turns to thoughts of his seed beds and preparations for the next season. He hopes for a

Picking tobacco

hazard-free eighteen-month growing season, which is a gamble from start to finish. His crops are threatened by storms, high winds and hail, or drought and periods of too much rain; from the time his seeds germinate they require spraying against blights, and the battle continues right through the entire growing season in a never-ending fight to the finish against disease to which tobacco is vulnerable. His investment is tremendous. Each spring the grower requires, for each acre of shade-grown tobacco, 5000 yards of cloth, 50 cedar posts, 350 pounds of wire and two tons of fertilizer — exclusive of labor.

If the grower is fortunate to have his crop reach the peak of the harvesting period, a freak storm might, and often does, destroy his crop by hail or high winds tear his tents to shreds.

Tobacco Growing in New England

Tobacco Valley is a narrow strip of fertile land in the Connecticut River Valley that extends northward from Portland, Connecticut, through western Massachusetts to the border towns of Vermont and New Hampshire. It occupies only sixty-one square miles.

The Mayan Indians of Yucatan were the first to raise tobacco for smoking and the habit spread to the Indians of South America and the Caribbean Islands and then to North America. Columbus found the natives of the West Indies inhaling the smoke from smoldering leaves of the tobacco plant. Explorers who followed Columbus carried the custom to Portugal and Spain; the rest of Europe, Africa and Asia became users of tobacco early in the sixteenth century.

The early colonists depended on tobacco as their prime commodity in trade and barter, and frequently tobacco was used as money. It is said that the first English brides shipped to Jamestown were paid for with tobacco — 120 pounds of tobacco for each bride.

In Tobacco Valley the tobacco raised is restricted to broadleaf Havana seed and shade-grown, used for the manufacture of cigars. Broadleaf and Havana seed are used for the binders and the shade-grown exclusively for the wrappers. The growers give their greatest attention to the cigar wrapper leaf, which is the costliest to raise.

Broadleaf and Havana seed tobacco are raised in open fields without protection from the elements; shade-grown tobacco is grown under cotton cloth coverings. Those who have traveled through the Connecticut River Valley in the summertime are well acquainted with the miles of white-cloth-covered fields, as well as the weathered barns in which the tobacco is cured and sorted.

Curing shed in Tobacco Valley

By 1825 Connecticut Valley broadleaf was of considerable importance, and up to that time it was the only wrapper tobacco used for cigars. With the switch in smoking from pipes to cigars, the introduction of Havana seed produced the ultimate in smooth smoking — besides, Havana seed could yield a higher percentage of wrappers.

Before much time passed the composure of the New England growers was ruffled by competition. A similar leaf was found to be growing on the island of Sumatra in the East Indies. It was smooth burning, mild in taste and finely textured. Soon it had reduced the Connecticut growers' product to use as fillers and binders, for the American cigar manufacturers who preferred the Sumatra leaf for their wrappers.

With the aid of the United States government, the Connecticut growers sought the secret of Sumatra-grown tobacco's special superiority. An experimental station was placed in Poquonock in Windsor to grow Sumatra tobacco under shade. The experiment proved so successful that the Sumatra leaf produced in Connecticut baffled the New York tobacco men — they couldn't tell the imported from the Poquonock product.

The tobacco industry in the Connecticut Valley quickly responded and cloth covered fields have been a commonplace sight since the turn of the century. The cloth tent over the growing plants creates artificial shade and reproduces the tropical conditions and the even temperature that protects the Sumatra plants on home soil by the low-lying heavy clouds.

The tobacco fields in all four New England states bordering on the Connecticut River grow "Connecticut" tobacco, three-quarters of which is raised in Connecticut and the other quarter in Massachusetts, except for a small amount raised in Vermont and New Hampshire.

Along the Housatonic River, around New Milford, tobacco was at one time a major crop, but it began to decline three decades ago and has entirely disappeared in recent times. The size of that tobacco industry is manifested in the number of huge tobacco barns that are scattered throughout the valley. They are stalwart, beautifully proportioned and a weathered gray, a color impossible to imitate. Many have suffered from vandalism by artists, who make picture frames from the siding, and decorators, who use the delightfully textured gray boards for panelling.

The Nathan Hale Homestead

COVENTRY

Coventry, Connecticut, ordinarily a quiet village, springs into life when the tourists start motoring through the countryside. Thousands of them each year seek out the Hale homestead to pay homage to their Revolutionary hero — Nathan Hale.

The Nathan Hale Homestead, Coventry

Nathan Hale was not born in the homestead; it was built by his father, Richard Hale, on the site of Nathan's birthplace. The present twelve-room house was completed and occupied in November 1776, two months after the news arrived of young Hale's death on British gallows in New York.

The legend of Nathan Hale is highlighted by the memorabilia contained in the house. There are, among numerous articles belonging at one time to young Hale, the silver buckles Nathan removed from his shoes before going behind the enemy lines on Long Island disguised as a Dutch schoolteacher; also on exhibition is a flintlock fowling piece that he used prior to his entry into Yale. The only known likeness of the hero — a shadow drawing — is there also, and numerous letters and diaries.

Nathan Hale's brothers distinguished themselves as educators, writers and ministers. Edward Everett Hale was among the notables of his time and several colleges had Hale professors.

Richard and Elizabeth Hale had twelve children, of whom Nathan was the seventh. When the American Revolution broke, five of their nine sons answered the call of duty — Nathan was the only one who did not survive.

Nathan chose a career of education and entered Yale at the age of fourteen, graduating with high honors. He delivered the valedictory address at his commencement in 1772 in Latin and English; after graduation he taught school at East Haddam for a brief time and in New London for about a year before joining the Continental Army in 1775 at the age of twenty. Hale was an intellectual dedicated to the cause of republicanism. When Washington was hard pressed for intelligence work behind the British lines, Nathan Hale volunteered, but his inexperience in espionage work betrayed him and he paid with his life for his bold patriotism.

The original Richard Hale estate consisted of 340 acres on the west shore of Lake Wamgumbaug, much of which became the Nathan Hale State Forest, one of the most beautiful preserves in Connecticut.

The L-shaped homestead is in an excellent state of preservation. In addition to a parlor, kitchen, dining room, six bedrooms and a central hall, there is a schoolroom where Nathan's brothers taught classes after the Revolution, and another room in which Richard Hale, as justice of the peace, held court. The windows, twelve panes over twelve, are the original hand-blown glass. Part of the stone walls that surround the house were laid by young Nathan.

Until 1914 descendants of Richard Hale owned the property, and then it passed into new hands. When George Dudley Seymour of New Haven died in 1948, he bequeathed the property and twenty acres, not acquired by the State for a forest preserve, to the Antiquarian and Landmarks Society of Connecticut.

New Haven

If Roger Sherman, New Haven's first mayor, and John Davenport, the city's early religious leader and one of its founders, Timothy Dwight, Yale's distinguished nineteenth-century president, and Eli Whitney, who spurred others on to adopting his mass production methods in manufacturing, returned to New Haven they would discover their city absorbed in the promulgation of modern efficiency and functional interests. Only at Yale University would there still be any vestige left of the fascination for the past; but Yale influences the cultural tone of New Haven, the arts and music, and lends its support to the tryouts of Broadway plays. Without Yale, New Haven would be just another large city engrossed in manufacturing for profit, devoid of aesthetic values.

Yale was chartered in 1701 and opened in 1702 as a Collegiate School of Connecticut at Clinton. It moved in 1707 to Old Saybrook and came to New Haven in 1716, at which time the name was changed to Yale College to honor Elihu Yale, whose father was David Yale, a first settler of New Haven. Elihu Yale's initial gift of $30,000 assured Yale's survival. All practical gentlemen, the trustees were misled into believing that Elihu Yale intended to leave the College a substantial gift upon his death. To their consternation his will left nothing further to the college that gave him immortality. If Cotton Mather's offer in 1718 had been accepted, the trustees might have struck a better deal. Mather offered to trump Yale's $30,000 if they would name the College after him. He previously made a similar proposition to Harvard, but they, too, were uninterested.

Yale College functioned as a Puritan school that grew to a renowned seat of learning years before the Colony became a state. John Davenport was persistent in arousing support for the College for the specific purpose of releasing the New Haven Colony from the dependence on Harvard for its ministers.

Among the early presidents of Yale were such outstanding men as Ezra Stiles and the elder Timothy Dwight. The younger Timothy Dwight, while president in 1887, changed the name to Yale University. Yale today functions as a nonsectarian university with noted schools in Medicine (1813), Divinity (1822), Law (1824), Sheffield Scientific School (1861), and Fine Arts (1869) — the first in any United States university. The Yale Art Gallery, established in 1830, contains collections of Early American and pre-Renaissance Italian Art.

Yale is a city within a city. I realized this the day I went down to New Haven to sketch Connecticut Hall in the Old Campus. The serenity that prevailed within the campus, encircled by University buildings, isolated me from the activities of bustling metropolitan New Haven.

The cornerstone of Connecticut Hall was laid in 1750. This ivy-covered red brick building is delightful for its contained simplicity and architectural charm. In front of the building is a well-executed full-length bronze of Nathan Hale as a young man. Hale occupied a room in Connecticut Hall when he attended Yale as a member of the class of 1773. The excellent restoration work was completed through the efforts of the graduates of the class of 1905.

Yale has numerous buildings of architectural merit, but none compare with Connecticut Hall for its simplicity, reminiscent of Yale's earliest years, of which far too little is still extant.

New Haven, originally called Quinnipiack, was founded in 1637–1638 by a group of wealthy immigrants who first sailed into Boston Harbor late in June 1637. It was their intention to look around before selecting a site for a settlement.

Among the group was a nonconformist London clergyman, John Davenport; another was a merchant, Theophilus Eaton, who once held a high position at the Danish Court in the name of the British Crown.

One day they received word from an officer who helped John Mason whip the Pequot Indians in Mystic. In pursuit of the stragglers and driving them further from Long Island Sound towards the Hudson Valley, the officer came upon Quinnipiack, which he described as so beautiful and idyllic. He also stressed the abundance of fish in the streams and the oysters beneath the Sound. In the woods there was plenty of game, and the meadows were fertile, to the north were high protecting cliffs — and the Indians in the area were friendly. All of this struck Eaton as worthy of investigation at once.

Theophilus Eaton was soon on his way; he sailed down the coast in a small boat and found the spot acceptable for the settlement. He departed for Boston, leaving seven men behind for the duration of the winter, which they spent in a hut near the shore.

The immigrants were obliged to live aboard their boat until homes were built and a meetinghouse erected according to the plan laid out by John Brackett, a civil engineer, after an agreement had been reached with the Indians.

A large tract was appropriated for a green and streets were plotted in squares surrounding it. The dwellings formed a motley assortment of huts and mansions, with Eaton's house the most ostentatious of them all with a creditable library. The present green in New Haven is the same one laid out by John Brackett.

In 1664 the New Haven Colony reluctantly united with Connecticut. New Haven was incorporated as a city in 1784, and from 1701 to 1875, it was joint capital with Hartford. As a colony, New Haven included Milford, Guilford, Stamford, Branford and Southold, Long Island.

During the Revolution, New Haven was invaded by British troops in July 1779 with the purpose of drawing Washington's attention to the defense of the Connecticut coast and thus weakening his position at West Point. Washington made a token counterattack at Stony Point but the British had by then completed their action at New Haven.

Connecticut Hall, Yale University

President Stiles of Yale spotted the British invaders landing at West Haven, from the steeple of the College chapel. Students immediately rose to the occasion and marched to meet the enemy. In the meantime beacon fires on the hilltops aroused the patriots in the surrounding towns, who converged upon New Haven to defend it.

The enemy succeeded in overpowering the defenders and started to plunder and destroy property with wanton delight; but General Garth, who intended to raze New Haven to the ground, decided that such action would encumber the Tories, who held vast properties, and gave the order that spared the town. It is generally conceded that it was Colonel Edmund Fanning, a Yale graduate with the British troops, and a Tory, who exercised his influence on the commanders to rescind the order to destroy New Haven. Small wonder that Yale gave Fanning an honorary degree in 1803.

General Tryon captured Fort Hale (formerly Rock Fort) but did not press on towards the town. By that time the patriots had increased in such numbers the enemy concluded it was wiser to transfer their military deviltry to the town of Fairfield, which they succeeded in burning so successfully that the oldest houses standing today in Fairfield date after 1779.

Colonel Aaron Burr was twenty-three when he took an active part in the defense of New Haven. Another young man, Benedict Arnold, who lived in the town, wrested the keys to the powderhouse away from the Tories and their sympathizers.

Center Church, near the center of the green on Temple Street, stands over part of the original burying ground, and very near the site of the first meetinghouse. Underneath is a crypt containing the remains and tombstones of many Puritan fathers and their families.

Old Saybrook on the Connecticut River

Six years before the *Mayflower* arrived at Plymouth, Adriaen Block, a Dutchman, discovered the Connecticut River. At Old Lyme on the east bank, and Old Saybrook on the west, Adriaen Block posted "No trespassing" signs. Here he found salt marshes covered with stands of water hemp, seaside goldenrod and beach grass. The place has changed little with time, and charming Lynde Point is truly land's end, where the bather who likes to feel the tang of tide-water will discover also a region of unperturbed peace.

Ahead lies Orient Point on Long Island, a mere mark on the horizon; all between Connecticut and Long Island is the Sound. Two lighthouses guide shipping

Breakwater Light, Old Saybrook

into the channel. One light, built in 1803 of white stone, towers 71 feet above the water on the west side of the mouth of the Connecticut River and is affectionately known as the outer light by the residents. The Saybrook Breakwater Light, which was built in 1886, is called the inner light — a white conical tower on a brown cylindrical pier rising 58 feet above the water.

Saybrook was considered a colony until 1644 with George Fenwick as its acting head; he was the only grantee to come to Saybrook and settle at the mouth of the Connecticut River in the spring of 1636. He left for England in the fall of the same year, returning several years later with his wife to represent the rest of the grantees of the Warwick Patent — this made him the acting head or governor of the colony. When Fenwick was unable to secure a confirmation of the Warwick Patent, he returned to England in 1646 and became governor of Leith and of Edinburgh.

Lieutenant Lion Gardiner arrived at Saybrook Point in 1636 with orders to build a fort at "Pequot River or the Connecticut." He selected the Connecticut River site and laid out homesites as well as the fort. Lieutenant Gardiner was greatly admired by Wyandanch, sachem of the Montauks, who gave him Smithtown around 1639, to which he received title from the Earl of Sterling. A bronze statue of Lion Gardiner was dedicated in 1930 as a gift to Saybrook from the family.

During the Revolutionary War no serious engagements took place at Saybrook, but British patrols went up and down the Sound daily. In April 1775, fifty-nine men answered the Lexington alarm and also went to the relief of Boston.

At the shipyard belonging to Captain Hayden, the *Oliver Cromwell* slid down the ways into the river in August 1776, the largest ship to go over Saybrook bar. As far back as 1777, David Bushnell experimented with submarine warfare at his Saybrook Ferry headquarters, constructing the *American Turtle* for experimental purposes.

George Washington passed through Old Saybrook February 23, 1756, and twenty years later, in 1776, he spent the night of April 10 at Old Lyme and passed through Old Saybrook the next day. Lafayette was honored in Saybrook August 21, 1824, with special ceremonies; he spent the night at the Pratt Tavern and the next day he left for New London.

Lynde Point Light, Old Saybrook

Mystic Village

Mystic Village lies on both sides of the Mystic River, parts of which are in Groton and Stonington. Old Mystic is a few miles north, at the junction of the Mystic River and Lantern Hill Brook. The Indians called the area Canemos, meaning the "river of the great sachem," for Sassacus, the Pequot sachem, whose stronghold overlooked the river. De Laet, the Dutch geographer, recorded the place on a map in 1616.

If any tribe of Indians were to be singled out as the most ruthless, wicked and powerful in Connecticut, the Pequots take first place in all three categories. They waged warfare continuously between 1632 and 1637 to dislodge the English from the country. The General Court at Hartford ordered an all-out war against the Pequots in May 1637, under the command of Captain Mason.

The battle of Mystic, which occurred May 26, 1637, was a fierce encounter between Captain Mason and the infuriated Pequots at their fort. Within an hour the fort and six or seven hundred Indians were destroyed. Mason, encouraged by the appearance of some English vessels sailing into Pequot harbor, moved in their direction — within range of the arrows of three hundred Indians who gathered on a hill from another fort. A short time after boarding the vessels, Mason disembarked and left the captains to wrangle among themselves over procedure. Captain Mason, with a plan of his own, soon reached the banks of the Connecticut River at sundown and was greeted by a salute from the fort at Saybrook — Lieutenant Gardner early the next morning arranged to bring Captain Mason across to the fort where Mason acquainted them with his success over the Pequots.

Four weeks later Captain Israel Stoughton joined Captain Mason's small force with his own, and they immediately began pursuit of the Pequots. Finally the English caught their quarry in Sasqua Swamp, near Southport, and defeated the Pequots so thoroughly that their remnants begged for mercy. Almost two hundred captured Pequots were divided among three Indian sachems and absorbed into their tribes.

The monument erected to Captain John Mason in 1889 at Mystic is on the site of the fort which he attacked so successfully 252 years before.

It has been estimated that more than one hundred deep-sea captains made their homes in Mystic, many of them born here. Captain William Edgar Wheeler, Niantic-born, took his eleven-year-old son on a trip to Foochow, China; he was the first white boy seen in China. Captain John E. Williams is credited with a record run in his Mystic-built sailing ship, the *Andrew Jackson* — New York to San Francisco in eighty-nine days and four hours.

The selection of Mystic as the site of the marine museum and the rebirth of its old-time seaport was similar to the restoration of Williamsburg. Mystic was once a great seaport and the museum has re-created a bygone era of cobbled streets, shipyards, lofts, shops and square-riggers alongside the wharf.

Entrance to the Marine Museum, Mystic Village

As early as 1662 the first ship, a small sloop, was built along the banks of the Mystic River. In the eighteenth century the shipyards were developed on a large scale. Mystic-built privateers harried the British during the War of 1812, but it was the clippers that brought her real glory; they were found everywhere on the high seas. The Mystic-built *Andrew Jackson* matched the record made by the *Flying Cloud* and the *David Crockett* made twenty-five voyages to San Francisco and continued to sail the high seas for another fifty years.

Among the interesting square-riggers permanently brought to rest at the marine museum is the whaler *Charles W. Morgan* — over one hundred years old. She grossed $2,000,000 in earnings as a whaler; her career came to an end in 1921.

The full-rigged ship *Joseph Conrad* is berthed near the *Charles W. Morgan*. She was built over eighty years ago in Copenhagen and served until the close of World War II. Other boats are constantly being added to the collection of this living museum.

During the Civil War the Mystic shipyards were busy building steamers. One curious-looking craft was the *Galena,* an ironclad which was sent against the Confederate batteries at Drewrys Bluff in 1862 to test her armor plate. The results were almost disastrous but the builders learned how much their ironclad could take.

During both World Wars Mystic made crash boats and minesweepers.

Mystic is tucked away in the southeastern corner of Connecticut and about ten miles from New London, where the U.S. Coast Guard Academy is located. The incredible Shaw Mansion in New London was built in 1756 by Nathaniel Shaw, who owned a fleet of trading ships and privateersmen. George Washington slept once in this granite house, which escaped destruction in the disastrous fire that ravaged New London in 1781.

Soaring over the River Thames at Groton is the monument to commemorate the massacre at Fort Griswold in 1781, during an attack led by Benedict Arnold after he changed uniforms.

The Civic Center
STONINGTON

The two guns in the square, 18 pound caliber, were not the largest available for a major job, but in the British bombardment of Stonington, during the War of 1812, the Stoningtonians used them effectively to pepper His Majesty's Navy with Yankee cannon balls in exchange for those dropped into the town by the British. Today the British balls serve as ornamental adjuncts atop sundry hitching posts about the town, and one is a finial on the monument in the square.

On August 9, 1814, the British fleet appeared and a note was sent from Captain T. M. Hardy ordering the citizens of Stonington to move out of the town to avoid annihilation. The inhabitants replied, "We shall defend," and readied their two 18-pounders and a 4-pounder for action. Colonel Randall's scattered regiment

The Civic Center, Stonington

was summoned by a signal of burning tar barrels to come to the aid of Stonington.

Colonel Randall and his men prevented the enemy from landing on the night of August 9. A three-day bombardment followed, but the Americans' remarkable resistance frustrated the attempt by the enemy to destroy Stonington. In the Old Stone Bank Building on the square may be seen the flag flown at the battle — it has sixteen stars and sixteen stripes.

Stonington is situated on a peninsula jutting into Long Island Sound. The first settler was Thomas Stanton, who was appointed special interpreter to the Indians and was permitted in 1649 to establish a trading post, as a concession, on the Pawcatuck River. He did not bring his family until 1657, by which time he had built a dwelling.

Stonington has long been identified with fishing and shipping. Recently there were forty "draggers" and numerous oyster boats that made Stonington their home port, the largest fleet in New England west of Gloucester, Massachusetts. The boats are manned and owned by Portuguese natives of Stonington, fishermen for generations.

As early as 1680, Joseph Wells was known to have built vessels there, and shipbuilding continued until the Revolution. The industry was revived after 1818 and square-riggers, schooners and sloops were built on a large scale. Later on side-wheelers and screw-driven boats of iron began to slide down the ways.

During the Revolution when Boston was besieged and hungry, the citizenry loaded a wagon with Stonington cheese and took it overland to Boston on March 27, 1777. Stonington cheese was an important part of Army rations.

The Stonington Lighthouse, where the Historical Society collections are housed, is one of the interesting buildings in town — a stone structure built in 1840 to replace the first light built in Connecticut by the Federal Government.

Before the Housatonic, Connecticut and Thames rivers were bridged, the Stonington Line of steamers picked up passengers at the Connecticut terminus of the railway line from Providence and Boston, to complete the trip to New York by water.

James McNeill Whistler lived in Stonington at one time. Edmund Fanning, born there in 1769, became famous for his exploits in foreign trade and exploration.

Captain Amos Sheffield's House
STONINGTON

The simple signs on the early homes bear the names of their former owners — a formidable list; many of whom were sea captains. The houses flank the narrow streets and lanes which no one would care to change. Here is the vital evidence of a way of life in early Stonington, and the honest exposure of men who played by the rules of the sea.

Captain Amos Sheffield's House, Stonington

Benjamin Franklin had an unusual experience while passing through the town on his way to Newport. He hired a horse in New London to continue his trip, but when he arrived in front of the Reverend Nathaniel Eells house on Hinckly Hill in Stonington, his horse balked and would go no further. Franklin was forced to borrow another horse from Eells to continue his journey to Newport.

Nathaniel Fanning was born in 1755 in a house on the old road between Mystic and Stonington. He was midshipman on the *Bonhomme Richard* under Captain John Paul Jones and saw action with the *Serapis* off Flamborough Head. He received a recommendation from Captain Jones for promotion. He died in 1805 while in command of the United States Naval Station at Charleston, South Carolina.

Paul Wheeler built his home on the corner of the road to North Stonington in 1750. He was one of the committee of safety to furnish supplies to the Revolutionary Army. It is said that Colonel Joseph Mason held his officers' drills in the house.

Richard Anson Wheeler, a descendant of William Chesebrough, who was one of the original settlers of Stonington, became noted as a genealogist and an historian. He died in 1904 at the age of eighty-seven.

George Denison (1620–1694) came to New England in 1631 but he returned to England twelve years later when his wife died. He came back to New England with his second wife; in 1654 he erected a mansion in Stonington a little to the west of the existing Denison house, now a museum, which was built in 1717 by his grandson, George.

Captain George Denison fought in Cromwell's army and later against King Philip's Narragansetts. The Denison Homestead built in 1717 in Mystic is one of New England's finest old houses, completely furnished and restored. Eleven generations of Denisons lived in the house, and it is still in family hands with all the Denison heirlooms under one roof.

Jeremiah Halsey was born in Stonington in 1744 and distinguished himself at the start of the Revolutionary War, in which he was actively engaged at Ticonderoga and Crown Point. He became captain of the *Enterprise* and commanded other boats on Lake George and Lake Champlain.

At the head of Wequetequock Cove is the old burying ground. Here is buried the Reverend James Noyes, who gave his library to help found Yale. Nearby is the grave of pioneer Walter Palmer.

The Palmer name is as indigenous to Stonington as any name could possibly get — the Palmers have been around a long time. At the time of the British bombardment we find Amos Palmer installed as chairman of the committee on defense. He reported that during the three days' bombardment that began August 10, 1814, His Majesty's ships sent on shore sixty tons of metal and wounded one man. The Stoningtonians inflicted death on twenty-one of the enemy and wounded fifty. If the

British had not withdrawn from our fire they might have been sunk since the men from Stonington, Mystic and Groton observed that the British vessels were seriously damaged.

Not far from the old custom house, the Amos Palmer house, built in 1780, is one of Stonington's distinguished landmarks.

The "Puritan Church"

BROOKLYN

Brooklyn is a stone's throw from the Rhode Island–Connecticut state line. General Israel Putnam made his home here in 1739. He bought the Governor Belcher farm located a short distance east of the highway on the Pomfret–Brooklyn road. To this place he brought his wife Hannah and their son Israel, Jr., in 1743.

Fame came early to Putnam in a strange way — he entered a cave and single-handed killed a predatory wolf which had harassed the farmers in the area. In 1755 Putnam was at the battle of Lake George as a second lieutenant and became a major two years later. He was at Ticonderoga in 1758 and became an aide to Abercrombie, who succeeded Lord Howe when the latter was killed. In 1758 Putnam was taken to Montreal as a prisoner where he won his release through exchange. He was made a lieutenant colonel in 1759 and was among the military at the surrender of Montreal when Canada became English territory. He lost his first wife and married Mrs. Deborah Avery Gardiner in 1767. Her social position brought many guests to their home, and then they moved into the Avery place, near the green, which they conducted as an inn. It became famous as the General Wolfe Tavern. The tavern sign is now owned by the Connecticut Historical Society.

The Lexington alarm terminated Putnam's peaceful farming interlude; he left his plow in the field when the news arrived, and without changing his clothes he started out for Cambridge.

Putnam was promoted to the rank of major general and participated in the battle of Bunker Hill, the siege of Boston and the battle of Long Island. General Putnam was in command of the Hudson Highlands when he was stricken with paralysis in 1779. Death came to him May 19, 1790, in the house located near the main road between Pomfret and Brooklyn.

The bronze equestrian statue of General Israel Putnam in Brooklyn, near the Mortlake Manor house on Main Street, was dedicated June 14, 1888. The sculptor of this outstanding statue was Karl Gerhardt.

The "Puritan Church" was erected in 1771 under the leadership of Israel Putnam, and he was elected caretaker and bell ringer in 1772 at a salary of £3 a year. In 1790, he was buried from this church; the bell that tolled that day was cast by another patriot — Paul Revere.

Owing to the Unitarian views of the pastor around 1817 the Congregational church became divided and the Congregationalists built an independent chapel in 1820; from that date to the present, the so-called "Puritan Church" has been occupied by Unitarians. The church also serves as the town hall.

The "Puritan Church," Brooklyn